AF608226

THE MARRIAGE OF MINORS

THE CATHOLIC UNIVERSITY OF AMERICA
CANON LAW STUDIES
No. 221

THE MARRIAGE OF MINORS

AN HISTORICAL SYNOPSIS AND COMMENTARY

BY
CLETUS FRANCIS O'DONNELL, M.A., J.C.L.
PRIEST OF THE ARCHDIOCESE OF CHICAGO

A DISSERTATION
SUBMITTED TO THE FACULTY OF THE SCHOOL OF CANON LAW OF THE CATHOLIC UNIVERSITY OF AMERICA IN PARTIAL FULFILLMENT OF THE REQUIREMENTS FOR THE DEGREE OF DOCTOR OF CANON LAW

THE CATHOLIC UNIVERSITY OF AMERICA PRESS
WASHINGTON, D. C.
1945

Nihil Obstat:
EDUARDUS G. ROELKER, S.T.D., J.C.D.,
Censor Deputatus
Washingtonii, D. C., die 15 maii, 1945

Imprimatur:
✠ SAMUEL A. STRITCH, D.D.,
Archiepiscopus Chicagiensis
Chicagiae, Illinois, die 16 maii, 1945

MURRAY & HEISTER—WASHINGTON, D. C.
PRINTED IN THE UNITED STATES

9

TO MY MOTHER
AND TO THE MEMORY OF
MY FATHER

TABLE OF CONTENTS

PART II

CANONICAL COMMENTARY

FOREWORD

The purpose of this dissertation is to present an historical treatment and canonical commentary on the Church's legislation concerning the marriage of minors. The general law of the Church on this subject has always been marked by a twofold characteristic, namely that of protecting the liberty of the child in contracting marriage, and that of moderating this freedom in order to prevent the minor from entering a hasty and ill-considered union. Never has the Church in her universal law strayed from this middle course, either by conceding full liberty of action to the minor, or by nullifying his freedom in completely subjecting him to the will of another. The writer in this work is not concerned with the diriment impediment of nonage, but only with that period which may be termed the "age of minority in marriage." This period begins after the child attains marriageable age, and it ceases when he reaches his majority.

This treatise is divided into two parts. The first section is an historical synopsis of the past legislation concerning the marriage of minors, while the second half presents a commentary on the present discipline of the Church in this matter. It is not intended that the first part be a complete history, but rather a consideration of the subject within two periods in the history of Canon Law. The first period is that of the *Corpus Iuris Canonici,* that is of Gratian, of the Decretal legislation, of the Glossators and the commentators of this period. Mention will be made, too, of the teachings of the Theologians, for they aided greatly in the clarification of the problems connected with the subject. The second period extends from the Council of Trent to the present day. However, at the very outset of this dissertation a brief consideration of the status of minors in regard to marriage as found in the Roman and Germanic law will be given. This will reveal the civil legislation which was not without influence on the legislation of the Church. Each of these two historical periods will be treated separately and distinctly. In the treatment of the first period the chronological approach will be used, for this will serve to indicate more clearly the evolution and development of the institute. In considering the second period, however, the subject will be treated analytically, and this period will be viewed as a whole with little or no consideration of chronology, except for the chapter dealing with the Council of Trent. This approach seems more advisable, since this second period offers for the most part merely a confirmation and clarification of the law of the Decretals and of the Council of Trent.

The second part of the work is a canonical commentary on the present law of the Church regarding the contraction of marriage by those who are of minor age. Therein is determined the meaning and extent of the term "minor." Consideration is also given to the exercise of rights by minors, especially of the exercise of their right to marry. A detailed account of the procedure on the part of the pastor and Ordinary in dealing with the marriage of minors is presented, and this consideration forms the principal section of the second part of this dissertation. The canonical commentary ends with an analysis of the penalty established by the legislator in canon 2353. Finally, the writer considers briefly the American civil law in so far as it affects the marriage of minors.

The writer wishes to express his sincere gratitude to His Excellency, The Most Reverend Samuel A. Stritch, Archbishop of Chicago, for the opportunity of graduate study in Canon Law, to the Right Reverend Monsignor George J. Casey, Vicar General of the Chicago Archdiocese, for his many acts of kindness, to the Right Reverend Monsignor John P. Campbell for his keen interest and encouragement, to the members of the Faculty of the School of Canon Law of the Catholic University of America for their help and guidance in the preparation of this work, and to his family and friends, especially the student priests at the Catholic University of America, for their generous assistance.

PART I

HISTORICAL SYNOPSIS

CHAPTER I

THE MARRIAGE OF MINORS IN ROMAN AND GERMANIC LAW

Article 1. In Roman Law

To understand adequately the subject of the marriage of minors in Roman Law some knowledge must be had of the Roman conception of the family. The word *familia* in Roman Law was much wider in its extension and meant far more than the present common usage of the term connotes. For in the legal system of the Romans the family included all the descendants of a living ancestor together with all adopted persons, servants, and slaves. It embraced all who were in any way under the legal power of the ancestor, or as he was termed, the *paterfamilias.*[1]

The legal power of the *paterfamilias* was called the *patriapotestas.* His power was absolute and it was exercised over all the members of his agnatic family. The *paterfamilias* was the absolute ruler and king of the family, and there was no appeal from his authority whether it was exercised with moderation or with despotic cruelty. This power was his as long as he lived, and it extended not only over his own children but also to his grandchildren and to all his other descendants. In early Rome the power of the *paterfamilias* was unlimited. It included then as its principal elements:[2] (1) the right of life and death over

[1] Buckland, *A Textbook of Roman Law from Augustus to Justinian* (2. ed., Cambridge: The University Press, 1932), p. 101; this work will hereafter be cited as *A Textbook of Roman Law.*

[2] Cf. Leage, *Roman Private Law Founded on the "Institutes" of Gaius and Justinian* (2. ed., by C. H. Ziegler, London: Macmillan and Co., 1937),

all who were subject to his power; (2) the right to sell into slavery or to imprison his children; (3) the right to forbid marriage and the power to divorce his children who were already married; (4) the right of ownership of everything acquired by the *filiusfamilias;* (5) the right to appoint in his will the guardians for his children.

In the progress of time his authority was greatly diminished but even to the last days of the Roman system the *paterfamilias* possessed great power over his children—more power than any legal system had ever granted to the father. Hence Justinian declared: "The power which we have over our children is peculiar to Roman citizens; for there are no other men possessing such power over their children as we have."[3] Therefore it is not surprising that in this Roman legal system the authority of the *paterfamilias* extended also to the disposal of his children in marriage.

In the early Roman Law the consent of the contracting parties was not demanded for a valid marriage and the *paterfamilias* gave his sons and daughters in marriage whenever and to whomever he willed. He was under no legal obligation to consult the wishes of his children regarding the intended marriage, and they, on the other hand, had no legal redress against the action of the *paterfamilias.* The marriage was arranged and executed by the fathers of the respective families and the consent of the bride and groom was entirely ignored.[4] However, in the Roman Law of the Classical era and throughout the subsequent periods the

---

pp. 90–94; this work will hereafter be cited as *Roman Private Law;* Burdick, *The Principles of Roman Law and Their Relation to Modern Law* (Rochester: The Lawyers Cooperative Publishing Co., 1938), pp. 254–259; Westermarck, *The History of Human Marriage* (London: Macmillan and Co., 1891), pp. 229–230.

[3] I. (1. 9) 2 pr. It may be noted that this observation had previously been made by Gaius and was merely repeated by Justinian in the same words. Cf. Institutiones Gai (1. 55)—*Collectio Librorum Iuris Anteiustiniani* (ed. Paulus Krueger, Theodorus Mommsen, Guilelmus Studemund, 7. ed., 2 vols., Berolini: apud Weidmannos, 1923), I, 15.

[4] Cf. Corbett, *The Roman Law of Marriage* (Oxford: Clarendon Press, 1930), pp. 53–55; Buckland, *A Textbook of Roman Law,* p. 113; Ferrero, *Ancient Rome and Modern America* (New York: G. P. Putnam's Sons, 1914), pp. 61–62.

consent of the contracting parties was necessary. The Roman Jurists of this Classical period declared time and time again that the essential element in marriage was the consent of the bride and groom. If such consent was lacking the marriage was invalid.[5] This consent of the parties, the Jurists declared, must be voluntary but the marriage was still valid even though the parties contracted it due to reverential fear of the parents because such fear did not constitute compulsion in the Roman Law.[6]

Besides this consent of the contracting parties the Roman Law required another consent which was equally essential for the validity of the marriage. For if the parties were not yet *sui juris* the consent of their *paterfamilias* was indispensable. This is seen from the law given by the Emperors Diocletian and Maximian (285) to Sabinus: "The policy of the law does not permit that even a son under paternal control shall be compelled to marry against his will. Therefore if you observe the ordinary legal precepts, you will not be prevented from marrying the wife whom you may choose, if you desire to do so, provided, however, that your father consents to the marriage." [7] The Emperors Honorius and Theodosius (408–409) likewise commanded that the wishes of the father were to be considered in the case of the marriage of daughters under parental control, and even when a girl was her own mistress but was under twenty-five years of age, the consent of her father had to be obtained. When she was deprived of the aid of her father, the consent of her mother and her kindred as well as of herself was necessary.[8] The *Digest* [9] and the *Institutes* [10] of Justinian stated similar laws which re-

[5] D. (23. 2) 2; D. (23. 1) 11; N. (22. 3) ; C. (5. 4) 9.

[6] C. (5. 4) 14.

[7] C. (5. 4) 12.

[8] C. (5. 4) 20.

[9] "Consistere non possunt nuptiae nisi consentiant omnes, id est qui coeunt quorumque in potestate sunt."—D. (23. 2) 2.

[10] "Iustas autem nuptias inter se Cives Romani contrahunt, qui secundum praecepta legum coeunt, masculi quidem puberes, feminae autem viripotentes, sive patresfamilias sint, sive filiifamilias, dum tamen filiifamilias consensum habeant parentum, quorum in potestate sunt. Nam hoc fieri debere, et civilis et naturalis ratio persuadet in tantum, ut iussus parentis praecedere debeat."—I. (1. 10) pr.

quired the consent of the *paterfamilias* for the marriage of those subjected to his power.

Notwithstanding the clearness of those texts in Roman Law which concerned the necessity of the knowledge and consent of the house-father to the marriage of his children, certain commentators claimed that those laws were merely prohibitive. Thus these authors taught that a marriage contracted by a *filiusfamilias* without parental consent was not invalid but only illicit.[11] In support of their opinion they called forth the statement of the Jurist Paul: "Eorum qui in potestate patris sunt, sine voluntate eius matrimonia iure non contrahuntur, sed contracta tamen non solvuntur. Contemplatio enim publicae utilitatis privatorum commodis praefertur."[12] But these words attributed to Paul cannot be allowed to militate against the clear texts mentioned in the Roman Law which declared that marriages contracted without the knowledge of or against the will of the *paterfamilias* were null and void. Indeed phrases expressed in this manner, "nuptiae consistere non possunt," "omnimoda patris auctoritas est necessaria," which are found in many texts of the Roman Law can have only the meaning of invalidating laws. Therefore this passage taken from the Sentences of Paul must be interpreted to mean that a marriage contracted with the express or even tacit consent of the *paterfamilias* cannot be annulled by his subsequent disapproval and hence the statement of Paul agrees, or can be understood to agree, with these texts.[13]

Therefore in Roman Law the consent of the fathers of both

---

[11] Cuiacius (*Opera Omnia, Opera ad Parisiensem Fabrotianem Editionem* [15 vols., Prati: Fratr. Giachetti, 1836–1843], V, in lib. XXV Pauli ad Edictum, p. 869, col. 2) stated: "Contractae tamen ita sine voluntate parentum in quorum potestate sunt, qui coeunt, invitis iis, qui hanc societatem coierunt, non dissolvuntur. Iustae non sunt nuptiae, fateor, contractae tamen non dissolvuntur"; Gothofredus in his remarks to the L. "filium" of the D., *de ritu nupt.* added: "Civiles hasce leges esse imperfectas, cum nuptias absque parentum consensu fieri prohibeant, contractas tamen non dissolvant . . ."—Cited from Vecchiotti, *Institutiones Canonicae* (19. ed., 3 vols., Taurini: Marietti, 1886), III, 231 inasmuch as the latter source was not available to the writer.

[12] Sent. Pauli (2. 19) 2—*Collectio Librorum Iuris Anteiustiniani,* I, 69.

[13] Corbett, *The Roman Law of Marriage,* p. 62.

the bride and groom was required for the validity of the marriage unless the contracting parties were *sui juris.* Moreover, if the groom was a grandson and his father was in *potestas,* the consent both of his grandfather and his father was needed before he could contract a valid marriage.[14] If, however, the grandfather was insane or was incapable of acting intelligently, the consent of the father alone sufficed.[15] Under certain circumstances a son or daughter under *potestas* could marry validly without the consent of the *paterfamilias.* This was true, for example, if the *paterfamilias* had fallen captive, or if he was absent and it was not known whether he was alive or, if alive, where he was. Justinian, however, in these cases required that the marriage be postponed for three years.[16]

The question arose as to whether the son or daughter of an insane father can validly contract marriage according to the Roman Law. The difficulty was that parental consent would be lacking since the *paterfamilias* was insane and hence incapable of positing an act of the will. This problem was settled by Justinian who decreed that the son or daughter in these circumstances could enter marriage without the paternal consent.[17]

If the *paterfamilias* refused without cause to give his consent for the marriage of his son or daughter the child had the legal right to appeal to the magistrate who had the authority to decide the issue. With the consent of the magistrate the child could validly marry even though the *paterfamilias* remained obstinate in his refusal to give his permission for the marriage.[18] If the father commanded an improper marriage, the child was not obligated in law to obey this mandate.[19] If the groom was no longer under the paternal authority but was *sui iuris* he did not need the consent of the *paterfamilias* in order to marry. The bride, however, was always under the paternal authority. If her father was dead she was subject to the authority of a guardian.

---

[14] D. (23. 2) 16. 1.
[15] D. (23. 2) 9 pr.
[16] D. (23. 2) 11.
[17] I. (1. 10) pr.; C. (5. 4) 25.
[18] D. (23. 2) 19.
[19] D. (23. 1) 12.

In theory this position of dependence of the woman was clearly demanded by the law but in practice it was not rigidly observed.[20]

When the *patriapotestas* of the father was extinguished the child became *sui juris*. But if the child was a grandson and his *paterfamilias* died the child did not immediately become *sui juris*, for he was now under the *potestas* of his father and his consent remained necessary for the validity of the child's marriage. Hence by the death of the *paterfamilias* only his immediate children became *sui juris*. The paternal power also ceased in other ways besides the death of the father. Thus the child became *sui juris* if his father emancipated him or if his father lost his status as a Roman citizen. In these instances the consent of the father was no longer needed for the marriage of his child.[21]

In the Roman Law puberty was the minimum age for marriage. The male must be *puber* and the female must be *viripotens* or of marriageable age before a marriage could be celebrated according to the law.[22] Justinian later determined the age of puberty as fourteen years in males and twelve in females.[23] If the parties were united before they reached those respective ages of fourteen years and twelve years the union became a legitimate marriage only after the spouses attained the necessary age.[24]

What was the attitude of the Church towards these Roman laws on the marriage of children? Because of the lack of adequate sources regarding the practice of the Church in the early centuries the question cannot be decided with sufficient certitude. Authors disagree. Esmein-Génestal seem to think that the Church accepted and followed faithfully the prescripts of the Roman Law in this matter.[25] Joyce, on the other hand, takes the opposite view. For he argues from the fact that Pope St. Callistus

---

[20] Cf. Burdick, *The Principles of Roman Law and Their Relation to Modern Law*, p. 216.

[21] Leage, *Roman Private Law*, pp. 94–96.

[22] I. (1. 10) pr.

[23] D. (23. 2) 4; I. (1. 22) pr.; C. (5. 60) 3.

[24] D. (23. 2) 4.

[25] "L'Eglise adopta tout d'abord ces principes sans difficulte et sans resistance, dans l'empire romain."—Esmein, *Le Mariage en Droit Canonique* (2. ed., 2 vols. [Vol. I rev. by R. Génestal, 1929; Vol. II rev. by R. Génestal and J. Dauvillier, 1935], Paris: Librairie de Recueil Sirey, 1929–1935), I, 169.

(218–223) permitted Christian marriages between free-women and slaves, a deed strictly forbidden by the civil law,[26] to the conclusion that the Church would have exhibited a similar independence regarding the law requiring parental consent.[27] However, the first opinion, which maintains that the Church conformed to the existing civil legislation, seems more likely in view of the teaching of Tertullian (d. 240–250 A. D.?)[28] and St. Basil the Great (d. 379).[29] Also earlier Church legislation decreed by various local councils made parental consent an essential requisite for the validity of the marriage of children.[30]

Article 2. In Germanic Law

In the fifth century the Church came into contact with the Germanic peoples. Their marriage law differed essentially from that of the Romans. For them consent was not the essential factor of marriage. Betrothal in Germanic law was the principal juridical element, and it was on this occasion that the parental authority intervened.[31] However, boys enjoyed more freedom under Germanic law than girls. A son on reaching puberty did not need the consent of the father in order to marry. The daughter, however, always remained subject to parental authority, and the consent of her father was needed for a *matrimonium plane legitimum*. If she married without such consent her marriage nevertheless was valid, but such a mode of action was punished severely.[32] Moreover, the Germanic law gave to the

[26] Hippolytus, *Philosophumena,* lib. IX, c. 12—Migne, *Patrologiae Cursus Completus, Series Graeca* (161 vols., Parisiis, 1856–1866), XVI, 3386. Henceforth this work will be cited *MPG.*

[27] Joyce, *Christian Marriage,* Heythrop Series: I (London and New York: Sheed and Ward, 1933), p. 71.

[28] *Ad Uxorem,* II, c. 8—Migne, *Patrologiae Cursus Completus, Series Latina* (221 vols., Parisiis, 1844–1864), I, 1302. Henceforth this work will be cited *MPL.*

[29] *Epist. 199 ad Amphilochium,* n. 42—*MPG,* XXXII, 730.

[30] I Council of Orleans (511), c. 2—*Monumenta Germaniae Historica, Concilia,* tom. I, *Concilia Aevi Merovingici* (ed. F. Maassen, Hannoverae, 1893), p. 3; IV Council of Orleans (541), c. 22—*ibid.,* p. 92; Council of Paris (556), c. 6—*ibid.,* p. 144.

[31] Esmein-Génestal, *Le Mariage en Droit Canonique,* I, 169.

[32] Cf. Wernz, *Ius Decretalium* (6 vols., Romae et Prati, 1898–1905), Vol. IV, *Ius Matrimoniale Ecclesiae Catholicae* (Romae, 1904), p. 482. Here-

parents the right to betroth validly a daughter against her will.[33]

The Church accepted the Germanic law regarding the marriage of boys, but reacted strongly against the legislation concerning girls. The Church forbade betrothal without the daughter's consent and, furthermore, if she was so betrothed she was free to disregard the contract.[34] However, in practice the civil laws were observed and their requirements for the validity of a marriage seem to have been followed entirely. This can be shown from a letter written by Bishop Atto of Vercelli, about 950 A. D., to a fellow Bishop;[35] also pope John VIII (872–882) in a letter to Emperor Louis II (850–875) stated: "What is done in defiance of the law may be set aside by the law," and stated that this principle ruled when marriage violated the civil law.[36]

Did the Classical Canon law accept and follow the Roman and Germanic laws regarding the necessity of parental consent for the marriages of children, or did it develop separately and proclaim its independence of the civil laws? The outcome will be shown in the following chapters of this historical synopsis: first, concerning Gratian and the doctrine of the Decretists; secondly, concerning the law of the Decretals together with the teaching of the Decretalists.

---

after this work will be cited *Ius Decretalium,* IV; Schröteler, *Das Elternrecht in der katholisch-theologischen Auseinandersetzung* (München: Neuer Filser-Verlag, 1936), p. 137. This work will hereafter be cited as *Das Elternrecht.*

[33] Dauvillier, *Le Mariage dans le Droit Classique de l'Eglise, depuis le Décret de Gratien (1140) jusq'a la mort de Clément V (1314)* (Paris: Recueil Sirey, 1933), p. 192. This work will hereafter be cited as *Le Mariage.*

[34] Joyce, *Christian Marriage,* pp. 51–52.

[35] Ep. ad Azonem (V): "Matrimonium enim est coniugium iusta conventio et condicio: eos vero qui nefario et exsecrabili coitu contra leges et mores permiscentur omnino separari oportet, quoniam nec vir nec uxor poterit esse in huiusmodi."—*MPL,* CXXXIV, 109.

[36] "Quod contra leges presumitur: per leges dissolvi meretur."—Ivo, *Decretum* IV, 179, and *Panormia,* II, 150; c. 10, D. X; Jaffé, *Regesta, Pontificum Romanorum* (ed. secundam et correctam et auctam auspiciis Gulielmi Wattenbach curaverunt Kaltenbrunner ad annum 590, Ewald 590–882, Löwenfeld 882–1198, Lipsiae, 1881) (henceforth JK, JE, JL will signify the authors of the several portions of this work), JE, n. 3011.

CHAPTER II

THE MARRIAGE OF MINORS FROM GRATIAN TO THE DECRETAL LEGISLATION

ARTICLE 1. THE MARRIAGE OF MINORS IN THE DECREE OF GRATIAN

Gratian frequently mentioned parental consent in relation to marriage,[1] but not with that clearness and preciseness one is accustomed to find in the *Decretum* of the Magister. It is not clear, therefore, whether Gratian required the consent of parents for the validity or merely for the licitness of the marriage. The question seems to admit of no certain solution. The core of the problem is simply this. If, on the one hand, it is admitted that Gratian in all cases required parental consent for the validity of the marriage, then how explain his clear teaching on the validity of clandestine marriages? Gratian without hesitancy or doubt affirmed that a clandestine union, though forbidden because of the difficulty in later proving that such a marriage actually took place, is nevertheless valid.[2] On the other hand, if it is stated that Gratian considered parental consent as an essential element not for the validity of the marriage but only for its licit celebration, then how explain his explicit teaching on *raptus?* If *raptus* had taken place, Gratian then demanded parental consent before a valid marriage could be celebrated.[3] An intermediate position on the part of Gratian appears, in the mind of the writer, to be more probable. With this position Gratian's teaching on clandestine marriage and *raptus* can be reconciled. Briefly his opinion seems to maintain that parental consent, except

[1] C. 33, D. 23; c. 1, 3, C. XXX, q. 5; c. 1, C. XXXI, q. 2; *Dict. Grat.* ad c. 4, C. XXXI, q. 2; c. un., C. XXXI, q. 3; cc. 12, 13, 14, 15, 16, C. XXXII, q. 2; c. un., C. XXXII, q. 3; c. 3, C. XXXVI, q. 1; cc. 2, 11, C. XXXVI, q. 2.

[2] C. 1, 3, C. XXX, q. 5; c. 17, C. XXVIII, q. 1.

[3] *Dict. Grat.* p. c. 11, C. XXXVI, q. 2; *Dict. Grat.* ad c. 7, C. XXXVI, q. 2.

in the case of *raptus,* is not required for the marriage to be *ratum,* that is to say valid, but that it serves simply to make the marriage *legitimum,* that is to say fully licit.[4]

As is usual in the second part of the *Decretum,* so also here in the thirty-first *Causa,* Gratian after positing a case proposed three questions for discussion in solving the case, two of which touched the subject of parental consent. He asked first of all whether a girl can be validly espoused by her parents without her consent; secondly, whether a girl validly espoused to someone by her parents can yet marry another person.[5] To the first question Gratian declared that a girl should never be forced to marry anyone against her will.[6] He answered the second question by stating that the betrothment binds both the parents and the daughter, but only if the girl has freely given her consent.[7]

Though Gratian maintained that the father cannot espouse his daughter without her consent, nevertheless he did not clearly state whether the girl is able to contract a valid marriage without parental consent, for the sense of the texts in Gratian which

[4] Köstler (*Die väterliche Ehebewilligung,* Ulrich Stutz' *Kirchenrechtliche Abhandlungen,* Heft 51 [Stuttgart: Verlag von Ferdinand Enke, 1908], pp. 106–107) defends this position, although Esmein-Génestal (*op. cit.,* p. 173, note 3) and Dauvillier (*Le Mariage,* p. 192, note 2) erroneously appeal to Köstler in defense of their opinion that Gratian in all cases required parental consent for the validity of the marriage. Also Mitterer (*Geschichte des Ehehindernisses der Entführung im kanonischen Recht seit Gratian,* Görres-Gesellschaft zur Pflege der Wissenschaft im katholischen Deutschland. Veröffentlichungen der Sektion für Rechts—und Sozialwissenschaft, Heft 43 [Paderborn, 1924], p. 32 [hereafter cited *Geschichte*]) incorrectly enumerates Köstler among those who consider that Gratian regarded parental consent as necessary in every case; Plöchl (*Das Eherecht des Magisters Gratianus,* [Leipzig: Franz Deuticke, 1935], p. 63) teaches the same doctrine as Köstler.

[5] C. XXXI: "Filiam . . . cuidam in coniugium se daturum promisit; illa assensum non praebuit; deinde pater alii eam tradidit; a primo repositur. Quaeritur . . . ; 2o an filia invita sit tradenda alicui; 3o an post patris sponsionem illa possit nubere alii."

[6] "Quod autem aliqua non sit cogenda nubere alicui": Gratian then offers four proofs and concludes with his *dictum* ad c. 4, C. XXXI, q. 2: "His auctoritatibus evidenter ostenditur, quod nisi libera voluntate nulla est copulanda alicui."

[7] *Dict. Grat.,* p. c. un., C. XXXI, q. 3.

touch this question is not clear.[8] Gratian considered the necessity of parental consent first of all in *c. 12, C. XXXII, q. 2.* In his *dictum* to this canon he affirmed that parental consent is a thing to be sought for in marriage, and without it the marriage is not legitimate. To confirm his statement he appealed to a letter supposed to have been sent to African bishops by Pope St. Evaristus (107 A. D.), which letter Gratian reproduced in *c. 1, C. XXX, q. 5,* but in reality it is a passage from Pseudo-Isidore (850).[9] Here the Pope is thought to have said that a *matrimonium legitimum* cannot otherwise be formed unless the woman is given in marriage by her parents.[10] Gratian continued the argumentation in *cc. 13, 14, 15,* of the same *causa* and question, and attempted to strengthen his former *dictum* with statements from St. Ambrose (ca. 340–397), the Book of Numbers of the Old Testament, and from St. Augustine (354–430). Not one of these canons helps to clarify the question of the necessity of parental consent.

Gratian again took up the question of parental permission in *c. un., C. XXXII, q. 3.* There he considered the case of a girl whose father is a church-slave, while her grandfather is a free man. Must the girl then receive the consent of the father, or of the grandfather, or of both? Gratian decided with a text from Pope Pelagius (555–560)[11] that the consent of the grandfather is to be sought.[12]

Now, those who hold that Gratian in all cases required the consent of parents for the validity of the marriage of their daughters enumerate the texts considered above among the arguments for their opinion.[13] However, these texts seem only to state that the marriage of a girl contracted without parental

---

[8] Cf. Mitterer, *Geschichte,* p. 32.

[9] JK, n. 19.

[10] *Dict. Grat.,* p. c. 12, C. XXXII, q. 2: "Cum dicitur: 'paterno arbitrio feminae iunctae viris,' datur intelligi quod paternus consensus desideratur in nuptiis, nec sine eo legitimae nuptiae habeantur, iuxta illud Evaristi Papae: 'Aliter non fit legitimum coniugium, nisi a parentibus tradatur.'"

[11] *Epist. incerti temporis (558–560)*—JK, n. 1004.

[12] *Dict. Grat.* p. c. un., C. XXXII, q. 3.

[13] Esmein-Génestal, *Le Mariage en Droit Canonique,* I, 173–174; Dauvillier, *Le Mariage,* p. 192.

consent is not a *matrimonium legitimum.* Nothing is stated there about the validity of the marriage.[14] The word *legitimum* means nothing more than fully licit, for when Gratian spoke about the validity of a marriage he used the word *ratum.*[15] Hence from *cc. 12 sq., C. XXXII, q. 2,* and *c. un., C. XXXII, q. 3,* the necessity of parental consent for the validity of the marriage cannot be conclusively proved.[16]

The Magister again mentioned parental consent when dealing with the question of *raptus.* In the thirty-sixth *Causa* Gratian posited this case for discussion. A certain youth gave a girl various gifts, and then invited her to dine with him. She accepted the invitation, and on the night of the dinner party he violated her. On hearing what had happened, the parents of the girl gave her in marriage to this same young man, who then publicly married her. Gratian proposed two questions for discussion, of which the second touched the question of the necessity of parental consent, namely, could the *raptor* marry the girl whom he violated if her father gave his consent.[17] Gratian, after having cited the authority of the Scriptures, of Conciliar legislation, and of the *dicta* of various Fathers, came directly to the point at issue and taught that the *raptor,* after he has performed the determined penance meted out for such a crime, may marry the girl whom he violated, unless the father of the girl forbade it.[18] Therefore under the point of view of *raptus,* and only for

[14] Plöchl, *Das Eherecht des Magisters Gratianus,* p. 63.

[15] *Dict. Grat.* ad c. 17, C. XXVIII, q. 1: "Legitimum coniugium est quod legali institutione vel provinciae moribus contrahitur . . . [Matrimoniorum ratorum] quaedam sunt legitima, veluti cum uxor a parentibus traditur, a sponso dotatur, et a sacerdote benedicitur. Haec talia coniugia legitima et rata appellantur. Illorum vero coniugia, qui contemptis omnibus solemnitatibus solo affectu aliquam sibi in coniugem copulant, huiuscemodi coniugium non legitimum, sed ratum tantummodo esse creditur." Mitterer (*Geschichte,* p. 32) upholds this distinction between "*ratum*" and "*legitimum*" as occurring in the *Decretum* of Gratian. Esmein-Génestal (*Le Mariage en Droit Canonique,* I, 173, note 3) seem to reject it.

[16] Cf. Mitterer, *Geschichte,* pp. 32–34; Köstler, *Die väterliche Ehebewilligung,* pp. 107–109.

[17] C. XXXVI: ". . . Quaeritur primo, an ille raptum admiserit. Quaeritur secundo, an rapta raptori nubere possit, patre assensum praestante."

[18] *Dict. Grat.* p. c. 11, C. XXXVI, q. 2: ". . . post peractam poenitentiam

the girl, did Gratian demand parental consent for the validity of the marriage.[19]

With this concludes the teaching of Gratian concerning the necessity of parental consent. Whether Gratian required the consent of the parents for the validity of the marriage, or whether he considered it necessary only that a marriage be licit remains doubtful. Strong arguments are present for either side of the controversy. The opinion of the writer, however, is that parental consent was not required by him in every case for the validity of the marriage (*matrimonium ratum*), but only that a marriage be licit (*matrimonium legitimum*). However, in the case of *raptus* a *matrimonium ratum* was impossible without parental consent. It may be remarked that arguments drawn from the *palea* appended to *c. 11, C. XXXVI, q. 2,* which relates Roman law texts demanding parental consent for the validity of the marriage in all cases,[20] cannot be used as a valid argument to demonstrate the thought of Gratian.[21] The reason is simply that these arguments are found in a *palea,* and therefore indicate something added to the *Decretum* beyond the personal writing of Gratian. However, they do indicate that even after Gratian later glossators judged parental consent as necessary for a valid marriage.[22]

Paucapalea, the first disciple of Gratian and the earliest glossator of the *Decretum,* in his *Summa* (1145–1148) followed closely the doctrine of the Magister. However, it is probable that Paucapalea demanded in every case parental consent for the validity of the marriage.[23] The *palea,* consisting of Roman

---

raptor poterit sibi copulare quam rapuit, nisi pater puellae illam raptori detrahere voluerit." Cf. *Dict. Grat.* p. c. 7, C. XXXVI, q. 2.

19 Plöchl, *Das Eherecht des Magisters Gratianus,* p. 63; Mitterer, *Geschichte,* pp. 32–35; Freisen, *Geschichte des canonischen Eherechts bis zum Verfall der Glossenlitteratur* (2. ed., Paderborn: Druck und Verlag von Ferdinand Schöningh, 1893), p. 316. This work will hereafter be cited as *Geschichte des canonischen Eherechts.*

20 C. (5. 4) 12; C. (5. 4) 20; D. (23. 2) 2; I. (1. 10) pr.

21 Esmein-Génestal (*Le Mariage en Droit Canonique,* I, 174), on the contrary, take the opposite view.

22 Köstler, *Die väterliche Ehebewilligung,* p. 111.

23 Dauvillier, *Le Mariage,* p. 193.

law texts, added by him after *c. 11, C. XXXVI, q. 2,* seems to indicate his views on the matter. Again, speaking of matrimonial consent, he stated that it must be "*licitus*" and "*manifestus,*" and in a new and separate sentence added that it must come about with the permission of the parents.[24] Thus from the sentence structure it would seem that he gave these words an added importance, so that one could suppose that the consent of the parents must always be present.[25] Paucapalea made special application of the necessity of parental consent in the marriages of girls. For in solving the case Gratian placed in *C. XXXII, q. 3,* (as to whether the girl was to seek the parental consent for marriage from her father who was a church-slave, or from her grandfather who was a free man) Paucapalea differed from Gratian and Pope Pelagius in demanding also the consent of the unliberated father.[26] On the question of the necessity of parental consent after *raptus* Paucapalea taught the same doctrine as Gratian.[27]

Article 2. Change in the Doctrine Effected by the Teachings of the School at Paris

This strict doctrine, however, was short-lived, for a change was brought about with the succeeding Decretists. Roland Bandinelli, Rufinus, and others clarified the doctrine and mitigated its severity as proposed by Gratian and Paucapalea, so that in no case was parental consent regarded essential for the validity of the marriage.[28] To understand this change in doctrine it is necessary to go beyond the *Corpus Iuris Canonici* and to seek

---

[24] Paucapalea ad C. XXVII, q. 2, ad vb. *consensus:* "Efficiens causa matrimonii est consensus. Consensus autem debet esse licitus et manifestus . . . ET CUM PARENTUM VOLUNTATE fieri debet."—Cited from Esmein-Génestal, *Le Mariage,* I, 174, n. 3. (Source is not available to the writer.)

[25] Köstler, *Die väterliche Ehebewilligung,* p. 112.

[26] ". . . Ergo magis est in nuptiis inquirendus paternus consensus quam avi, cum sine paterno arbitrio nuptiae non habeantur. . . . Auctoritas illa Pelagii, scilicet patrem puellae . . . loquitur de famulo et non de originario servo."—Cited from Esmein-Génestal, *Le Mariage,* I, 174–175, n. 4.

[27] Cf. Köstler, *Die väterliche Ehebewilligung,* p. 111.

[28] Dauvillier, *Le Mariage,* p. 193.

the causes for such a change in the rapid growth and development of theology during this period.

The doctrinal change was brought about by the teachings of the Theologians at Paris. The great dispute between the Schools of Bologna and of Paris concerning the essence of marriage touched also the question of parental consent. The School of Bologna held that a carnal union was requisite for the full constitution of marriage, while the French school taught that consent alone was sufficient. Thus the French Theologians developed and clarified the consent theory, and in so doing expressly stated that the consent of the contracting parties alone effected the marriage, thereby eliminating as an essential requisite the consent of the parents. Moreover, the Scholastic doctrine of the Sacraments was being developed at this time. As regards the Sacraments theologians taught that no one, when qualified, should be denied the Sacraments and, at the same time, that no one could be forced to receive a Sacrament. The will of the recipient had to be absolutely free. Now, marriage was a Sacrament, and hence the whole theology of the Sacraments concerning *consensus liber,* matter and form was applied to it.[29]

The leading figure of the French School was Peter Lombard (d. 1160). In his treatment of marriage in his *Book of the Sentences* he was the first who clearly taught that the consent of parents was never an essential requisite for a valid marriage. To obtain parental permission was desirable and praiseworthy, and, if possible, it was to be present, but it was in no way necessary for the validity of the marriage. The mutual consent of the parties themselves effected the marriage.[30]

---

[29] Dauvillier, *Le Mariage,* p. 193.

[30] Sententiae, IV, d. XXVIII, 1, 2: "Illi etiam sententiae, qua dictum est, solum consensum facere coniugium, videtur contradicere quod Evaristus Papa ait: Aliter coniugium legitimum non fit, nisi ab eis, qui super feminam dominationem habere videntur, et a quibus custoditur, uxor petatur et a parentibus sponsetur. . . . Hoc autem non ita intelligendum est, tamquam sine enumeratis non possit esse legitimum coniugium, sed quia sine illis non habet decorem et honestatem debitam. In huius enim Sacramenti celebratione, sicut in aliis, quaedam sunt pertinentia ad substantiam Sacramenti, ut consensus de praesenti, qui solus sufficit ad contrahendum matrimonium; quaedam vero pertinentia ad decorem et solemnitatem

Two other factors—one acting directly, the other indirectly—helped to eliminate the further continuance of the doctrine which pointed to the necessity of parental consent. The direct factor was Lombard's distinction between betrothal and marriage, that is, *consensus per verba de praesenti* and *consensus per verba de futuro. Verba de praesenti* constituted marriage, while *verba de futuro* did not.[31] The other factor, acting indirectly, was the historical fact that the consent of the parents according to popular custom was exercised at the time of the *desponsatio,* and not at the time of the actual marriage.[32] This was true because during the Middle Ages marriages were looked upon as alliances of families, and through them peace and concord was to be established and maintained. Hence to attain this objective they had to take place when the parties espoused were still at an early age.[33] Now this *desponsatio* bound both the children and the parents.[34] When the time had come for the promise to be fulfilled, the parents did not give a new consent, for the consent previously given sufficed for the mere execution of the contract.

The interplay of these two factors effected the following result. By the distinction between *sponsalia de praesenti* and *sponsalia de futuro* the harmony which had previously existed in the popular procedure was shattered. The contract of marriage now became separated and could exist independently of the *sponsalia de futuro.* The two became separate juridical institutes. Now, since the tradition and practice had been for the parental consent

---

Sacramenti, ut parentum traditio, sacerdotum benedictio, et huiusmodi; sine quibus legitime fit coniugium, quantum ad virtutem, non quantum ad honestatem sacramenti."—*Petri Lombardi Libri IV Sententiarum studia et cura PP. Collegii S. Bonaventurae in lucem editi* (2. ed., 2 vols., Ad Claras Aquas: Typographia Collegii S. Bonaventurae, 1916), II, 926–927; hereafter this work will be cited as *Petri Lombardi Libri IV Sententiarum.*

[31] Sententiae, IV, d. XXVII, 3, 7: "Efficiens autem causa matrimonii est consensus, non quilibet, sed per verba expressus, nec de futuro sed de praesenti. . . . Est et desponsatio habens consensum de praesenti, id est pactionem coniugalem, quae sola facit coniugium."—*Petri Lombardi Libri IV Sententiarum,* II, 917, 921.

[32] Dauvillier, *Le Mariage,* p. 193.

[33] C. 2, X, *de desponsatione impuberum,* IV, 2; c. 1, C. XXX, q. 2.

[34] *Dict. Grat.* p. c. un., C. XXXI, q. 3.

to intervene at the time of the *sponsalia de futuro,* the conclusion was manifest that, since marriage could exist without the *sponsalia de futuro,* it could also be valid without the consent of the parents.[35]

ARTICLE 3. COMMENTARIES AND GLOSS ON THE DECREE OF GRATIAN

The change and development of the doctrine effected by the theologians of the School of Paris is evident in the writings of the subsequent Decretists. They took up the consent theory of marriage, and hurried to interpret the *Decretum* in the light of this new doctrine.

Among the Decretists Roland Bandinelli (d. 1181) was the first to note the change in the doctrine. Between 1150–1158 Roland wrote the *Sententiae* in which he clearly taught that the mutual consent of the contracting parties constituted the essence of marriage.[36] The thought of Roland should be noted well, for he was later destined to wear the Fisherman's Ring as Alexander III (1159–1181), and thereby was able to give this doctrine the force of law.

In his *Stroma* (ca. 1148) Roland commented on the *dictum* of Gratian to *c. 12, C. XXXII, q. 2* and therein he clearly taught that parental consent was in no way necessary for a valid marriage. True, it was an element that should be present, for it pertained to the licit celebration of the marriage. However, if for some reason it was lacking, the marriage was nevertheless valid.[37] Concerning the question of *raptus,* Roland denied the impediment of *raptus in parentes* as proposed by Gratian and Paucapalea,[38] and stated that if the girl was abducted in view

[35] Bernard, *Étude Historique et Critique sur le Consentement des Ascendants au Mariage* (Paris: Librairie de la Société de Recueil Général des Lois et des Arrêts, 1899), pp. 89–90; Freisen, *Geschichte des Canonischen Eherechts,* p. 317.

[36] Joyce, *Christian Marriage,* p. 63.

[37] "Quod hic dicitur, non usque adeo necessarium est ut, si non sit ibi consensus parentum, non sit matrimonium: sed ad verecundiorem honestatem coniugii paternum consensum expedit inquiri."—Cited from Esmein-Génestal, *Le Mariage en Droit Canonique,* I, 175, n. 1. (Source is not available to the writer.)

[38] Cf. *supra,* pp. 12–14.

of marriage and freely consented, even though the parents were unwilling, the marriage was valid.[39]

Rufinus (d. ca. 1190) in his *Summa* (1157–1159) followed the doctrine of Roland. He upheld the validity of clandestine marriages as did Roland and Gratian before him. For him a clandestine marriage was one that lacked one or all of the various solemnities, among which was parental permission. The contracting of such a marriage was forbidden; if, however, contrary to the laws of the Church it was contracted, its validity was certain, for it was recognized that the consent of the contracting parties alone effected the marriage.[40] In his explanation of Gratian's *dictum post c. 12, C. XXXII, q. 2* Rufinus used the same words as Roland did in his *Summa,* and hence stated that parental consent was not necessary for the validity of the marriage.[41] In his treatment of *raptus* Rufinus was explicit when he stated that a girl who was abducted against the will of her parents could nevertheless contract a valid marriage with her abductor without the consent of her parents, provided that she was otherwise capable of marrying, that the abduction took place with a view to marriage, and that she freely gave her consent.[42] Hence, for such a case Rufinus stated that there was no impediment of *raptus in parentes,* and therefore the marriage was to be regarded as valid.

In his *Summa* (c. 1160) Stephen of Tournai (d. 1203) followed and developed the doctrine of Roland and Rufinus. In commenting on *c. 2, C. XXVII, q. 2* [43] which reports the letter of Pope Nicholas I to the Bulgarian Christians,[44] Stephen taught

[39] Rolandus, ad c. 32, C. XXVII, q. 2, ad vb. *raptus*—Cited from Köstler, *Die väterliche Ehebewilligung,* pp. 118–119.

[40] *Summa Decretorum* (ed. Singer, Paderborn, 1902), c. 1, C. XXX, q. 5, ad vb. *quod autem.*

[41] *Summa Decretorum, dict. Grat.* p. c. 12, C. XXXII, q. 2, ad vb. *cum dicitur: paterno arbitrio.*

[42] *Summa Decretorum, dict. Grat.* p. c. 3, C. XXXVI, q. 1, ad vb. *vis infertur.*

[43] "Sufficiat secundum leges solus consensus eorum, de quorum coniunctionibus agitur. Qui consensus si in nuptiis solus forte defuerit, cetera omnia etiam cum ipso coitu celebrata frustrantur."

[44] Nicolas Papa ad consulta Bulgarorum: a. 866—Mansi, *Sacrorum Conciliorum Nova et Amplissima Collectio* (53 vols. in 60, Parisiis, 1901–1927), Vol. XV, 403, c. 3. This work will hereafter be cited as Mansi.

that, even though paternal consent for the marriage was demanded by the civil laws, the law of the Church declared otherwise. He likewise stated that the solemnities were not required for the validity of the marriage.[45] Its validity depended on the free consent of the contracting parties alone.[46] Concerning the question of *raptus* Stephen stated that personal consent was not necessary for the validity of the marriage if the girl was of age and freely gave her consent.[47]

The Magister Simon de Bisiniano reaffirmed in his *Summa* (1177–1179) the doctrine of his contemporaries, and expressly declared that parental consent, according to ecclesiastical law, was not necessary, even though Roman civil law demanded such consent for the validity of the marriage.[48]

Sicard of Cremona (d. 1215) in his *Summa* (1179–1181) distinguished between the *causa operans* and the *causa cöoperans* of the Sacrament of Matrimony. He designated the free consent of the will of the parties as the *causa operans,* while he regarded the parental consent merely as a *causa cöoperans* or a solemnity.[49] The will of the parties had to be entirely free; no force from the outside could be brought to bear on it. Hence parental permission as an essential requisite for the validity of the marriage was to be excluded.[50] Sicard in discussing the necessity of

---

[45] Stephanus ad c. 2, C. XXVII, q. 2, ad vb. *sufficiat solus:* "Solus dicit ad remotionem consensus patris, sine quo secundum leges, si filius est in potestate, non erit ratum matrimonium eius; vel excludit solemnitates, quae requiruntur in coniugio, et non pactionem coniugalem. Nam substantiam quidem sacramenti non solemnitates faciunt, sed consensus de praesenti expressus secundum leges ecclesiasticas, nam matrimonia reguntur hodie iure poli, non iure fori."—Cited from Köstler, *Die väterliche Ehebewilligung,* p. 121, n. 1. (Source is not available to the writer.)

[46] Köstler, *op. cit.,* p. 121, n. 2.

[47] Köstler, *op. cit.,* pp. 121–122.

[48] "Secundum leges subaudi canonicas, quae solum contrahentium consensum esse necessarium dicunt, non secundum romanas leges, quae parentum consensum valde necessarium exigunt et requirunt."—Cited from Köstler, *op. cit.,* p. 124, n. 2. (Source is not available to the writer.)

[49] Cf. Sicardus ad C. XXVII, ad vb. *cooperans*—Cited from Köstler, *op. cit.,* p. 124, n. 5. (Source is not available to the writer.)

[50] Sicardus ad C. XXVII, ad vb. *operans ut consensus.*—Cited from Köstler, *op. cit.,* p. 125, n. 1.

parental consent after the girl had been abducted against the will of her parents followed the doctrine of the preceding Decretists. In explaining the words of Gratian about the right of the father to forbid his daughter to marry her abductor,[51] Sicard maintained that this was to be understood for the case of a girl who was not yet of age, or of one who was of age but who refused to marry her abductor.[52]

With Huguccio (d. 1210), who completed his great *Summa* between 1188–1190, the period of the early Decretists came to an end. His work was a complete summary of this period and his opinions received added importance, since many of them were later given the force of law by his pupil Lotario de' Conti, who became Pope Innocent III (1198–1216).

Huguccio insisted that the consent of the contracting parties alone effected the marriage, and that neither for the engagement nor for the marriage was parental consent necessary.[53] In considering the necessity of parental consent after *raptus,* he presented the same teaching as the other Decretists. If the girl was *nubilis* and freely gave her consent, the marriage could take place, even though the father of the girl was decidedly opposed to it.[54] Thus Huguccio, together with Roland, Rufinus, Stephen and others, rejected the necessity of parental consent for the validity of the marriage. Nothing more remains to be considered but the *Glossia Ordinaria* to the *Decretum.*

---

[51] *Dict. Grat.* p. c. 11, C. XXXVI, q. 2.

[52] Sicardus ad C. XXXVI, ad vb. *Nam vis.*—Cited from Köstler, *op. cit.,* p. 125, n. 4.

[53] Huguccio ad c. 2, C. XXVII, q. 2, ad vb. *aliter:* "Notandum, quod in sponsalibus contrahendis unum solum exigitur, scilicet consensus utriusque. . . . Secundum leges humanas consensus patris exigitur, sed non secundum divinas. Honestum est, ut intersit et adhibeatur, sed non exigitur . . . et in hoc canones prevalent, cum hodie matrimonium tractetur iure poli et non iure fori."—Cited from Köstler, *op. cit.,* p. 128, n. 3. (Source is not available to the writer.)

[54] Huguccio ad *dictum Grat.* p. c. 3, C. XXXVI, q. 1, ad vb. *ex hac:* "Si autem est nubilis et tunc vel post consensit in matrimonium, non est reddenda, quia matrimonium est inter eos et tenet, licet forte patri puelle sit molestum et displiceat. Et in quocumque (casu) non est reddenda, non iudicatur ille tamquam raptor nisi forte, ubi illa non consensit in matrimonium."—Cited from Köstler, *op. cit.,* p. 129, n. 6.

The *Glossia Ordinaria* stated that parental consent was in no way necessary for the validity of the marriage.[55] Indeed, children were to seek their parents' permission, since it was a duty which they owed to their parents, but if parental consent was lacking the marriage was nevertheless surely valid.[56] No one could be forced to marry against his will.[57] Moreover, the Gloss interpreted the words *legitimae nuptiae* simply as a marriage contracted with all the solemnities. There was no question about its validity.[58] With regard to marriage those who had reached the age of puberty, which was fourteen years for the boy and twelve for the girl, *nisi malitia suppleat aetatem,* were exempt from the authority of the father.[59] Therefore, according to ecclesiastical law, parental consent was not required for the validity of the marriage, even though for entering marriage the child was to ask his parents' permission. It was to be sought, then, out of decency and not through necessity.[60] In considering the question raised by Gratian, whether a girl should receive the consent of her slave father or her free grandfather, the Gloss decided that the consent was to be asked of the grandfather, inasmuch as the father, since he was not free, had no power over his daughter. But the Gloss significantly added that this consent of the parents or the guardians was never required for the validity

---

[55] *Glossa Ordinaria* ad c. 1, C. XXX, q. 5, ad vb. *Quod autem.*

[56] *Glossa Ordinaria* ad c. 2, C. XXVII, q. 2, ad vb. *solus:* "Consensus parentum an sit in matrimonio requirendus? Sed haec dictio, 'solus,' non excludit consensum parentum immo tantum alias solemnitates quae fiunt circa matrimonium quasi dicat solus eorum consensus est causa effectiva matrimonii, et ideo non sunt contrariae leges illae in Cod. *de Nupt.* L. *nec filium,* ff. *de rit. nupt.* L. *Nuptiae* (C. [5. 4] 12; D. [23. 2] 2) quae dicunt, quod in matrimonio requiritur consensus parentum. Sed dic quod requiritur ex honestate, non ex necessitate, 30, q. 5 'nostrantes'; hoc tamen ad honestatem referas."

[57] *Glossa Ordinaria* ad C. XXXI, q. 2, ad vb. *Quod.*

[58] *Glossa Ordinaria* ad c. 12, C. XXXII, q. 2, ad vb. *legitima.*

[59] *Glossa Ordinaria* ad c. 14, C. XXXII, q. 2, ad vb. *pater.*

[60] *Glossa Ordinaria* ad c. 16, C. XXXII, q. 2, ad vb. *parentum:* "Secundum canones licet filiae praeter voluntatem parentum nubere. Unde nec est necessaria patris voluntas quantum ad hoc, quin teneat matrimonium, licet non adsit voluntas eius. Alias bene dico requirendum eius consensum, maxime si est minor. . . . Hoc de honestate dictum est, non de necessitate."

of the marriage.[61] Concerning the necessity of parental consent after *raptus* the Gloss disposed of the matter in the same manner as Huguccio and the other Decretists.[62]

---

[61] *Glossa Ordinaria* ad c. un., C. XXXII, q. 3, ad vb. *De tertia,* et ad vb. *avi magis.*

[62] *Glossa Ordinaria* ad *dictum Grat.* p. c. 3, C. XXXVI, q. 1; *Glossa Ordinaria* ad *dictum Grat.* p. c. 11, C. XXXVI, q. 2, ad vb. *auctoritas.*

CHAPTER III

THE MARRIAGE OF MINORS FROM THE TIME OF THE DECRETALS TO THE COUNCIL OF TRENT

Article 1. The Law of the Decretals and the Teaching of the Decretalists

From the previous chapter it is manifest that the doctrine regarding the necessity of parental consent for the marriage of minors underwent an essential change in the writings of the Decretists. But as yet this change had occurred only in the doctrine of the Schools without obtaining the authentic force of law. It now remains to examine the status of this doctrine in the Decretals and to note its explanation in the teachings of the Decretalists.

At the very outset let it be stated that as part of the *Corpus Iuris Canonici* no pope ever issued a decretal which *ex professo* decided the extent of the necessity of parental consent. However, many decretals indirectly rejected the notion that parental permission was required for the validity of the marriage. Hence, for the most part, the arguments brought forward from the decretals will of necessity be indirect.

The letter of Pope Adrian IV (1154–1159) to the Bishop of Salzburg offers the first argument against the necessity of parental consent. Here the pope declared that the permission of the lord was not requisite for the marriage of his slaves. Indeed, Pope Adrian stated that a slave could marry validly even against the will of his master.[1] Therefore it seems that children could also marry without the consent of their parents, since the power of a parent over them was far less than the power which a master enjoyed over his slaves. Indeed, the reason given by Pope Adrian for his decision applied equally well to the question of children,

[1] C. 1, X, *de coniugio servorum,* IV, 9; JL, n. 10445.

for he stated that none of the faithful should be excluded from matrimony, since it is a Sacrament. Concerning the marriages of slaves Bernard of Pavia (d. 1213) noted (c. 1173–1179) that such marriages held good *novo iure,* for the consent of the contracting parties was sufficient to constitute marriage.[2]

Pope Alexander III (1159–1181) indirectly helped to clarify the question regarding the necessity of parental consent by giving to the consent theory of marriage the force of law. For, when the Archbishop of Salerno asked if a woman might marry a second man when to the first she had given a marital consent *per verba de praesenti,* though no sanction of an oath had been attached to the promise, and the union furthermore had remained unconsummated, the Pope replied: "If a lawful consent *de praesenti* has been exchanged between a man and a woman (with the formalities which are usually observed, namely, in the presence of a priest, or even of a notary as is also the custom in certain parts) . . . it is not lawful for the woman to marry a second man, and if she should have married him, even though this second union be consummated, she must be separated from him, and compelled by the threat of ecclesiastical censures to return to the first, even though the contrary opinion is maintained in some quarters, and likewise some judgments to the contrary have been given by some of our predecessors."[3] Again in a letter to the Bishop of Pavia Alexander III stressed the truth that marriage is effected by the free consent of the contracting parties alone.[4] Here the Gloss concludes that other elements, such as parental consent, the blessing of the priest, and the veiling, are to be counted only as solemnities which do not touch the substance of the marriage.[5] Therefore, since the consent given by the parties in marriage must be absolutely free, Hostiensis (d. 1271) taught that children are not bound to follow

---

[2] *Bernardi Papiensis Summa Decretalium* (ed. E. A. T. Laspeyres, Ratisbonae, 1860), p. 395, § 6: *de conditione.*

[3] C. 3, X, *de sponsa duorum,* IV, 4; JL, n. 14091.

[4] C. 14, X, *de sponsalibus et matrimoniis,* IV, 1; JL, n. 9866.

[5] *Glossa Ordinaria* ad c. 14, X, *de sponsalibus et matrimoniis,* IV, 1, ad vb. *solo consensu.*

the will of their parents.[6] In commenting on this decretal letter of Alexander to the Bishop of Pavia, Panormitanus (d. 1453) clearly stated that the consent of the contracting parties alone was sufficient for the essence of the marriage.[7] He presented the same doctrine in other places.[8] In still another pasage Panormitanus stated explicitly that parental consent was not required in order that the marriage be valid.[9] From his teaching on the decretal of Pope Alexander to the Bishop of Pavia [10] it is evident that a girl could contract a valid marriage without parental permission. And he further stated that if such a case happens, and her parents abuse her on this account, then the ecclesiastical judge should remove the girl from the parents' home and take her to a safe place.[11]

Lucius III (1181–1185), in deciding a case sent to Rome, indirectly rejected the notion that parental consent was necessary for a valid marriage. The case involved a soldier who wished to marry. The parents of the girl involved were opposed to such a union and so refused to give their permission. The couple, however, went off to be married, and the marriage thereupon was consummated. After some time the girl without the soldier's permission entered a convent. He then demanded that

---

[6] *Summa Aurea* (Venetiis, 1570), lib. IV, tit. *de sponsa duorum,* p. 300, § 7: "Filii non tenentur sequi voluntatem parentum in matrimoniis contrahendis."

[7] *Commentaria in Quinque Libros Decretalium* (5 vols. in 7, Venetiis, 1588), lib. IV, *de sponsalibus et matrimoniis,* c. 14—tom. VII, p. 10, § 3. This work will hereafter be cited as *Commentaria.*

[8] *Commentaria,* lib. IV, *de sponsa duorum,* c. 3—tom. VII, p. 29, § 4; *Commentaria,* lib. IV, *de sponsalibus et matrimoniis,* c. 1—tom. VII, p. 3, §§ 1, 3, 4; also lib. IV, *de clandestina desponsatione,* c. 1—tom. VII, p. 27, § 2.

[9] *Commentaria,* lib. IV, *De sponsalibus et matrimoniis,* c. 10—tom. VII, p. 7, § 2: "Nota ibi, consentiente patre, quia filia non contrahit etiam sponsalia, nisi patre consentiente, quod intellige de honestate (C. XXXII, q. 2 'honoratur'). Sed ad substantiam matrimonii seu sponsaliorum non requiritur parentum consensus, ut in C. XXVII, q. 2: 'sufficiat.'" Cf. also *Commentaria,* lib. IV, *de desponsatione impuberum,* c. 1—tom. VII, p. 21, § 4.

[10] C. 14, *X, de sponsalibus et matrimoniis,* IV, 1.

[11] *Commentaria,* lib. IV, *de sponsalibus et matrimoniis,* c. 14—tom. VII, p. 10, § 5.

she return to him, since she was his wife. She, however, protested and claimed she was not his wife, inasmuch as he had abducted her, and an abductor was not able to contract marriage with the one he abducted. The Pope decided the case by saying that there was no *raptus* here, since the girl had freely given her consent, and that after the consummation of the marriage she was unauthorized to embrace the religious life as long as her husband was unwilling.[12] Thus, from the case and the solution given, it was clear that the lack of parental consent did not invalidate the marriage. The Gloss here noted that parental dissent does not touch the validity of the marriage.[13] Hostiensis likewise taught the same doctrine.[14] And in this connection Panormitanus enunciated the principle that children are not under parental authority in spiritual things.[15]

That parental consent was not regarded as an essential requisite for a valid marriage is evident also from a letter of Pope Urban III (1185–1187) in 1186.[16] In this letter there was question of a boy and a girl who entered marriage under the condition, namely, "si pater eius suum praestaret assensum." In his response Pope Urban mentioned that such a condition was *honesta* and in no

---

[12] C. 6, X, *de raptoribus et incendiariis, et violatoribus ecclesiarum,* V, 17. This decretal is also found in c. 4, Comp. I, *de raptoribus et incendiariis, et violatoribus ecclesiarum,* V, 14; JL, n. 15184. (The exact date and the identity of the Bishop to whom the decretal was addressed are uncertain.)

[13] *Glossa Ordinaria* ad c. 6, X, *de raptoribus et incendiariis, et violatoribus ecclesiarum,* V, 17, ad vb. *parentes reclamarent.*

[14] *Commentaria in Quinque Libros Decretalium* (5 vols. in 3, Venetiis, 1581), lib. V, *de raptoribus et incendiariis, et violatoribus ecclesiarum,* c. 6, ad vb. *reclamaret:* "Talis reclamatio non impedit matrimonium, quia secundum canones solus consensus contrahentium exigitur et spectatur." This work will hereafter be cited as *Commentaria.* Cf. also *Summa Aurea,* lib. V, tit. *de raptoribus,* p. 366, § 1.

[15] *Commentaria,* lib. V, *de raptoribus, incendiariis, et violatoribus ecclesiarum,* c. 6—tom. VII, p. 226, § 4; also lib. IV, *de desponsatione impuberum,* c. 1—tom. VII, p. 21, § 5; and lib. IV, *de sponsalibus et matrimoniis,* c. 11—tom. VII, p. 8, §§ 1, 2.

[16] C. 5, X, *de conditionibus appositis in desponsatione vel in aliis contractibus,* IV, 5. This decretal is found also in c. 4, Compilatio I, *h.t.,* IV, 5. JL, n. 15729.

way forbidden by law. Now, the very fact that parental permission could be made a condition by the contracting parties demonstrated that it was legally unessential. For, if parental consent was placed as a condition for marriage, it followed that it was extrinsic to the requirements set by law for the validity. A *conditio honesta* of its very nature had to be dependent on the will of the contracting parties and consequently could not be one of the essential elements required by law.[17] If an essential requisite were made a condition it would not suspend the validity of the marriage, but the marriage would be valid or invalid from the very beginning, and that independently of the will of the contracting parties. The fact that the parties themselves could place parental consent as a condition to marriage shows that in law such a permission was unessential for the validity of the marriage in question.

That parental consent could be made a condition, and hence was regarded as an unessential element in marriage, can be further established from a letter of Pope Innocent III (1198–1216) in 1203, in which he decided a case brought to Rome for a solution.[18] The case concerned a man designated N. and a woman designated P., who exchanged consent *per verba de praesenti* under the condition that the father of the man would consent to the marriage. Later there was a carnal intercourse. The man, however, refused to take the woman as his wife, asserting that his father had refused to give his permission, and that in consequence the condition remained unfulfilled. The Pope nevertheless decided for the validity of the marriage, since inasmuch as a carnal union had followed, "*videtur a conditione opposita recessisse.*" Thus paternal consent was not regarded as necessary for the validity of the marriage.

---

[17] Hostiensis, *Summa Aurea,* lib. IV, tit., *de conditionibus appositis in desponsatione vel aliis contractis,* p. 301, § 12, *quae conditio in sponsalibus.*

[18] C. 6, X, *de conditionibus appositis in desponsatione vel in aliis contractibus,* IV, 5. This decretal is found also as c. 4, Compilatio I, *h.t.,* IV, 5. Cf. also Potthast, *Regesta Pontificum Romanorum, inde ab anno post Christum natum MCXCVIII ad MCCCIV* (2 vols. in 1, Berolini: Rudolphi De Decker, 1874–1875), n. 1968. Hereafter this work will be cited Potthast.

Hostiensis, in commenting on the permission of the parents as being made a condition in marriage, taught that even though the civil law required the consent of the parents for the validity of the marriage, Canon law did not, and in this point the Canon law was to be observed.[19]

Joannes Andreae (d. 1348) taught the same doctrine as Hostiensis.[20]

Innocent III in 1198, the first year of his pontificate, sent a letter to the Archbishop of Arles, in which he declared that everyone who was not expressly prohibited by law could marry, and only the consent of the contracting parties was necessary.[21] The Gloss added that all are admitted who are not expressly prohibited.[22] Now, the law did not expressly prohibit children from marrying without the consent of their parents, for such a prohibition was not found in any decretal. Also the Decretalists enumerated the impediments which prohibited one from contracting a valid marriage, yet among these impediments lack of parental consent was not expressly mentioned. Bernard of Pavia in his *Summa Decretalium* (c. 1191–1198) enumerated fourteen impediments, but lack of parental permission was not listed.[23] Also St. Raymond of Pennafort (d. 1275), when commenting in his *Summa* (1222–1230) on the words "*nisi expresse prohibeatur,*" as used by Pope Innocent in the decretal mentioned above, stated that, since the law about contracting marriage is

---

[19] *Commentaria,* lib. IV, *de conditionibus appositis,* c. 5, ad vb. *non improbent.*

[20] *In Sex Decretalium Libros Novella Commentaria* (6 vols. in 5, Venetiis, 1581), lib. IV, tit. V, *de conditionibus appositis,* ad vb. *leges:* ". . . leges in tantum hoc requirunt, quod volunt matrimonium aliter non valere, nisi parentes consentiant; sed canones hoc requirunt de honestate."

[21] C. 23, X, *de sponsalibus et matrimoniis,* IV, 1; Potthast, n. 329.

[22] *Glossa Ordinaria* ad c. 23, X, *de sponsalibus et matrimoniis,* IV, 1, ad vb. *prohibitorium:* "Unde omnes admittuntur, qui non expresse prohibentur: et id quod non prohibetur concessum videtur."

[23] "Sunt autem quae impediunt matrimonium XIV: votum, ordo, habitus, dispar cultus, error personae, conditio, cognatio, ligatio, enormitas delicti, impossibilitas coeundi, coactio, causa publicae honestatis, tempus feriarum et ecclesiae interdictum."—*Summa Decretalium,* IV, 1, § 6, p. 131. (In the Appendix to this edition there is given *Bernardi Summa de Matrimonio,* and on p. 287, § 3, these XIV impediments are again listed.)

prohibitory, all who are not expressly forbidden by law are able to contract marriage.[24] Yet, when St. Raymond listed his enumeration of the impediments which invadidate or merely impede marriage, he did not mention the lack of parental consent.[25] So also Hostiensis in his *Summa* (1250–1253) listed thirteen impediments to the contracting of a valid marriage, but did not include mention of the lack of parental consent.[26] Also in his teaching on the decretal sent by Pope Innocent III to the Archbishop of Arles,[27] he stated that the consent of the contracting parties was sufficient to the exclusion of parental consent.[28] There, too, he taught that all persons not expressly prohibited by law were able to contract marriage.[29] In another passage Hostiensis listed the requirements for the contracting of a valid marriage, and he foregoes all mention of parental consent as at all requisite.[30]

Joannes Andreae presented the same doctrine, for in explaining that marriage was effected by the consent of the parties he expressly stated that parental permission was not included, and hence was not necessary for the validity of marriage according to the law of the Church.[31]

Also Panormitanus in commenting on this same decretal of Innocent III taught that to the essence of marriage pertains only

---

[24] *Summa* (Veronae, 1744), lib. IV, tit. II, *de matrimonio,* p. 473, § 5: "Quod vero dictum est, 'nisi expresse prohibeatur,' ideo additum est, quoniam edictum de matrimonio contrahendo est prohibitorium, id est, omnis qui non prohibetur, admittitur et contrahere potest. Prohibeatur enim aliquis propter votum, propter ordinem, et propter alia impedimenta de quibus infra dicetur."

[25] *Summa,* lib. IV, tit. II, *de matrimonio,* p. 481, § 9.

[26] *Summa Aurea,* lib. IV, tit. *de matrimoniis,* p. 291, §§ 24, 25, 26.

[27] C. 23, X, *de sponsalibus et matrimoniis,* IV, 1.

[28] Hostiensis, *Commentaria,* lib. IV, *de sponsalibus et matrimoniis,* c. 23, § 3, ad vb. *coniunctionibus.*

[29] *Commentaria,* lib. IV, *de sponsalibus et matrimoniis,* c. 23, § 3, ad vb. *prohibitorium.*

[30] *Summa Aurea,* lib. IV, tit., *quis possit contrahere matrimonium,* p. 328.

[31] *In Sex Decretalium Libros Novella Commentaria,* lib. IV, tit. I, *de sponsalibus et matrimoniis,* § 8, ad vb. *solus:* "Non excludit verba quae sunt necessaria in his, qui loqui possunt, sed excludit solemnitates et consensum dominorum, et parentum, licet contrarium videatur secundum leges."

the mutual consent of the parties themselves, and that parental consent is not required.[32] In another place Panormitanus stated that according to civil law parental consent was necessary for the validity of the marriage, but that according to Canon law the same did not hold true;[33] and the Canon law was to be observed in this matter.[34]

Article 2. The Teaching of the Theologians

That parental consent was not necessary for the validity of the marriage was clearly enunciated by the theologians of the thirteenth century. They viewed marriage as a Sacrament, and when the contracting parties gave their consent the Sacrament of marriage came into existence.[35] Thus St. Thomas (d. 1274), arguing from the fact that marriage is a Sacrament, taught that whenever the proper matter and form were present marriage was effected.[36] Nothing else was required. Again the Angelic Doctor with great clearness distinguished between what was required for the essence of a Sacrament and that which pertained to the solemnity, so that if the latter was absent the Sacrament nevertheless existed. The omission of these solemnities without cause, however, he regarded as sinful. Moreover, he taught that

---

[32] "Secundo nota ibi sufficit solus consensus, quoad substantiam matrimonii verba non sunt necessaria, nec solemnitates patriae, nec consensus parentum, vel dominorum, sed sufficit solus consensus contrahentium. Hoc denotat hoc verbum, sufficit."—*Commentaria,* lib. IV, *de sponsalibus et matrimoniis,* c. 23—tom. VII, p. 14, § 2.

[33] *Commentaria,* lib. IV, *qui matrimonium accusare possunt,* c. 3—tom. VII, p. 76, § 4; also *Commentaria,* lib. IV, *de sponsalibus et matrimoniis,* c. 13—tom. VII, p. 9, § 4.

[34] *Commentaria,* lib. IV, *de desponsatione impuberum,* c. 1—tom. VII, p. 21, § 4; also *Commentaria,* lib. IV; *de desponsatione impuberum,* c. 2—tom. VII, p. 23, § 2; *Commentaria,* lib. V, *de raptoribus, incendiariis, et violatoribus ecclesiarum,* c. 7—tom. VII, p. 227, § 2.

[35] Dauvillier, *Le Mariage,* p. 193.

[36] "Ubicumque est debita forma et debita materia, ibi est sacramentum. Sed in occulto matrimonio servatur debita materia, quia sunt personae legitimae ad contrahendum; et debita forma, quia sunt verba de praesenti consensum exprimentia. Ergo est ibi verum matrimonium."—*Commentarium in IV Libros Sententiarum Magistri Petri Lombardi* (ed. Mandonnet, Parisiis: Lethielleux, 1929), dist. XXVIII, q. 1, art 3, sed contra.

the children were free persons and not slaves, and that the parents held only the rôle of educators. Hence the children had the inalienable right to choose their state of life—whether they wished to dedicate their lives to God in religion or to serve Him in the married state.[37] On reaching puberty children are emancipated from parental authority concerning the choice of their state of life, and so could enter the married state even against the wishes of their parents.[38]

In the *Liber Sextus* (1298) nothing is stated about the consent of parents in the marriages of their children. However, Pope Boniface VIII in 1295 declared that a *puber* is authorized both for the "*agere et defendere*" not only in a spiritual cause, but also in those things which flow from and are dependent upon such a cause, without the consent of his parents. Indeed, he could act against the will of his parent in such matters.[39] The Gloss stated that one over fourteen years of age could prosecute and defend a spiritual matter either by himself or through a procurator; and that a *filiusfamilias* could act in spiritual matters without the consent of his father.[40] The Gloss added that marriage is to be considered a spiritual matter.[41]

The *Clementinae* and the *Extravagantes* are silent concerning this question of parental consent in marriage. Hence there was no new development in the doctrine from the promulgation of the *Liber Sextus* until the Council of Trent, when the whole question was reconsidered and finally settled.

But before considering this Tridentine legislation it is necesary to examine the effects of this teaching of the Church, namely,

---

[37] ". . . puella non est in potestate patris quasi ancilla, ut sui corporis potestatem non habeat, sed quasi filia ad educandum; et ideo secundum hoc, quod libera est, potest se in potestatem alterius absque consensu patris dare, sicut etiam potest aliquis vel aliqua intrare religionem absque consensu parentum, cum sit persona libera."—*IV Sent.*, dist. XXVIII, q. 1, art. 3, solutio.

[38] *IV sent.*, dist. XXXVIII, q. 1, art. 1, quaestiuncula 3, solutio 3, ad secundum.

[39] C. 3, *de iudiciis*, II, I, in VI°; Potthast, n. 24064.

[40] *Glossa Ordinaria* ad c. 3, *de iudiciis*, II, I, in VI°, ad vb. *si annum.*

[41] *Glossa Ordinaria* ad c. 3, *de iudiciis*, II, I, in VI°, ad vb. *spiritualibus.*

that a marriage contracted by a minor without the knowledge of his parents or against their will is a valid and true marriage.

Article 3. The Effect of the Church's Teaching

The teaching of the Church which regarded the simple consent of the contracting parties as the constituent element of marriage occasioned many difficulties, especially with regard to the marriage of children who were still subject to the authority of their parents. Previous to the Council of Trent (1545–1563) the Church did not require any special form for the validity of a marriage. Since a marriage, then, was effected solely by the consent of the contracting parties it followed logically that, if they exchanged consent even privately and secretly—with neither priest nor witnesses present and without the knowledge or consent of the parents—the marriage nevertheless was valid and held to be such by the Church. For, provided the parties were not hindered by any impediment, nothing more was demanded by the Church for the validity of marriage than the giving and accepting of mutual consent.[42]

In practice this doctrine led to the great evil of clandestine marriages which plagued the Church up until the time of the Council of Trent. For secret unions brought with them a whole host of evils. Since the marriage was celebrated secretly, all proof of the fact of marriage was lacking save the testimony of the spouses themselves. Hence, if one of the parties to such a marriage deserted the other spouse and entered a second union publicly and before witnesses this latter adulterous union was judged in the external forum a true marriage. For the protests of the true wife against the validity of this second contract could not be entertained as conclusive proof. Even if the guilty party later on repented of his evil act he could not receive any relief

---

[42] However, the marriage was to be celebrated in the presence of a priest who would bless and solemnize the union and generally speaking this was usually observed; but the presence of the priest or witnesses was in no way necessary for the validity of the marriage. Cf. Triebs, *Praktisches Handbuch des geltenden kanonischen Eherechts in Vergleichung mit dem deutschen staatlichen Eherecht* (Teil I–IV in einem Band, Gesamtausgabe, Breslau: Ostdeutsche Verlagsanstalt, 1933), p. 561.

from the ecclesiastical courts. This necesarily led to the difficult and intricate problem of the conflict between the internal and external forums.

These secret marriages contracted by minors were widespread, and this evil practice wreaked havoc with rightful parental authority. Thus, if children desired to enter marriage but their parents refused to give them permission, a valid marriage was still possible and easy to effect. For the boy and girl had only to exchange matrimonial consent in order to become man and wife. True, if they did so act, they sinned but their marriage was valid. Parents, too, often refused to believe their children when they were informed by them of their marriage. Hence valid marriages between minors were often disrupted and the common matrimonial life destroyed by forceful separations imposed by outraged parents. In these cases the minor spouses usually had no proof other than their own testimony that a true matrimonial consent had been exchanged between them. In the year 1526 Erasmus of Rotterdam, in a work dedicated to Queen Catherine of Aragon, called attention to these difficulties and lamented the fact that the Church had not decreed the invalidity of marriages contracted by children without the knowledge and consent of parents. He remarked that the Church had previously proclaimed the validity of such unions entered into by children in order to remedy an evil caused by tyrannical parents but in reality this remedy brought about a far worse condition than had formerly existed.[43] Ten years later, in the year 1536 the First Provincial

[43] "Deinde ne parentes impii, vel ob quaestum, vel ob aliam quamcumque causam detinerent liberos suos in coelibatu, aut obtruderent eos conjugibus quibus nollent, in favorem liberorum pronunciavit humana constitutio, ratum esse matrimonium quod insciis etiam et invitis parentibus inter puberes contractum esset per verba praesentis temporis. . . . Opinor autem humanum esse decretum, solo consensu coire matrimonium, ut qui legem pro ratione temporum statuit, possit eandem pro ratione temporum vel abrogare vel moderari. Atqui jam ex hac lege, quot adolescentes bene natos, quot puellas etiam summo loco natas, vidimus et videmus implicari infaustis perplexisque conjugiis, ingenti luctu parentum ac propinquorum, nonnumquam et summo reip. discrimine? Ab exemplis prudens tempero. . . . Non haec refero quod damnem constitutionem: sed quo cautiores reddam juvenes ac puellas in contrahendis matrimoniis. Nam receptis ab Ecclesia legibus adversari, non arbitror esse consultum. Caeterum illius est mutare legem e

Council of Cologne expressed the desire that the Church would soon declare invalid by general law all marriages contracted by children without the knowledge and consent of parents. The same Council punished with excommunication not only those who dared to contract such a marriage, but also all who advised or aided the parties in entering this sinful union.[44]

The Church had been long cognizant of the great evil of clandestine marriages and for many centuries had legislated against this abuse. The IV Lateran Council (1215) prescribed that when marriages are to be contracted they were to be announced publicly in churches by priests during a suitable and fixed time, so that if any impediments existed they might be made known. Furthermore the Council decreed that severe penalties should be imposed for any infraction of this law.[45] Similar legislation was

---

re nata, qui legem condidit."—*Christiani Matrimonii Institutio* (Lug. Batavorum: Ex Officina Joh. Maire, 1650), pp. 65–67. (The writer has seen fit to give the complete text of Erasmus's teaching regarding the marriages of children entered into without parental knowledge and consent, for the position of Erasmus on this question has been commonly misunderstood. Canonists as Gasparri (*Tractatus Canonicus de Matrimonio* [2. ed., 2 vols., Romae: Typis Polyglottis Vaticanis, 1932], I, 114), (hereafter cited *De Matrimonio*), Vlaming (*Praelectiones Iuris Matrimonii ad Normam Codicis Iuris Canonici* [3. ed., 2 vols., Bussum in Hollandia: Sumptibus Societatis Editricis Anonymae Olim Paulus Brand, 1919–1921), I, 220 (hereafter cited *Praelectiones Iuris Matrimonii*), Ayrinhac-Lydon (*Marriage Legislation in the New Code of Canon Law* [2. ed., New York: Benziger Brothers, 1943], p. 50), (hereafter cited *Marriage Legislation*), consider Erasmus among those authors who held for and taught the invalidity of these marriages of minors which were contracted without parental knowledge and consent. From the text as given above it is clear that Erasmus did not deny the validity of such marriages nor did he wish to contradict the authority and teaching of the Church in this matter.

[44] Concilium Coloniense I, canon 43: "Optandum ut canon Evaristi pontificis concilio generali renovetur, tollanturque illa clandestina matrimonia, quae invitis parentibus et propinquis, Veneris potius quam Dei causa contrahuntur: nam quanta ex his clandestinis matrimoniis mala suboriantur in aperto est. Interea vero donec ecclesia de hoc prospiciat, si non irrita, prohibita saltem sint, et poenae canonicae hoc est excommunicationi, contrahentes, et qui his ope et consilio adfuerint, subjaceant: . . . Quantum fieri potest, cavebit parochus, ne liberos citra parentum auctoritatem conjungat."—Mansi, XXXII, 1267–1268.

[45] IV Concilium Lateranense, canon 51—Mansi, XXII, 1038–1039; cf.

enacted by numerous provincial councils and local synods in an effort to end all secret unions. They ordered that marriages were to be celebrated in church, that witnesses were to be present, and that a priest should bless and solemnize the union. They condemned in harsh terms every clandestine marriage as gravely sinful.[46]

However this abundance of legislation did little to eradicate the abuse of clandestine marriages.[47] Even though the Church forbade these secret unions and punished severely those who disobeyed, nevertheless the legislation always acknowledged these marriages as valid. The contracting parties were guilty of serious sin, but the validity of their marriage was never questioned. This was the weak point in all these laws. More stringent regulations were sorely needed if the evil of secret marriages was to be overcome. But before the Church found an effective answer to this difficulty the Protestant Revolt had broken over Europe.

Article 4. The Doctrine of the Reformers

Luther (1483–1546) and the other leaders of early Protestant thought attacked the Church's teaching on almost every point of

---

Schroeder, *Disciplinary Decrees of the General Councils: Text, Translation, and Commentary* (St. Louis: B. Herder Book Co., 1937), pp. 280–281; 578–579.

[46] Council of London (1102), c. 22—Mansi, XX, 1152 b ; Council of London (1174), c. 18—Mansi, XXII, 151-152; Council of London (1200), c. 11—Mansi, XXII, 719; Provincial Council of Scotland (1225), c. 65—Mansi, XXII, 1241-1242; Council of Treves (1227), c. 5—Mansi, XXIII, 29; Council of Langeais (1278), c. 3—Mansi, XXIV, 212–213; Synodal Statutes of the Church of Liége (1287), cc. 1–6—Mansi, XXIV, 904–905; Synodal Statutes of the Church of Cahors (1289), c. 18—Mansi, XXIV, 1011-1012; Council of Salzburg (1291), c. 1—Mansi, XXIV, 1075–1076; Council of Padua (1350)—Mansi, XXVI, 234c; Provincial Synod of Prague (1355), c. 50—Mansi, XXVI, 401–402; Council of Magdeburg (1370), c. 32—Mansi, XXVI, 583–584; Council of Narbonne (1374), c. 22—Mansi, XXVI, 605; Council of Lyons (1449), c. 14—Mansi, XXXII, 97; Council of Avignon (1509), c. 28—Mansi, XXXII, 546; Council of Treves (1310), cc. 95–96—Mansi, XXV, 273–274.

[47] Friedberg, *Das Recht der Eheschliessung in seiner geschichtlichen Entwicklung* (Leipzig: Verlag von Bernhard Tauchnitz, 1865), p. 106. This work will hereafter be cited as *Das Recht der Eheschliessung.*

faith and morals. Certain Catholic doctrines, however, received more attention from the so-called Reformers than others, and among these doctrines was the teaching of the Church on the validity of clandestine marriages. Against this doctrine of the Church the Reformers directed their most bitter attacks. They condemned this teaching, namely, that a secret marriage while illicit remained valid as a doctrine which contradicted both the natural law and the revealed Word of God as contained in the Scriptures.

These Protestant leaders understood by a clandestine or secret marriage one which was contracted by children unknown to their parents or against their will. Lack of parental knowledge of and consent to the marriage constituted for the Reformers clandestinity. This, of course, was a different concept of clandestinity from that which was understood and accepted in Catholic circles. For amongst Catholic jurists it was recognized that a clandestine marriage was still possible even though the children had obtained the permission of their parents. The term "clandestine" had been given at different times in the history of the Church's law various meanings by Catholic canonists. The term was used to signify a union for which the banns of marriage had not been announced previous to the solemnization of the marriage. It also was employed to designate a marriage for which no objective proof existed except the testimony of the contracting parties. A marriage was also referred to as clandestine if it was contracted before witnesses but not celebrated *in facie ecclesiae.* But the Church never understood the absence of parental knowledge of and consent to the marriage as the essential element which brought about clandestinity.

The fact, however, was that children who entered marriage unbeknown to their parents or against their will generally contracted a clandestine union. The chief offenders in this matter of clandestine marriages were minors. The Reformers seized upon this abuse and proclaimed that the very essence of clandestinity consisted in contracting a marriage without the knowledge and approval of parents or guardians. Hence the whole emphasis in the thought of the Reformers on clandestine marriages was against marriages entered into by minors without parental knowledge and permission, and an understanding of their teaching is necessary in order to comprehend why this question of the marriage of minors caused so much difficulty and occupied so great a rôle in the deliberations of the Council of Trent.

Three reasons can be given to explain the origin of this doctrine of the Reformers that a marriage contracted by children without the knowledge and consent of parents was null and void. (1) It could not be gainsaid that clandestine unions caused great evils and were widespread at this time. Hence it was to be expected that the Reformers should blame the Church for this evil, and should strive to prove that it was the logical result of the Church's teaching that the consent of the contracting parties alone formed the essence of marriage. Since the majority of clandestine unions involved parties both of whom were minors, the Reformers preached that the Church had no respect for parental authority and that Catholic dogmatists sought to disrupt the family. Luther and his satellites called for a change in this evil teaching and gave as their solution the declaration that marriages contracted by children without parental knowledge and consent were by that very fact invalid. (2) The revival of Roman Law studies within the German States, which was the birthplace of Protestantism, had great influence on the thought of the Reformers. For in Roman Law the marriage of a person who was not *sui iuris* without the consent of the *paterfamilas* was null and void.[48] (3) The Reformers denied the sacramentality of marriage. In this way they undermined and destroyed the very basis of the Church's teaching that a minor could validly marry without the consent of his parents or guardians. For the Church maintained that since marriage was a Sacrament the recipient must be left perfectly free in his decision to enter the married state. He can in no way be subjected to and made dependent on the will of another person even though that person be his parent. In the eyes of the Church marriage could be forced upon no one; nor could anyone be prevented from receiving this Sacrament if he was qualified. Since, then, marriage in the teachings of the Reformers ceased to be considered as a Sacrament and was looked upon as only a natural contract, the consequence was that the Church's principal arguments, which were based upon the sacramentality of the marriage contract, ceased

[48] Friedberg, *Das Recht der Eheschliessung,* p. 105.

to be cogent reasons for the freedom and independence of minors in contracting marriage. Furthermore, this doctrine of the Protestant School withdrew marriage from the exclusive authority of the Church and denied the absolute right of the Church to legislate concerning it.[49]

Martin Luther was outspoken in his condemnation of all clandestine unions which were entered into by children. He clearly defined a clandestine union as one which a minor child contracted without the knowledge and consent of his parents and guardians. Furthermore he declared that a contract of this nature lacked all possibility of proof and that no one could know with certainty if it had actually taken place.[50] These unions which children entered into unknown to their parents or guardians or against the will of the latter were according to Luther null and void.[51] Moreover, he taught that, where such unions have taken place, the parents possessed the power to dissolve them.[52] While Luther denied the validity of a marriage contracted by children without

---

[49] Bernard, *Étude Historique et Critique sur le Consentement des Ascendants au Mariage,* p. 96.

[50] "Wo aber sich zwei mit einander heimlich verloben, kann niemand gewiss sein, obs wahr sei oder nicht, weil Mann und Weib (so auch Braut und Brautigam) ein Leib und ein Mund sind; auf welcher Bekenntniss und Zeugniss nicht zu bauen, noch solch ungewisse Ehe zu bestätigen ist. Auf dass aber nicht jemand hie ein Wortgezänk anrichte, heisse ich das heimlich Verlöbniss, das da geschieht hinter Wissen und Willen derjenigen, so die Oberhand haben, und die Ehe zu stiften Recht und Macht haben, als Vater, Mutter, und was an ihrer Statt sein mag."—Luther, *Sämmtliche Werke,* nach den ältesten Ausgaben kritisch und historisch bearbeitet von Dr. Johann Konrad Irmischer (67 vols. in 25, Erlangen: Verlag von Carl Heyder, 1831–1883), XXIII, 96. This work will hereafter be cited as *Sämmtliche Werke.*

[51] "So sei dies der endliche Beschluss dieses ersten Artikels, dass heimliche Verlöbniss, weil da noch keine Ehe im Werk, und der Magd und ihren Eltern noch keine thätliche Verletzung geschehen, sondern noch ganz in der Eltern Verbot und Gewalt stehet, soll gänzlich verhindert, und für keine Ehe gehalten werden."—*Sämmtliche Werke,* XXIII, 110.

[52] "Darum sollen die Eltern wissen, dass sei Gewalt und Recht haben, die heimlichen Verlöbniss ihrer Kinder zu reissen; und die Kinder sollen wissen, dass sei in diesem und allem, was nicht wider Gott ist, Gehorsam zu leisten schuldig sind, und dass ihre heimliche Verlöbniss nichts ist: . . ."—*op. cit.,* XXVIII, 122. Cf. *op. cit.,* LIII, 237.

the knowledge or consent of their parents and taught that the parents had the power to dissolve such a contract, nevertheless he never went so far as to teach that the parents could force their children to marry.[53] Furthermore, he advised those parties, who had as children entered into a secret union without the knowledge and approval of their parents or guardians and then later on had contracted another marriage publicly and with the approval of their parents or tutors, not to worry or have troubled consciences for fear that they were living in adultery as the Church taught. Luther instructed them that they were not living in sin, since their previous secret union was null and void because it was entered into by them without parental knowledge and consent.[54]

Luther ridiculed the Catholic position which maintained that marriages contracted by children without the consent of their parents are valid though gravely illicit. He declared that the Church in teaching this doctrine was openly advocating disobedience of children towards their parents. He held that, if the Church, on the one hand, preached to children the obedience they owed their parents and, on the other hand, left the power of the parents untouched and undiminished, there would have been no need for any legislation on clandestine marriages because these secret unions would never have existed. For fear of parents together with the knowledge that such clandestine marriages were null and void would have kept children from entering these secret unions.[55]

---

53 "Es ist gar viel anders, die Ehe hindern oder wehren, und zur Ehe zu zwingen oder dringen; und ob die Aeltern gleich im ersten, nämlich die Ehe zu wehren, Recht und Macht hätten, so folgt draus nit, dass sei auch Macht haben, darzu zu zwingen: . . ."—*op. cit.*, LIII, 237.

54 "Ich will doch hiermit getröstet und berichtet haben all, die in solchen Gewissen, des heimlichen Verlöbniss halben, durch Papst, Bischoffe, Official, Prediger, Beichväter verstrickt und verwirret sind, dass sie fröhlich und sicher solch päpstlich Gesetze verachten, lassen das heimlich Verlöbniss nichts sein, und halten sich nach der offentlichen Ehe zusammen, wie rechte Eheleute, ohn alle Scheu und Furcht des Ehebruchs, es sei mit fordern oder leisten die Eheschuld. . . ."—*op. cit.*, XXIII, 100–101.

55 *Op. cit.*, XXVIII, 121–122.

He decried the sacramentality of matrimony as a papal invention designed to bring marriage within the legislative and judicial competency of the Church. For him marriage was only a natural contract and thus it was not the concern of the Church and its ministers.[56]

Calvin (1509–1564), too, was in complete agreement with Luther in condemning the Church's doctrine on the validity of marriages contracted by minors who had not informed their parents or guardians or who had entered marriage without the latter's consent. He called such marriages clandestine, and he taught that these unions were null and void. Like Luther, he maintained that the parents or guardians possessed the power to dissolve all unions of this nature. Moreover, he vehemently denied that marriage was a Sacrament; consequently, he declared that the Church had no right to legislate concerning it.[57]

The doctrine and teaching of the other Reformers as Melanchton, Brenz, and Beza was substantially the same as that of Luther and Calvin.[58]

An effective solution to the problem of clandestine marriages was sorely needed at this time by the Church. Catholic leaders called upon the Church to re-examine her teaching on the subject of a minor contracting marriage unknown to his parents or against their will. This attitude of unrest and disquiet which was manifest within Catholic circles together with the position and teaching of the Reformers on the subject forced the Church to consider the question at great length in the Council of Trent. The efforts of the Council in meeting this problem will be considered in the following chapter.

---

[56] *The Table Talk of Martin Luther,* translated and edited by William Hazlitt (London: George Bell and Sons, 1890), p. 304, n. DCCXLI; p. 306, n. DCCXLVIII; cf. *Sämmtliche Werke,* XXVIII, 122.

[57] *Joannis Calvini Opera Quae Supersunt Omnia,* ed., Guilielmus Baum-Eduardus Cunitz-Eduardus Reuss (59 vols. in 58, Brunsvigae, Berolini: Apud C. A. Schwetschke et Filium, 1863–1900), II, 1091–1092; *op. cit.,* XXXVIII, 586; *Calvin's Institutes of the Christian Religion,* translated by John Allen (6. ed., 2 vols., Philadelphia: Presbyterian Board of Publication and Social Work, 1902), II, 632.

[58] Cf. Joyce, *Christian Marriage,* pp. 118–119; Friedberg, *Das Recht der Eheschliessung,* pp. 226–228.

CHAPTER IV

THE COUNCIL OF TRENT AND THE MARRIAGE OF MINORS

On January 18th, 1562, the Council of Trent reassembled under Pius IV after an interruption of nearly ten years. The Fathers of the Council had as yet to deal with the problem of marriages contracted by children without the consent of their parents. This question proved a difficult one and led to many heated debates.[1] In the Council it was linked to the question of clandestine marriages, not only because in the thought and terminology of the Reformers a clandestine marriage was precisely a union entered into without parental consent, but also because in practice these two questions were closely connected as was pointed out in the preceding chapter. On February 4th, 1563, eight articles on the Sacrament of Matrimony were drawn up to be proposed to the *theologi minores*. In order to secure a thorough treatment of these propositions, the theologians were divided into four groups, each group receiving two articles to examine and later on to submit their report.[2] The second of these propositions stated the Protestant tenet that marriages contracted by minors without the consent of their parents are null and void.[3] On February 9, 1563, the theologians commenced the examination and discussion of these propositions.

The result of the sessions proved beyond doubt that there was no agreement in Catholic thought as to the necessity of parental

[1] Waterworth, *The Canons and Decrees of the Sacred and Oecumenical Council of Trent* (London: C. Dalman, 1848), p. ccxxiii.

[2] *Concilii Tridentini Diariorum, Actorum, Epistolarum Tractatuum Nova Collectio* (ed. Societas Gorresiana, 13 vols., Friburgi Brisgoviae: B. Herder, 1901–1938), IX, 380. This work will hereafter be cited as *Acta Concilii Tridentini.*

[3] "Parentes posse irritare matrimonia clandestina nec esse vera matrimonia, quae sic contrahuntur, expedireque, ut in ecclesia huiusmodi in futurum irritentur."—*ibid.*, p. 380, n. 2.

consent in marriage. One group of theologians including Salmerón,[4] Vigur,[5], Coquier,[6] and Antonio de Grignano,[7] maintained that the Church had always recognized as valid, though gravely illicit, marriages of children contracted without parental consent. Yet this entire group, with the exception of the Franciscan de Grignano, conceded to the Church the power whereby it might render such consent essential and necessary in the future. De Grignano taught, contrary to the opinions of the others, that, even though parental consent was lacking for a marriage, the marriage, nevertheless, was a true matrimonial union and a Sacrament. Hence, inasmuch as it was a Sacrament, the Church was powerless to modify it in any degree, since such a power was not given to the Church by Christ.[8] Other theologians, however, declared that the marriages contracted without parental consent were invalid, and in this group the most vehement in his contention was the Sorbonnist, Nicholas de Brys.[9]

After the theologians had discussed the matter, a draft of the proposed legislation containing eleven Canons and a Decree on clandestine marriages was submitted to the Fathers of the Council on July 20th, 1563. In Canon 3 of this draft it was dogmatically affirmed that parents were incapable of confirming or annulling clandestine marriages of their children.[10] This canon was inserted to condemn the current Protestant teaching that marriages entered into without parental consent were invalid. The Decree, however, on clandestine marriages was divided into two sections,

---

[4] *Ibid.*, p. 385.

[5] *Ibid.*, p. 397.

[6] *Ibid.*, p. 398.

[7] *Ibid.*, p. 407.

[8] *Ibid.*, p. 407.

[9] "Matrimonia igitur quae clam contrahuntur absque consensu parentum nulla sunt. . . . Itaque matrimonium neque iure naturae, neque iure gentium, neque civili, neque divino clam contrahi debet, sed palam et publice adhibitis adhibendis praesertim consensu patris, et alias contractum non est ratum neque validum neque firmum matrimonium, neque a Deo est sed a satana."—*ibid.*, p. 387.

[10] "Si quis dixerit, clandestina matrimonia quae libero consensu contrahentium fiunt, non esse vera et rata matrimonia, ac proinde esse in potestate parentum, ea rata vel irrita facere: anathema sit."—*ibid.*, p. 640.

the second of which declared null for the future marriages contracted by boys before the completion of their eighteenth year, and girls before the completion of their sixteenth year without parental consent.[11]

This first draft occasioned much discussion among the Fathers in the Council. A delegation sent by King Charles IX of France (1560–1574) appeared on the first day of the discussion and solemnly petitioned the Council to declare invalid all marriages contracted by children without the consent of their parents, since the outcome of such marriages was usually harmful both to parents and spouses alike. However, the petition stated that a certain age limit should be set, namely the twentieth year for the boy and the eighteenth year for the girl, so that when the child reached this determined age, he could marry without the consent of his parents. This would be a remedy for the child against parents who would unreasonably refuse their permission.[12]

Some of the Fathers, guided by the teaching of the theologians Nicholas de Brys [13] and Delgado,[14] maintained that this first draft of the Decree, which declared that for the future marriages of children before they have completed their eighteenth year and sixteenth year of age if contracted without parental consent were invalid, was in keeping with the Canon law of the previous centuries, and so it met with their approval. The Bishop of Segovia claimed that the Church had taught for centuries that such marriages were invalid, and that this teaching was supported by Scripture and the natural law.[15] Many at the Council

---

[11] "Insuper eadem sacrosancta synodus ea quoque matrimonia, quae filiifamilias ante decimum octavum, filiae vero ante decimum sextum suae aetatis annum completum sine parentum consensu de cetero contraxerint, praesenti decreto irritat et annullat."—*ibid.*, p. 640.

[12] Pallavicini, *Historia Concilii Tridentini*, trans. by Joannes Baptista Giattini (3 vols., Antwerpiae: 1670), III, lib. 22, cap. 1, n. 16. Friedberg, *Das Recht der Eheschliessung*, p. 122.

[13] *Acta Concilii Tridentini*, IX, 387.

[14] *Ibid.*, p. 401.

[15] Episcopus Segobiensis: "Per 1200 annos ecclesia tenuit, clandestina non esse matrimonia, neque matrimonia esse rata, antequam succedat consensus parentum, probavitque patres habere potestatem super filios ex dictis Pauli: Si quis tradet virginem nuptui, bene facit: si servat virginem melius

agreed with this opinion.[16] However, the Bishop of Verdun, while declaring that he held the same view, suggested that the Decree should be changed to read thus: "*decernit sancta synodus, matrimonia irrita et nulla quae contrahuntur . . . insciis parentibus.*"[17] Others again gave their approval to this first draft of the Decree without advising any change.[18]

The majority, however, of those who favored the proposed legislation desired that the Council modify it in certain respects. Some, while affirming the necessity of parental consent, asserted that if the parents refused to give their permission the child had a right to appeal to the Bishop. This right would become operative if the parents were unreasonable in withholding their consent,[19] or if the denial of marriage would lead to sin on the part of the child,[20] or, finally, if the child was separated from his parents by so great a distance that parental consent could not be asked or received.[21]

Others, however, wanted to raise the age, but were not agreed among themselves as to what age limit should be determined. One group, and that by far the largest, set eighteen years of age for the girl and twenty years for the boy, so that those below this age could not marry validly without parental permission.[22] Another group placed the ages at twenty years for the

---

facit. Et hoc esse de iure naturae quia filii sunt in potestate parentum et ideo non possunt habere legitimum consensum in re maximi momenti, quale est matrimonium."—*ibid.*, 656.

[16] Episcopus Feretranus (Montefeltro, in Italy)—*ibid.*, p. 658. Cf. also *ibid.*, pp. 660, 663, 678.

[17] Episcopus Virodunensis—*ibid.*, p. 658.

[18] Episcopus Canomanensis (Le Mans, in France)—*ibid.*, p. 663; Episcopus Salamentinus (Salamanca, in Spain)—*ibid.*; p. 673.

[19] Archiep. Niochensis (Nicosia, in Italy)—*ibid.*, p. 671; Episcopus Uxentinus (Ugento, in Italy)—*ibid.*, p. 667; Episcopus Veneciensis (Vence, in France)—*ibid.*, p. 670.

[20] Episcopus Nemausensis (Nîmes, in France)—*ibid.*, p. 667; cf. also *ibid.*, pp. 673, 676.

[21] Episcopus Almeriensis (Almeria, in Spain)—*ibid.*, p. 666; Episcopus Barcinonensis (Barcelona, in Spain)—*ibid.*, p. 670.

[22] Archiep. Granatensis (Granada, in Spain)—*ibid.*, p. 644; Episcopus Caiacensis (Caiazzo, in Italy)—*ibid.*, p. 653; Episcopus Tarvisinus (Treviso, in Italy)—*ibid.*, p. 653; Episcopus Suessionensis (Soissons, in France)—

girl and twenty-two for the boy.[23] A few of the Fathers, however, demanded twenty-four years for the boy.[24] A considerable number of the Bishops, led by the Cardinal of Lorraine, fixed the age of twenty for the girls and twenty-five for the boys.[25] Two of the Fathers demanded twenty-five years of age for both boys and girls.[26]

Several of those who supported this Decree differed regarding the person who was to give this permission for the marriage. Some wanted to restrict the giving of this permission to the father alone.[27] If the father was dead, then the mother was to give the needed consent.[28] If both parents were dead then the right was to cede to the Bishop.[29] Others extended the granting of this necessary permission even to the guardians.[30] A singular opinion in this matter was advanced by the General of the Dominicans, who stated that minors were always to receive for their marriage the permission of the Bishop, since he was their spiritual father and guardian. This consent, he contended, was sufficient, and parental consent need not be obtained.[31]

Though this first draft of the Decree, which declared invalid for

---

ibid., p. 665; Episcopus Dolcnsis (Dol, now joined with Rennes, in France) —*ibid.*, p. 667; Episcopus Pampilonensis (Pamplona, in Spain)—*ibid.*, p. 674.

23 Episcopus Aurelianensis (Orleans, in France)—*ibid.*, p. 660; Episcopus Cauriensis (Coria, in Spain)—*ibid.*, p. 659; Episcopus Guadiscensis (Gozo, Island of Malta)—*ibid.*, p. 672.

24 Episcopus Leiriensis, (Leiria, in Portugal)—*ibid.*, 661; Episcopus Metensis (Metz, in France)—*ibid.*, p. 662.

25 Lotharingus (Cardinal of Lorraine)—*ibid.*, p. 643; Episcopus Nucerinus (Nocera, in Italy)—*ibid.*, p. 673; cf. also *ibid.*, pp. 651, 662, 663, 664.

26 Episcopus Oppidensis (Oppido Mamertina, in Italy)—*ibid.*, p. 673; Episcopus Pennensis (Penne, in Italy)—*ibid.*, p. 673.

27 Lotharingus (Cardinal of Lorraine): "Dicaturque in canone *sine patrum consensu* loco illius, quod dicitur *parentum*, etc."—*ibid.*, p. 643.

28 Episcopus Senonensis (Sens, in France): ". . . defuncto autem patre sit consensus matris, et hoc probavit lege naturali"—*ibid.*, p. 653.

29 Episcopus Ilerdensis (Lerida, in Spain): ". . . potest dici quoad parentes quod ubi ipsi deficiunt, episcopi provideant"—*ibid.*, p. 666.

30 Episcopus Senonensis (Sens, in France): "Et hoc decretum extendatur etiam ad eos, qui sunt sub tutoribus."—*ibid.*, p. 653; Archiep. S. Severini (San Severino, in Italy)—*ibid.*, p. 645; Archiep. Iadrensis (Zara, in Italy)—*ibid.*, p. 645.

31 *Ibid.*, p. 679.

the future marriages contracted by boys before their eighteenth year and by girls before their sixteenth year of age without parental consent, had many ardent defenders, opposition to it was not lacking. Many of the ablest Fathers at the Council objected to the proposed legislation, and called forth Scripture, history, dogma, tradition, and various practical reasons to support their condemnation.

For the most part only two texts of Scripture were used by the Fathers in opposing this draft of the Decree. They argued that to demand parental consent for the validity of the marriage of children was contrary to the teaching of Genesis, where it is written that for marriage "a man shall leave father and mother and shall cleave to his wife."[32] From this they concluded that a child is not under the paternal authority in regard to the contracting of marriage.[33] Use was made also of a text of Saint Paul in which the Apostle stated that, if one is not able to live chastely, it is better to marry than to burn.[34] Now these Fathers argued that, if parental consent was necessary for the validity of the marriage, the child would not be free to follow out the words of Saint Paul, but would depend entirely on the will of another, namely, his parents.[35] And this, they asserted, would be contrary to the divine law.[36] These two texts from Scripture were strengthened by the citation of the example in the Old Testament of the marriage of Esau,[37] and it was pointed out that,

---

[32] Gen. ii, 24.

[33] Episcopus Hyprensis (Ypres, in Belgium)—*Acta Concilii Tridentini,* IX, 729.

[34] I Cor., vii, 9.

[35] Archiep. Rossanensis (Rossano, in Italy)—*Acta Concilii Tridentini,* IX, 648; Episcopus Namurcensis (Namur, in Belgium)—*ibid.,* p. 670; Episcopus Coimbricensis (Coimbra, in Portugal)—*ibid.,* p. 705.

[36] Episcopus Hyprensis (Ypres, in Belgium): "Contra ius tum humanum tum divinum id esse; atque idcirco universe dicit ab Apostolo: *Si se non continent, nubant;* non ab ipso dici, *nubant post talem aetatem,* neque *nubant si genitores consenserint;* sed, *nubant, absque exceptione.* Non esse igitur ad annos aut ad permissionem restringendum hoc remedium, a Deo concessum humanae cupidini. . . ."—Pallavicini, *Historia Concilii Tridentini,* III, lib. 22, cap. 4, n. 15.

[37] Gen. xxvi, 34.

even though he sinned in marrying against the wishes of his parents, nevertheless the marriage was valid.[38]

Many of the Fathers denied the statements of those who claimed that in the previous Canon law the Church had required parental permission as an essential requisite for the marriage of children. They maintained that the Church had always deplored marriages entered into by children without parental knowledge or consent, but nevertheless considered them as valid. For proof they re-examined the texts concerning this question as found in Gratian, and brought forth arguments based on the decretal legislation.[39] Thus they maintained that their predecessors for hundreds of years had held that such marriages were valid; and so they appealed to the Council to respect the judgment of the Church throughout the centuries, for, they added, in such an important matter innovations should not be lightly made.[40] For this reason Cardinal Ludovico Madruzzo (1530–1600) opposed the Decree, stating that he was against any alteration in the actual law and practice of the Church.[41]

A few of the Fathers offered as an argument against this first draft of the Decree that the Church had even recognized as valid the marriage of slaves, who contracted marriage against the wishes of their master. Hence for a greater reason the Church should recognize as valid the marriages of children entered into without parental consent, since the power of a father over his children is far less than that which an owner possessed in relation to his slaves.[42]

Many of the Bishops appealed to the teachings of the Theo-

---

38 Generalis Iesuitarum—*Acta Concilii Tridentini,* IX, 740.

39 Archiep. Rossanensis (Rossano, in Italy)—*ibid.,* p. 648; Episcopus Lucerinus (Lucera, in Italy)—*ibid.,* p. 660; Episcopus Montisfalisci (Montefiascone, in Italy)—*ibid.,* p. 663; Episcopus Hyprensis (Ypres, in Belgium)—*ibid.,* p. 729.

40 Episcopus Pientinus (Pienza, in Italy)—*ibid.,* p. 652; Archiep. Hydruntinus (Otranto, in Italy)—*ibid.,* p. 688; Archiep. Rossanensis (Rossano, in Italy)—*ibid.,* p. 694.

41 Pallavicini, *Historia Concilii Tridentini,* III, lib. 22, cap. 4, n. 7.

42 Episcopus Urbevetanus (Orvieto, in Italy)—*Acta Concilii Tridentini,* IX, 677; Episcopus Minorensis (Minorca, Balearic Islands)—*ibid.,* p. 677; Episcopus Coimbricensis (Coimbra, in Portugal)—*ibid.,* p. 705.

logians, especially Saint Thomas, to prove the absolute freedom that all men enjoy as regards the reception of the Sacraments and concerning the choice of a state of life. In spiritual matters they held that children were not bound to follow out the will of their parents, but were independent of them.[43] It was declared that under the natural law all who were capable of marrying had a right to do so, and this right could be exercised even in opposition to the will of the parents.[44] The Patriarch of Venice contended that the essence of matrimony consisted in the mutual consent of the contracting parties; everything else had to be counted among the solemnities, the absence of which cannot affect the validity of the contract. This argument was all the more forceful, he maintained, in the case of children marrying without the consent of their parents; for in addition to annulling a Sacrament, there was a violation of that natural liberty which all possess upon coming to the age of puberty.[45]

Practical arguments were advanced by a good number of the Fathers who condemned the proposed draft of the Decree to annul for the future marriages of children contracted without parental consent. Some held that, if the Council would declare invalid the marriages contracted by children in the past without parental consent, or if they would state that for the future such marriages were to be considered null, support would thereby be given to the heretics of that day. For the Reformers had vigorously attacked the teachings of the Church of Rome especially on the question that the lack of parental permission did not invalidate a marriage.[46] Others stated that such a law would lead

[43] Episcopus Clusinus (Chiusi, in Italy)—*ibid.*, p. 667; Episcopus Dertusensis (Tortosa, in Spain)—*ibid.*, p. 671.

[44] Episcopus Hyprensis (Ypres, in Belgium)—*ibid.*, p. 669; Episcopus Coimbricensis (Coimbra, in Portugal)—*ibid.*, pp. 655, 705; Episcopus Clusinus (Chiusi, in Italy)—*ibid.*, p. 725.

[45] ". . . minus quoque irrita effici posse matrimonia, contracta a filiis familias absque parentum voluntate, cum per hoc libertas ab illis tollatur, accepta ab ipsa natura."—Pallavicini, *Historia Concilii Tridentini,* III, lib. 22, cap. 4, n. 8.

[46] Patriarcha Venetiarum (Venice)—Pallavicini, *op. cit.*, III, lib. 22, cap. 4, n. 8; Archiep. Rossanensis (Rossano, in Italy)—*Acta Concilii Tridentini,* IX, 646–647, 690, 693; Generalis Iesuitarum—*ibid.*, p. 741; Archiep. Hydruntinus (Otranto, in Italy)—*ibid.*, p. 688.

to sin, for, if the parents refused their consent, it was then impossible for the children to contract a valid marriage. The result in many cases would be that the parties, no longer able to contain themselves, would commit the sin of fornication. This argument was supported by two of the most prominent figures at the Council, Archbishop John Baptist Castagna of Rossano in Calabria, who in 1590 was elected to the Chair of Peter as Urban VII,[47] and by the Spanish priest, James Laynez, General of the Society of Jesus.[48] The Archbishop of Rossano presented also as an additional argument the practical difficulty of receiving parental consent when the child is living away from home, separated from the parents by a great distance, and the marriage is urgent.[49]

Many of the Fathers who opposed the proposed legislation, on the grounds of one or all of the above reasons, suggested, however, that severe penalties be inflicted on those who without reason married without the knowledge or consent of their parents. This group admitted that marriages contracted by children unknown to their parents or against their will, though always valid, are gravely illicit, and hence the parties to this deed should be punished. No specific penalty was indicated by the majority of the Fathers comprising this group.[50] A few, however, maintained that such children should be disinherited,[51] and one bishop wished to see them punished with excommunication.[52]

---

[47] Archiep. Rossanensis: ". . . sed dico, quandoque malum esse, filios sine patris consensu nubere, sed semper peius est, si non nubentes fornicentur; cuius rei occasionem ne praestet decretum hoc, vereor, cum non tantum prohibeat, sed matrimonium ipsum, si contractum fuerit, irritet."—*ibid.*, p. 648.

[48] Generalis Iesuitarum: ". . . si enim edetur hoc decretum frequenter violabitur praeceptum Dei quia pluries incident in fornicationem. Nam quando aliquis est liber, non tenetur ad remedia castitatis."—*ibid.*, p. 741.

[49] Archiep. Rossanensis—*ibid.*, p. 648.

[50] Archiep. Hydruntinus (Otranto, in Italy)—*ibid.*, p. 644; Episcopus Castellanetensis (Castellaneta, in Italy)—*ibid.*, p. 654; Episcopus Commensis (Como, in Italy)—*ibid.*, p. 668; Patriarcha Hierosolymitanus (Jerusalem)—*ibid.*, p. 687.

[51] Episcopus Recinatensis (Recanati, in Italy)—*ibid.*, p. 655; Episcopus Lesinensis (Lesina, on the island of Lesina off the Dalmatian Coast)—*ibid.*, p. 659.

[52] Episcopus Theanensis (Teano, in Italy)—*ibid.*, pp. 663–664.

The majority of the Fathers who rejected the Decree gave no reasons for their opposition, but simply stated that the proposed legislation should be abandoned by the Council.[53]

Thus no agreement was reached by the Fathers concerning this first draft of July 20, 1563. It was evident that a new draft of both the Canons and the Decree had to be drawn up—one which would more likely meet with the approval of the Fathers. Therefore it was agreed to omit the dogmatic Canon condemning the Protestant teaching that marriages already contracted by children without the knowledge and approval of their parents were invalid, and that parents had the right to validate or annul them. This Canon was deleted and its subject matter was placed in the preamble to the disciplinary Decree, for in a matter involving so much dispute it was impossible that the Council would continue to propose it as a dogma to be defined.[54] So on August 7th a new draft was presented to the Fathers. In the preamble to the Decree, as was mentioned above, it was stated that the Council condemned those who taught that marriages contracted in the past either clandestinely or in any other manner by children without parental consent can be rendered invalid by the parents.[55] It was also decreed that for the future boys or girls could not enter marriage without the consent of their parents before they had competed their twentieth and eighteenth years respectively. If they attempted to do so against the provisions of this law the contract by this decree was rendered null and void. It permitted, however, that a marriage could take place could not enter marriage without the consent of their parents had been asked and had given their consent. If the parents unjustly refused to give their permission, the case could be referred

[53] Episcopus Barensis (Bari, in Italy)—*ibid.*, p. 652; Episcopus Cavensis (Cava, in Italy)—*ibid.*, p. 652; Episcopus Umbriaticensis (Umbriatico, in Italy)—*ibid.*, p. 656; Episcopus Nicensis (Nice, in France)—*ibid.*, p. 658; Episcopus Marsicanus (Marsico Nuovo, in Italy)—*ibid.*, p. 677; Episcopus Amerinus (Amelia, in Italy)—*ibid.*, p. 677.

[54] Pallavicini, *Historia Concilii Tridentini*, III, lib. 22, cap. 4, n. 2.

[55] ". . . iure damnandi sunt illi, prout ab hac sacrosancta synodo damnantur, . . . qui falso affirmant, matrimonia a filiisfamilias clam sive alio quocumque modo sine parentum consensu facta parentum voluntate irritari posse."—*Acta Concilii Tridentini*, IX, 683.

to the Bishop; and if he judged that there was sufficient cause present to warrant the marriage, then a valid and licit marriage could be celebrated.[56] Moreover, to this Decree on clandestine marriages there were added various "*Canones super abusibus circa sacramentum matrimonii*"—twelve in number, of which the last directed bishops to admonish parents never to force their children to contract marriage.[57]

From the 7th to the 23rd of August the Fathers examined this second draft and proposed their reasons for and against this Decree. The substance of the argumentation remained the same as that which was presented by them in their voting on the previous draft. Hence it is not necessary to examine in detail and to classify the different reasons offered by the individual Fathers.[58] However, it is of interest to note the opinion advanced by the Bishop of Città di Castello, in Italy, who claimed that the problem under discussion did not even exist in France, for there the children were not under the *patria potestas*.[59] This statement is difficult to reconcile with the urgent petition sent by the French King to the Council on July 20th, 1563, asking the bishops to invalidate marriages contracted by children without parental consent. And Pallavacini (1607–1677) noted that the main reason leading Charles IX to make such a request was that in his kingdom such marriages often occurred and caused no little harm.[60] The status of the Civil law of France, too, is

[56] "Insuper eadem sancta synodus filios quoque familias, qui ante 20., filias vero familias, quae ante 18. suae aetatis annum completum sine parentum consensu de cetero matrimonium sive sponsalia contrahere attentaverint, ad matrimonium sive sponsalia sic contrahenda inhabiles reddit, atque huiusmodi contractum irritat et annullat, nisi parentibus per se vel per alios requisitis, ut nuptiis ab eis honeste optatis assentiantur, illis inique (praelati iudicio) renuentibus, de eiusdem praelati licentia id fecerint."—*ibid.*, p. 683.

[57] "C. 12. Curent episcopi, . . . parentes quoque moneant, ne filios filiasve invitas ad matrimonium contrahendum compellant."—*ibid.*, p. 685.

[58] For the reasons proposed by the different Fathers for and against this second draft, confer *ibid.*, pp. 685–747.

[59] Episcopus Civitatis Castellanae (Città di Castello, Italy): "Quoad id, quod dicitur de filiisfamilias, dixit, quod Galli non sunt sub patria potestate. Et quod non est disputandum an ecclesia possit . . ."—*ibid*, p. 728.

[60] *Historia Concilii Tridentini*, III, lib. 22, cap. 1, n. 16.

opposed to the dictum of the bishop, for in the sixteenth and seventeenth centuries in France marriages contracted by children without the knowledge and consent of their parents were declared invalid and the parties attempting such unions were severely punished.[61] The Bishop of Brugnato also added a singular opinion, for in his *votum* he desired to include the grandfather of the children among the persons who were competent to give the necessary marriage permission.[62]

When the voting ended on August 23rd more than fifty bishops were still opposed to the legislation contained in this Decree. So on September 5th a third draft was drawn up, and this included a few necessary changes. It embodied two different Decrees on clandestine marriages, in which Decrees the question under consideration was treated. In the first of these forms nothing else was stated than that the Council condemned those who maintained that marriages contracted by children in the past without the consent of their parents were void. The Decree also stated that parents had no power to validate or invalidate the marriages of their children.[63] However, the alternate draft contained all the provisions of the first form, and there was added to it a provision concerning the marriages of children in the future. The age was now set at eighteen years of age for the boy, and sixteen years of age for the girl. Before this age it was impossible for them to contract a valid marriage, or even valid *sponsalia,* unless they had received the consent of their father. The decree added that this permission might also be asked from the grandfather. This consent was necessary only if the parents were Catholic. If the parents refused their permission or were absent for a long time, then it remained for the Ordinary to judge whether or not the marriage might be celebrated.[64]

---

[61] Wernz, *Ius Decretalium,* IV, 487, nota 98.

[62] Episcopus Brugnatensis (Brugnato, in Italy)—*Acta Concilii Tridentini,* IX, 708.

[63] *Ibid.,* p. 761.

[64] "Eadem sancta synodus filios familias, qui ante decimum octavum, et filias familias, quae ante decimum sextum suae aetatis annum perfectum sine patris vel avi paterni catholici consensu matrimonium sive sponsalia in futurum contrahere attentaverint, ad matrimonium sive sponsalia sic contrahenda inhabiles reddit, atque huiusmodi contractus invalidat et an-

On the 7th of September the Fathers began to examine and to submit their vote on this third draft. By September 10th the voting was complete.[65] But since this third proposal brought no further agreement among the Fathers, it was decided to postpone the next general session of the Council until November 11th. Meanwhile, a fourth and altered draft was presented to the Fathers to be examined by them and voted upon in the next general session. It was this draft that met with the approval of the Council on the 11th of November.[66] In the preamble to the Decree it was stated that marriages contracted by children without the consent of their parents are not invalid, and that parents are not able to annul marriages thus contracted.[67]

On the 26th day of October the Fathers began the examination of this proposed legislation. A few wished to re-insert the requirement of parental consent for the validity of the marriage, but the majority of the previous proponents of this requirement remained silent. So the Decree was presented unchanged at the general session on the 11th of November. Thus the twenty-fourth session of the Council of Trent embodied in the famous Decree, known from its opening word as the *Tametsi,* this statement concerning the marriages of children contracted without parental consent: ". . . and consequently, that those persons are justly to be condemned, as the holy Council does condemn them with anathema, who . . . falsely assert that marriages contracted by children (minors) without the consent of parents are invalid, and that parents can make such marriages either valid or invalid; nevertheless, the holy Church of God has, for reasons most just, at all times detested and prohibited such marriages."[68] In this final draft it is evident that the omission of the clause which required parental consent for the marriage of sons under eighteen

---

nullat, nisi patre vel ave per se vel per alios requisitis, ut nuptiis honeste optatis assentiantur, et illis renuentibus, vel longe et diu absentibus, de Ordinarii licentia id fecerint."—*ibid.*, pp. 763–764.

[65] For the arguments of each bishop, confer *ibid.,* pp. 779–795.

[66] *Ibid.,* p. 889.

[67] *Ibid.,* p. 889.

[68] Conc. Trident., sess. XXIV, *de ref. matrim.,* c. 1; Waterworth, *The Canons and Decrees of the Sacred and Oecumenical Council of Trent,* p. 196.

years of age and of daughters under sixteen was motivated by the desire on the part of the Fathers to ensure the passage by the Council of the new provisions concerning clandestine marriages. On account of the opposition the two reforms could not be passed, and so it was elected to sacrifice the proposed reform concerning the marriage of minors. Thus the old law of the Church was retained and confirmed by the Council of Trent.

CHAPTER V

POST-TRIDENTINE TEACHING AND PROBLEMS REGARDING THE MARRIAGE OF MINORS

Though the law itself remained substantially unchanged from the time of the Decretals, nevertheless subsequent confirmation of this teaching along with a fuller analysis and clarification of problems was effected in the post-Tridentine period through treatises by commentators, through decisions and responses by the Congregations of the Holy See, and through judicial decisions in general. This confirmation of the law and the various problems connected with it will now be considered.

ARTICLE 1. CONFIRMATION OF THE TEACHING OF THE COUNCIL OF TRENT

After the Council of Trent the law remained unchanged, and so parental consent was in no way made necessary for the validity of the marriage of children. Such was the unanimous teaching of all Catholic authors who wrote after the year 1563,[1] and this doctrine time and time again found expression in various provincial councils.[2]

---

[1] Gonzalez-Téllez, *Commentaria Perpetua in Singulos Textus Quinque Librorum Decretalium Gregorii IX* (5 vols. in 4, Lugduni, 1715), tom. IV, tit. II, cap 1, n. 10; Sanchez, *Disputationum de Sancto Matrimonii Sacramento Tomi Tres* (Antiverpiae, 1626), lib. III, disp. 22, n. 3 (hereafter cited as *De Matrimonio*); Pirhing, *Jus Canonicum in Quinque Libros Decretalium Distributum Nova Methodo Explicatum* (5 vols. in 4, ed. novissima, Dilingae, 1722), lib. IV, tit. I, n. 90 (hereafter cited as *Jus Canonicum*); Reiffenstuel, *Jus Canonicum Universum* (5 vols. in 7, Parisiis, 1864–1870), lib. IV, tit. I, n. 23; Schmalzgrueber, *Jus Ecclesiasticum Universum* (5 vols. in 12, Romae, 1843–1845), lib. IV, tit. II, n. 71.

[2] Provincial Council of Rheims (1583)—Mansi, XXXIV A, 694e; Provincial Council of Bordeaux (1583)—Mansi, XXXIV A, 761b; Provincial Council of Bourges (1583)—Mansi, XXXIV A, 909a; Provincial Council of Mount Lebanon (1736)—*Acta et Decreta Sacrorum Conciliorum Recentiorum, Collectio Lacensis* (7 vols., Friburgi, Brisgoviae, 1870–1890) (hereafter cited as *Coll. Lac.*), II, 174a, b; Provincial Council of New Granada (1868)—*Coll. Lac.*, VI, 520c.

Likewise Pope Benedict XIV (1740–1758) declared that, even though the Church in earlier centuries had either made her own or at least tolerated laws which required the consent of the parents for the validity of the marriage, nevertheless it was clear that this parental consent was no longer required; the validity of marriage depended solely on the consent of the contracting parties to the exclusion of the will of the parents.[3]

Moreover, whenever the civil laws of the various nations, especially France,[4] decreed the invalidity of marriages contracted by minors without parental knowledge and consent, the Church always refused to acknowledge these laws as just and continuously voiced her opposition to them. Thus in the year 1629 King Louis XIII of France declared that marriages contracted by minors without the knowledge and approval of parents or guardians were null and void according to the civil law of France. This proclamation of the King demanded that the invalidity of these marriages be recognized and upheld also by ecclesiastical judges in all the ecclesiastical courts throughout the French kingdom. This edict of King Louis XIII was merely a renewal of a former decree which had been issued in 1556 by Henry II, King of France.[5] The General Assembly of the French Clergy met at Paris in the same year 1629 and there lodged a strong protest against this edict of King Louis XIII. They petitioned the King to change the force of his decree and limit it to the civil effects of marriage, for they informed him that ecclesiastical judges are obligated in conscience to observe only the Canon law in deciding the validity or invalidity of Christian marriages. Furthermore they reiterated the solemn declaration of the Council of Trent that marriages entered into by minors unknown to their parents or in opposition to their will are illicit but nevertheless valid, for lack of parental knowledge and consent is not considered by the Church as a diriment impediment to marriage.[6]

[3] Benedictus XIV, *De Synodo Dioecesana* (libri 13 in 2 tom., Lovanii, 1763), tom. I, lib. IX, cap. XI, n. IV.

[4] Bernard, *Étude Historique et Critique sur le Consentement des Ascendants au Mariage, pp.* 106–147.

[5] Roskovány, *Matrimonium in Ecclesia Catholica* (4 vols., Pestini [Nitriae]: Typis Athenaei, 1870–1882), I, 3.

[6] Roskovány, *op. cit.,* I, 4, 94–95.

Two years later, in the year 1631, King Louis XIII declared invalid the marriage of his brother Gaston, Duke of Orleans, to Margaret, sister of the Duke of Lorraine, because they married without his permission. In support of his action the King appealed to an age old custom which was in vogue amongst royal families whereby the King or head of the royal household must know of and consent to the marriages of all the members of his family. Otherwise, if the King remained uninformed or having been informed refused his consent, a valid marriage was impossible. King Louis XIII petitioned Pope Urban VIII to uphold this custom and to declare null the union of Gaston and Margaret. The Pope, however, refused to do so and in 1635 informed King Louis that neither the civil laws of his kingdom nor customs proper to the royal family could affect the validity of a Christian marriage. Furthermore, the Pope declared that the laws of the Council of Trent concerning marriage were to be observed. Consequently the marriage of Gaston and Margaret was upheld by the Pope as a valid union, since this lack of consent on the part of the head of the family in no wise constituted a diriment impediment to marriage.[7]

Early in the nineteenth century this teaching of the Council of Trent, namely, that a marriage contracted by a minor without parental knowledge and consent is a valid and true marriage, was again upheld and ratified by the Roman Pontiff. This time the Pope was Pius VII and the marriage in question likewise involved a brother of a French monarch, who at this time was Napoleon. The Emperor's brother, Jerome Bonaparte, married Eliza Patterson, a Protestant, in Baltimore, Maryland, on December 24, 1803, when he was only nineteen years of age. The marriage was celebrated without the knowledge and consent of Jerome's mother. Napoleon on learning of his brother's marriage was displeased and prevailed upon his mother to protest the validity of the marriage on the ground that Jerome Bonaparte

[7] Cf. Bauduin, *De Consuetudine Iure Canonico Dissertatio Canonica* (Lovanii: Universitatis Catholicae Typographi, 1888), pp. 200–203; *Analecta Juris Pontificii* (Romae, 1855–1869; Parisiis, 1872–1891), XII (1873), 937–969; Roskovány, *Matrimonium in Ecclesia Catholica,* I, 4, 89, 95; Wernz, *Ius Decretalium,* IV, n. 336.

was a minor and had married without her consent. Thus on February 22, 1805, Madame Bonaparte acceded to her Emperor son and protested the marriage. Then on May 24, 1805, Napoleon wrote to Pope Pius VII and petitioned the Pope to declare the marriage null and void.[8] In this letter Napoleon pointed out to the Pope that according to the civil law of France the marriage was invalid because it was contracted while his brother was still a minor and it was entered into without parental knowledge and consent. Furthermore, he explained to the Pope that if the Church declared this marriage null the best interests of the Church and France would be thereby served. For if this marriage remained a valid one a Protestant would of necessity be admitted into the ruling family of France. The Emperor instructed the Sovereign Pontiff that, after the Church had declared the invalidity of the marriage, then he himself as the ruler of France would immediately issue a declaration of nullity in accordance with the civil law of his nation. On June 27, 1805, Pope Pius VII responded to the plea of the Emperor Napoleon.[9] The Pope declared that it was beyond his power and authority to dissolve the marriage of Jerome Bonaparte and Miss Patterson since this marriage was surely a valid union. The lack of parental consent, the Pope declared, did not invalidate the marriage, for in Canon law absence of parental knowledge and consent is not recognized as a diriment impediment for the marriage of minors. Even though the civil laws of France required the knowledge and consent of parents or guardians for the validity of a marriage in which a minor is involved, nevertheless these civil prescripts cannot invalidate a Christian marriage. For the Church is exclusively competent with regard to the marriages of the baptized because matrimony is a Sacrament. The civil power of France, then, had no right to establish the lack of parental knowledge and consent as a diriment impediment for the marriage of Christians.[10] Therefore Pope Pius VII refused the request of the

[8] The letter of Napoleon to Pope Pius VII is given by Roskovány, *op. cit.*, I, 598–599.

[9] This letter of Pope Pius VII to Napoleon is recorded by Roskovány, *op. cit.*, I, 598–604; it may also be found in Artaud de Montor, *Histoire du Pape Pie VII* (2 vols., Louvain, 1836), II, 53–58.

[10] Roskovány, *Matrimonium in Ecclesia Catholica,* I, 600–601.

powerful and influential Napoleon and upheld the validity of the marriage between Jerome Bonaparte and Eliza Patterson.

In the year 1835 this teaching, which declared valid a marriage contracted by a minor without the knowledge and consent of his parents, was again confirmed by the Sacred Congregation of the Holy Office in response to two questions proposed by the Bishop of Quebec. The Sacred Congregation was asked: (1) whether a marriage contracted by minors according to the form prescribed by the Church but against the will of the parents was valid; and (2) whether a marriage between a Catholic and a baptized non-Catholic, if both were minors and contracted without parental consent, was to be considered valid. An affirmative answer was given to both questions. To the first it was pointed out that in the current legislation of the Church neither minor age nor dissent of the parents could be considered diriment impediments to marriage, even though the civil law recognized them as such. In answer to the second question it was affirmed that the same teaching was to be understood as affecting Protestants, since they, too, were bound by the laws of the Church; even in their case the civil law could not establish lack of parental consent as an invalidating impediment.[11]

Article 2. Post-Tridentine Problems

A. Whether Parents Incur an Excommunication if They Interfere with the Freedom of Marriage

One of the problems discussed by the authors was whether parents, who unjustly impeded their children from contracting marriage, or who forced them to enter the married state, incurred the excommunication established by the Council of Trent against those who attempted anything contrary to the freedom of marriage.[12] Sanchez (1550–1610) stated that authors were not in agreement, since some held that parents did incur this penalty.[13]

[11] S. C. S. Off. (Quebecen.), 17 nov. 1835—*Collectanea S. Congregationis de Propaganda Fide* (2 vols., Romae: Typographia Polyglotta S. C. de Propaganda Fide, 1907), I, n. 842. (This work will hereafter be cited *Collectanea S. C. P. F.*); *Acta Sanctae Sedis* (*ASS*), XXVI (1893), 383.

[12] Conc. Trident., sess. XXIV, *de ref. matrim.*, c. 9; cf. Waterworth, *The Canons and Decrees of the Sacred and Oecumenical Council of Trent*, p. 203.

[13] *De Matrimonio*, lib. IV, disp. XXII, n. 9 .

They argued that the Council, in stating this excommunication, wished to include all persons who impeded marriage, and that this could clearly be seen from the words of the Council, "all of whatsoever grade, dignity, and condition they may be."[14] The better opinion, however, held that parents did not incur this penalty.[15] The reason was that the decree of the Council of Trent concerned only temporal lords and magistrates and others who had jurisdiction in the external forum. That was clearly to be seen from the preface to the decree, which stated that temporal lords or magistrates should not attempt anything contrary to the freedom of marriage.[16] Thus the whole decree was to be understood in the light of this preface. Again the particle "*quare*" placed a casual connection between the first part of the decree, which spoke about temporal lords, and the second part, which condemned and punished with excommunication any interference with the freedom of marriage. Hence this penalty was to be restricted to those persons who are mentioned expressly in the first section of the decree.[17] To extend this penalty so as to include parents would have been contrary to the laws of interpretation, since in all matters that are odious and in which penalties are involved a strict interpretation must be given.[18] Sanchez noted that any bishop who unjustly forced children to marry incurred this excommunication, since a bishop had jurisdiction in the external forum over his subjects. However, if a pastor

---

[14] Gutierrez (*Canonicarum Quaestionum Libri Duo* [3 vols. in 2, Lugduni, 1661], tom. II, lib. I, cap. XX, n. 31) mentions Aegidius Alvarez Alborñoz (ca. 1300–1367) as holding this opinion. (Original source is not available to the writer.)

[15] Engel, *Collegium Universi Juris Canonici* (ed. nova, annotationes Barthel Beneventi, Venetiis, 1760), lib. IV, tit. V, n. 10.

[16] "Ne Domini Temporales aut Magistratus Quidpiam Libertati Matrimonii Contrarium Moliantur"—Conc. Trident., sess. XXIV, *de ref. matrim.*, c. 9.

[17] Sanchez, *De Matrimonio*, lib. IV, disp. XXII, n. 9; Pichler, *Jus Canonicum Secundum Quinque Decretalium Titulos Gregorii IX* (2 vols., Venetiis, 1741), I, lib. IV, tit. I, n. 83; hereafter this work will be cited as *Jus Canonicum.*

[18] Gutierrez, *Canonicarum Quaestionum Libri Duo*, tom. II, lib. I, cap. XX, n. 31; Schmalzgrueber, *Jus Ecclesiasticum Universum*, lib. IV, tit. II, n. 90.

acted in such a manner he did not incur the penalty, since in the external forum he lacked this jurisdiction.[19]

B. CLARIFICATION OF THE DECREE "TAMETSI"

A second problem considered by the authors was whether the words of the decree "*Tametsi*," "nevertheless the holy Church of God has, for reasons most just, at all times detested and prohibited such marriages," referred only to clandestine marriages or also to marriages contracted by children without the knowledge or the consent of their parents.[20] Estius (1542–1613) maintained that these words of necessity referred only to marriages entered into clandestinely, and not, therefore, to marriages contracted by children without parental consent. He argued that the particle "*nihilominus*" in the latter section of the chapter had reference to the particle "*tametsi*" in the former section, in which part the Council treated simply of clandestine marriages. He stated, therefore, that what the Council taught concerning the marriages of children entered into without parental permission should be read, as it were, within parenthesis, and was something entirely separate from the condemnation which immediately followed.[21]

This same opinion was expressed in a note in the *Acta Sanctae Sedis,* which note was appended by the editor to a decision rendered by the Sacred Congregation of the Council. The author of this note reasoned that the words embodying the condemnation by the Council of Trent could refer only to clandestine marriages; for it would be absurd for the Council to affirm that the Church recognizes marriages contracted by children without parental consent as valid and true marriages, and at the same time, in the same decree and context, to mention that the Church forbids and detests such marriages. To strengthen his argument he also appealed to decisions in which the Sacred Congregation of the Council confirmed and declared as valid marriages

---

[19] *De Matrimonio,* lib. IV, disp. XXII, n. 10.

[20] "Nihilominus Sancta Dei Ecclesia ex iustissimis causis illa semper detestata est atque prohibuit"—Conc. Trident., sess. XXIV, *de ref. matrim.,* c. 1.

[21] *In Quatuor Libros Sententiarum Commentaria* (4 vols. in 2, Parisiis, 1680), tom. III, Lib. IV, dist. 28, n. 3e.

contracted by children without parental knowledge or consent.[22] Vecchiotti (d. 1870) likewise cited the teaching of Estius with approbation, and added that it would be altogether absurd to maintain otherwise.[23]

However, the above mentioned interpretation of the decree "*Tametsi*" of the Council of Trent cannot be sustained, for the history of the acts of the Council demonstrates that the Church had always prohibited and detested marriages contracted by children without a just cause and against the will of their parents.[24] It seems evident, too, that it is an unwarranted conclusion to state that, since the Council declared valid the marriages entered into by children without parental consent, therefore the Church did not prohibit and detest such marriages. For there is a great difference between the validity and the licitness of marriage, and it is not a contradiction for the Council to affirm the validity of certain classes of marriages and yet at the same time to detest them. Moreover, the general teaching of the authors was opposed to this interpretation, for they declared that marriages contracted by children without a just cause and without the knowledge and consent of their parents, while valid, were nevertheless gravely illicit and truly detestable. Hence the Church has always prohibited them.[25] Thus, the most that can be ad-

[22] "In quo decreto particula '*nihilominus*' relationem habere videtur ad illam 'tametsi' ita ut Tridentinum detestaverit atque prohibuerit matrimonia clandestina, non ea quae ineuntur sine parentum consensu. Ista enim valida et rata pronuntiat; et absurdum foret dicere quod eodem contextu eadem detestetur et prohibeat Tridentina Synodus, quae matrimonia S. C. Concilii ipsa rata habet et confirmat"—*ASS,* XIII (1880), 444, nota 1.

[23] *Institutiones Canonicae,* III, 233.

[24] Cf. *Acta Concilii Tridentini,* IX, 380–409, 633–747, 779–795, 898–906, 958–977.

[25] Laymann, *Theologia Moralis in Quinque Libros Distributa* (ed. nova, Venetiis, 1630), lib. V, tract. X, pars I, cap. I, n. 14 (hereafter cited *Theologia Moralis*); Bellarminus, *De Controversiis Christianae Fidei Adversus huius Temporis Haereticos* (6 vols. in 7, Neapoli, 1856–1860), tom. III (Neapoli: 1858), lib. I, cap. XIX, propositio tertia; Fagnanus, *Commentaria Super Quinque Libros Decretalium* (5 vols. in 3, Venetiis, 1709), lib. IV, tit. II, n. 11; Gutierrez, *Canonicarum Quaestionum Libri Duo,* tom. II, lib. I, cap. XX, n. 3, 7–8; Cosci, *De Sponsalibus Filiorumfamilias*

mitted is that this passage proximately and expressly condemns clandestine marriages, and only secondarily and less clearly marriages contracted by children without parental consent.[26]

C. PENALTY OF DISINHERITANCE INCURRED BY THOSE CONTRACTING MARRIAGE WITHOUT PARENTAL CONSENT

Whether parents could lawfully disinherit children who married without their knowledge or consent is a question which was disputed at great length by all the authors. Many of the canonists considered the same problem from a different point of view, and asked whether the civil laws, which disinherited children for so marrying, were lawful and just. Authors in responding to these questions stated that it depended on the character and status of the person whom the child married, that is, whether the person was respectable and honorable, or unworthy and disreputable. Thus, if the child married a respectable spouse against the wishes of his parents, was it lawful to disinherit him? Even on this point authors did not agree. Those who denied such power to the parents appealed to Roman law to support their contention. They maintained that in the law of Justinian's *Novels* only fourteen reasons were set forth for which parents could lawfully disinherit their children.[27] Furthermore, it was pointed out that an all inclusive enumeration was given in this law; hence, parents were not able to disinherit their children for any other reason.[28] Now, the fact that children entered marriage without parental knowledge or consent was not listed among these fourteen causes. Therefore, since disinheritance could have ensued only as a penalty, a strict interpretation had to be employed, and no extension of the law to make it comprise similar cases was permissible. Engel (ca. 1634–1674) noted that this was the common opinion.[29]

As a supplementary argument Reiffenstuel (1642–1703) taught that one who employed his own rights did injury to no one, and

(Romae, 1766), Votum IX, n. 215–216; Devoti, *Institutionum Canonicarum Libri IV* (Romae, 1830), lib. II, tit. II, sectio X, § CXLIX, n. 1.

[26] Wernz, *Ius Decretalium,* IV, 483, nota 90.

[27] N. (115. 3).

[28] ". . . ut praeter ipsas nulli liceat ex alia lege ingratitudinis causas opponere nisi quae huius constitutionis serie continentur."—N. (115. 3).

[29] *Collegium Universi Juris Canonici,* lib. IV, tit. V, n. 7.

in law one was permitted to contract marriage, especially with an honorable person, without parental consent.[30] He stated that this was in accord with the rule of law as found in the *Digest.*[31] Sanchez proposed the argument that children could not be disinherited for marrying against the wishes of their parents, since this would be opposed to the liberty conceded by law to those contracting marriage. Moreover, he taught that civil laws which permit parents to disinherit their children were unjust and had been corrected by the Canon law. For to make laws regarding matrimony did not pertain to the secular power.[32] The same opinion, supported with the same arguments, was held by a number of authors.[33]

This position, however, was opposed by Dominic de Soto (1494–1560) and by John Gutierrez (fl. 1617). Soto stated that he could not see the worth of the opposing arguments, namely, that the civil laws, which disinherited children who enter marriage without the consent of their parents, were abrogated by the Canon law. Matrimony, even though it was a Sacrament, was also a contract, and under this aspect it has civil effects. From this angle it also pertained to the civil forum, not in the sense that the secular power was capable of changing the substance of marriage, but that it was competent to punish parties who in contracting marriage did harm to the public good of society. But children who married without a just cause against the wishes of their parents were guilty of a crime punishable by the civil law.[34] He added that the freedom of contracting marriage was not

---

[30] *Jus Canonicum Universum,* lib. III, tit. XXXVI, n. 499.

[31] ". . . non videtur vim facere, qui iure suo utitur et òrdinaria actione experitur."—D. (50. 17) 155.

[32] *De Matrimonio,* lib. IV, disp. XXV, n. 2.

[33] Navarrus, *Opera Omnia in Sex Tomos Distincta* (6 vols., Venetiis, 1618), lib. I, cap. XIV, n. 15 (hereafter cited *Opera Omnia*); De Molina, *De Primogeniorum Hispanorum Origine ac Natura* (Venetiis, 1757), lib. II, cap. XVI, n. 6; Ferraris, *Prompta Bibliotheca Canonica, Iuridica, Moralis, Theologica, necnon Ascetica, Polemica, Rubricistica, Historica* (9 vols., Romae: 1885–1889), tom. III, ad vb. *exheredatio,* p. 487, n. 26 (hereafter cited *Bibliotheca*).

[34] *In Quartum (quem vocant) Sententiarum* (2 vols., Venetiis, 1575), II, dist. 29, quaest. 1, art. 4, ad argumentum 4um.

impeded by this right of the civil power to disinherit children if they married against the wishes of their parents.[35] Gutierrez simply denied the argument brought forward from the law of the Novels. He asserted that children could be disinherited for other reasons not explicitly mentioned in the law.[36]

On the other hand, most authors agreed that parents could lawfully disinherit their children when without a just cause they attempted marriage with a disreputable or unworthy person, or with one belonging to a lower class of society. Hence they affirmed that civil laws which enacted such legislation were valid and just. The civil power in this case did not interfere with the law of the Church nor with the freedom of the parties to marry, but rather aided the Canon law by punishing a crime which was detrimental both to Church and State.[37] And Laymann (1574–1635) argued that such action did not impede the freedom of marriage, since a liberty which led to sin was a false liberty and one that could scarcely be defended by the Sacred Canons.[38]

Schmalzgrueber (1663–1735), in defending this view, argued that acts which are illicit and prohibited by the divine and natural law may be punished by the State. But marriages contracted by children against the will of their parents with an unworthy person are illicit, and are prohibited by ecclesiastical, natural, and divine law. For children, in such a grave matter as marriage, which affects not only the spouses but also the families of the contracting parties, are gravely bound to respect the just judgment of their parents. He concluded, therefore, that laws, which conceded to parents the right to disinherit their children under these circumstances were licit and just.[39]

However, many authors denied that parents could lawfully disinherit their children, even though they married an unworthy person without a just cause and against the will of the parents.

[35] Soto, *loc. cit.*

[36] *Canonicarum Quaestionum Libri Duo,* II, lib. I, cap. XIV, n. 4: "Exhaeredari possunt filii, non solum una ex quattuordecim causis a iure expressis, sed etiam ex similibus."

[37] Pichler, *Jus Canonicum,* lib. IV, tit. I, n. 83.

[38] *Theologia Moralis,* lib. V, tract. X, pars I, cap. I, n. 15, ad vb. *dicendum tertio.*

[39] *Jus Ecclesiasticum Universum,* lib. IV, tit. II, n. 101.

The arguments employed in proving their position were based on the liberty due the contracting parties, and the incompetence of the civil power to legislate concerning matrimony.[40] Reiffenstuel[41] and Ferraris (d. ca. 1763),[42] while denying that parents had a right to disinherit their children, even though they married an unworthy person, nevertheless conceded that the opposite opinion was truly probable.

However, it is to be noted that in cases actually heard and decided by the Sacred Congregation of the Council the dissent of the parents generally was judged to be unreasonable. These cases, in which the parents prohibited the marriage because the spouse was from a lower class of society, were overruled by the Sacred Congregation.[43] An interesting case was referred to the Sacred Congregation of the Council from the Diocese of Mileto, in Italy. The son of a noble family desired to marry a girl of ordinary means. The mother of the boy objected to the marriage, and appealed to the Curia of the diocese to sustain her objection on the grounds that her son was marrying a girl of inferior rank, who belonged to the common working class. Hence, she would not consent to such a marriage, for it would cause irreparable damage to the honor and dignity of her noble family. The local Curia rejected this request of the mother, and declared that her dissent was unreasonable and therefore null in law. The mother then appealed to the Sacred Congregation of the Council against the sentence of the diocesan Curia. After hearing the arguments of both sides, which were supported by the teachings of various authors, the Sacred Congregation on July 9th, 1881, confirmed the sentence of the episcopal Curia, and permitted the

---

[40] Sanchez, *De Matrimonio,* lib. IV, disp. XXV, n. 2–3; Vallensis, *Paratitla Juris Canonici sive Decretalium* (Venetiis, 1732), lib. IV, tit. I, § 9, n. 2; Navarrus, *Opera Omnia,* tom. I, cap. XIV, n. 15; De Molina, *De Primogeniorum Hispanorum Origine ac Natura,* lib. II, cap. XVI, n. 8.

[41] *Jus Canonicum Universum,* lib. III, tit. XXVI, n. 501.

[42] *Bibliotheca,* tom. III, ad vb. *exheredatio,* pp. 487–488, nn. 27–28.

[43] *Thesaurus Resolutionum Sacrae Congregationis Concilii* (167 vols., Romae: 1718–1908) (hereafter cited as *Thesaurus S. C. Concilii*), III, 251; V, 318; XLVII, 168; LXII, 222; CXXXIX, 116; *ASS,* XIII (1880), 440.

boy to marry the girl of lower rank against the wishes of his parents.[44]

The Curial practice, then, did not favor the petition of parents to prohibit the marriages of their children on the basis that the child's choice was a person of inferior social rank and condition. Hence, in the cases in which the Sacred Congregation of the Council permitted the celebration of the marriage, the parents could not lawfully disinherit their children.[45]

D. MARRIAGES CONTRACTED BY PARENTS IN THE NAME OF THEIR CHILDREN WHO ARE PRESENT AND DO NOT OBJECT

A final difficulty considered by the authors was whether a marriage contracted by the parents in the name of their children, but without their command, was valid if the children were present at the time of the contract and voiced no objection to the action of their parents. Authors disagreed. Those who held for the validity of these marriages based their arguments on a law of Boniface VIII.[46] This law declared that *sponsalia* contracted by the parents in the name of the children who, though present, did not object, were to be considered valid because of the presumed consent of the children. This presumption was founded on the fact that parents love their children more than themselves; hence, it was presumed that they would always provide in the best possible way for them. Since the children were present and did not object, their consent, then, had to be presumed.[47] Now, these authors extended this law of Boniface VIII so as to include *sponsalia de praesenti,* or marriage. For, they argued, the same reasons by which the *sponsalia de futuro* were presumed valid held also for marriage. Moreover, they maintained that one who remained silent was presumed to consent, especially when there was an obligation to speak out and contradict; and a child would be bound to voice his objection to a marriage planned and executed for him by his parents if it was contrary to his liking.[48] How-

[44] *Thesaurus S. C. Concilii,* CXL, 502; *ASS,* XIV (1881), 455; *Analecta Juris Pontificii,* XXI (1882), 126–128.

[45] Wernz, *Ius Decretalium,* IV, 486.

[46] C. un., *de desponsatione impuberum,* IV, 2, in VI°.

[47] Sanchez, *De Matrimonio,* lib. I, disp. XXIII, n. 3.

[48] Sanchez, De *Matrimonio,* lib. I, disp. XXIII, n. 2–3; Pirhing, *Jus*

ever, the same authors limited this right to the parents, so that, if another person, even a brother, a sister, or a relative contracted marriage in the name of the children and without their permission, the marriage was considered invalid. Silence on the part of the child in this case did not suffice, but his internal consent had to be manifested externally.[49] Sanchez noted that this right was common to both parents, and did not belong exclusively to the father. For the right was based, not on the civil law of the *patriapotestas,* but rather on the natural love of parents for their children, which is even stronger in the mother than in the father.[50]

On the other hand, many authors denied that parents could contract marriage in the name of their children. Mere silence on the part of the child, even though he was present, did not give rise to the presumption of consent. The child had to manifest this consent by some external sign. Schmalzgrueber stated that the right enjoyed by parents to engage their children without their command was something altogether singular and exceptional. Therefore it was not to be extended to include also their right to contract marriage for their children.[51] He also denied the parity between *sponsalia* and marriage, which furnished the basis of all the arguments for the opposite opinion. With great clearness he pointed out that marriage effected the assumption of a much graver obligation and also established an indissoluble status. Therefore complete freedom was demanded in the contracting parties, which freedom was not so necessary for the *sponsalia,* since they could later be dissolved for many reasons.[52] Pichler (1670–1736) strengthened the force of this argument by pointing to a rule of law which stated that one who remained

---

Canonicum, lib. IV, tit. II, § 3, n. 16; Mascardus, *Conclusiones Omnium Probationum Quae in Utroque Iure Quotidie Versantur* (3 vols., Venetiis, 1593), III, Concl. MCCLV, n. 34.

[49] Sanchez, *De Matrimonio,* lib. I, disp. XXIII, n. 7; Engel, *Collegium Universi Juris Canonici,* lib. IV, pars III, cap. V, § 3, n. 5; Pirhing, *Jus Canonicum,* lib. IV, tit. XVI, n. 5.

[50] *De Matrimonio,* lib. I, disp. XXIII, n. 9.

[51] *Jus Ecclesiasticum Universum,* lib. IV, tit. I, n. 247.

[52] Schmalzgrueber, *op. cit.,* lib. IV, tit. I, n. 247.

silent neither affirmed nor denied.[53] A child, then, who remained silent while his parents contracted marriage in his name neither consented nor dissented, and thus he did not express his personal consent through any certain and definite sign, as the nature of matrimony required.[54] Wernz (1842–1914) approved this position of Schmalzgrueber and Pichler.[55]

ARTICLE 3. THE DUTY OF PASTORS AND ORDINARIES REGARDING THE MARRIAGE OF MINORS

The Council of Trent in the twenty-fourth session commanded that a Catechism of Catholic doctrine be drawn up, and placed both bishops and pastors under a grave obligation to explain its contents to their people.[56] This Catechism demanded, among other things, that pastors frequently warn children not to enter marriage without consulting their parents, or in defiance of their express wishes. Pastors were to explain to the young that they owed this honor and respect to their parents or guardians.[57] The statutes of many provincial councils placed upon the pastor a serious obligation to exhort children in public sermons always to consult their parents before entering marriage. He was to make known to them that they were thus bound by the laws of God and of the Church.[58]

Pope Benedict XIV demanded that, when the contracting parties approached the pastor to make arrangements for their

[53] "Is, qui tacet, non fatetur; sed nec utique negare videtur"—Reg. 44, *R. J.* in VIº.

[54] Pichler, *Jus Canonicum,* lib. IV, tit. I, n. 81.

[55] *Ius Decretalium,* IV, 483–484.

[56] Conc. Trident., sess. XXIV, *de ref.,* c. 7; cf. Waterworth, *The Canons and Decrees of the Sacred and Oecumenical Council of Trent,* p. 213.

[57] *The Catechism of the Council of Trent,* translated by J. Donovan (Dublin, 1829), p. 339.

[58] Provincial Council of Siponto (1567)—Mansi, XXXV, B, 886-b; Provincial Council of Besançon (1571)—Mansi, XXXVI (bis), 60-c; VI Provincial Council of Milan (1582)—Mansi, XXXIV, A, 527-c; Provincial Council of Avignon (1725), cap. V—*Coll. Lac.,* I, 551; Provincial Council of Ravenna (1855), Pars II, cap. VIII, n. 2—*Coll. Lac.,* VI, 166-c; Provincial Council of Prague (1860), Tit. VI, cap. IX—*Coll. Lac.,* V, 517-c; Provincial Council of Vienna (1858), Tit. III, cap. XII—*Coll. Lac.,* V, 175-c; Provincial Council of Venice (1859), Pars III, cap. XXII, § 8—*Coll. Lac.,* VI, 337-c.

marriage, the pastor diligently had to inquire and receive proof from them that their parents had been consulted and had given their consent. If, however, the pastor learned that the children had not consulted their parents about the marriage, or that the parents, having been consulted, remained unwilling, then he was not to assist at the marriage, but was to refer the case to the Ordinary.[59] The same teaching was expressed by various authors,[60] and likewise was inserted in the legislation of many provincial councils.[61]

As Wernz indicated, it was within the bishop's power to forbid pastors to assist at these marriages, for in such cases the bishop did not unjustly and absolutely forbid the marriage because of lack of parental consent, but merely reserved to himself the judgment as to whether parental opposition was founded on a just and canonical reason.[62] If it was discovered that the parents were unjustly opposed to the marriage, no dispensation, properly considered, was given by the bishop, but simply a declaration that there was nothing present in this particular case to hinder the valid and licit celebration of the marriage.[63] If, however, the objection of the parents was deemed reasonable and just, then the bishop could not licitly permit the celebration of the mar-

---

[59] Benedictus XIV, ep. encycl. "*Nimiam licentiam,*" 18 maii 1743—*Codicis Iuris Canonici Fontes cura Emi Petri Card. Gasparri Editi* (9 vols., Romae: Typis Polyglottis Vaticanis, 1923–1939, Vols. VII–IX ed. cura et studio Emi Iustiniani Card. Serédi) (hereafter cited as *Fontes*), n. 337.

[60] Muscettula, *Dissertatio de Sponsalibus et Matrimonio Parentibus Insciis vel Invitis cum Adnotationibus Mazochii et Zech* (Venetiis, 1772), Dubium III, n. 95–105; Cosci, *De Sponsalibus Filiorumfamilias,* Votum IX, n. 91; Zitelli, *Apparatus Juris Ecclesiastici juxta Recentissimas S. S. Urbis Congregationum Resolutiones* (Romae, 1886), p. 369-d; Feije, *De Impedimentis et Dispensationibus Matrimonialibus* (3. ed., Lovanii: Carolus Peters, 1885), n. 537; Wernz, *Ius Decretalium,* IV, 484; Bangen, *Introductio Practica de Sponsalibus et Matrimonio in Usum Sacerdotum Curatorum* (4 vols., Monasterii, Typis et Sumptibus Librariae Aschendorffianae, 1858–1860), II, 7.

[61] Provincial Council of Rouen (1581)—Mansi, XXXIV, A, 626-e; I Provincial Council of Sienna (1599)—Mansi, XXXVI (bis), 540-c; Provincial Council of Cambray (1631)—Mansi, XXXVI (ter), 180-d; I Provincial Council of New Granada (1868), Tit. IV, cap. XI—*Coll. Lac.,* VI, 520-c.

[62] *Ius Decretalium,* IV, 484–485.

[63] Wernz, *ibid.,* p. 484.

riage.[64] Indeed, Benedict XIV warned bishops to be strict in this matter, lest they become co-operators in the sin of the children, or easily offer them the occasion for disobedience towards their parents.[65] And Gutierrez advised bishops not to scruple about prohibiting such marriages, since it were far better to forego the use of the Sacrament than to stir up hatred and quarrels between the father and his child.[66]

[64] Cosci, *De Sponsalibus Filiorumfamilias,* Votum IX, n. 14–25, 60–62.

[65] Benedictus XIV, ep. encycl. "*Satis vobis,*" 17 nov. 1741—*Fontes,* n. 319.

[66] *Canonicarum Quaestionum Libri Duo,* Lib. I, cap. XX, n. 23.

PART II

CANONICAL COMMENTARY

CHAPTER VI

PRELIMINARY DISCUSSION

Before considering in detail the canonical legislation with regard to the marriage of minors the writer deems it both helpful and necessary to insert this preliminary chapter. Herein the writer will consider the division of persons according to age, for, since this dissertation concerns the marriage of minors, it is imperative that a clear understanding of the term "minor" be had. Furthermore, the writer will treat of the juridical effects of age in relation to the acquisition and exercise of rights and will point out the legislation of the Code of Canon Law which is proper to minors concerning this point. Hence the first two articles of this preliminary chapter will be nothing more than an analysis of canons 88 and 89 of the Code of Canon Law. Canon 88 classifies persons into various age groups, while canon 89 enacts the basic principle concerning the exercise of rights by those who are of minor age. In a third and separate article the writer will discuss the exercise of a minor's right in marriage.

Article 1. Classification of Persons According to Age

At the outset it will be helpful to consider the division of persons as found in the Roman Law, for this legislation concerning the matter under consideration served as a model for the present law of the Church. The Roman Law divided persons into four age periods, namely infancy, impuberty, puberty, and majority. At the time of Justinian those who had not completed their seventh year of age were considered infants.[1] However, in the

[1] C. (6. 30) 18; D. (23. 1) 14.

earlier Roman Law, when all juridical acts, such as contracts, were performed by speaking solemn words, infants were held to be those who could not speak. Hence, in that period the etymological significance of the term "infant" (*in- fari*) was understood.[2]

The next period of age was that of impuberty, which extended from the end of the seventh year of age to the completion of the fourteenth year for boys and the twelfth for girls.[3] In the earlier Roman Law both boys and girls were considered as *impubes* up to the time that they actually possessed the power to procreate, and this fact was to be established by means of corporal inspection. Therefore, in this early period of Roman Law it is impossible to speak of an age at which puberty is attained. Gradually it came to pass that girls were no longer subject to this corporal examination. They were now considered as *impubes* up to the completion of their twelfth year. Boys, however, were continued to be examined, and this examination probably took place when they assumed the dress and political status of men.[4]

In the classical period of Roman Law there was not full agreement among the Romans as to when impuberty ended and puberty began in regard to boys. In fact, there were three different schools of thought. The Sabinian school held that the boy reached the age of puberty when he appeared to have done so from his bodily development, that is, when he was able to procreate. Therefore, the Sabinians maintained that before the boy could be considered *pubes* a corporal inspection was necessary. The Proculians, on the other hand, declared that the age of impuberty lasted until the boy had completed his fourteenth year. Age alone was the deciding factor, and no corporal inspection was necessary. Still a third view was advanced by Priscus. This opinion stated that the age of impuberty for males lasted until both factors, namely the actual development of the body ascer-

---

[2] Institutiones Gai (3. 109)—*Collectio Librorum Iuris Anteiustiniani,* I, 126; cf. also D. (40. 5) 30. 1.

[3] C. (5. 60) 3; I. (1. 22).

[4] Corbett, *The Roman Law of Marriage,* p. 51; Ojetti, *Commentarium in Codicem Iuris Canonici* (4 vols., Romae: Apud Aedes Universitatis Gregorianae, 1927–1931), II, 15; this work will hereafter be cited as *Commentarium in Codicem.*

tained by inspection and the necessary age of fourteen years were present.[5] Before the time of Justinian the common opinion was that of Priscus.[6] This age-old dispute was authoritatively settled by Justinian in the year 529 when he declared that henceforth the age of impuberty for males was presumed to end and the period of puberty to begin after the completion of their fourteenth year of age.[7] In favoring the opinion of the Proculians, Justinian rejected the necessity of corporal inspection and declared that such an examination was an indecency unworthy of the decorum of his times.[8]

The third period of age according to Roman Law was that of puberty, which extended from the end of the twelfth year in girls and the fourteenth in boys up to the completion of their twenty-fifth year.[9] After the twenty-fifth year was completed, the period of majority for the Romans began. This age of twenty-five years was the same for both men and women, and, when completed, these persons were called majors or adults.[10]

The law of the Church regarding the division of persons by reason of age is given in canon 88. Here for the first time in the history of Canon law there is provided definite legislation treating of the general classification of persons according to age.[11] It is true that in pre-Code law the ecclesiastical lawgiver had determined a necessary age in regard to the acquisition of certain

---

[5] Ulpian (11. 28)—Muirhead, *The Institutes of Gaius and the Rules of Ulpian* (Edinburgh: T. & T. Clark, 1904), p. 387; Institutiones Gai (1. 196)—*Collectio Librorum Iuris Anteiustiniani,* I, 44.

[6] I. (1. 22); C. (5. 60) 3.

[7] C. (5. 60) 3.

[8] I. (1. 22).

[9] D. (4. 4); C. (5. 60) 3; I. (1. 22) pr.; cf. Burdick, *The Principles of Roman Law and Their Relation to Modern Law,* pp. 262–263.

[10] D. (38. 2) 14 pr.; C. (6. 45) 5; D. (33. 1) 21. 5.

[11] Wernz-Vidal, *Ius Canonicum ad Codicis Normam Exactum* (7 vols. in 8, Romae: Apud Aedes Universitatis Gregorianae; Vol. II, *De Personis,* 3. ed., recognita Philippo Aguirre, 1943; Vol. III, *De Religiosis,* 1933; Vol. V, *Ius Matrimoniale,* 2. ed., 1928; Vol. VII, *Ius Poenale Ecclesiasticum,* 1937), II, n. 2; this work will hereafter be cited *Ius Canonicum;* Michiels, *Principia Generalia de Personis in Ecclesia* (Lublin–Polonia: Universitas Catholica (1932), p. 24; this work will hereafter be cited as *De Personis.*

rights as, for example, the right to marry,[12] but nowhere in Church law was there set forth a complete and accurate system of age. This lacuna in pre-Code law was filled by having recourse to Roman Law and using the principles concerning age as found therein. But when Roman Law ceased to be regarded as a subsidiary source of Canon law, the Church was compelled to bring forward her own principles and establish a definite system of classifying persons by reason of age. Such a need on the part of the Church was accentuated because the civil codes of the various nations greatly differed in their division of persons according to age. Because of this divergence the Church could not follow the civil law in this regard.[13]

The Code of Canon Law classifies persons according to age into two main groups, namely, majors and minors. A person who has completed his twenty-first year is a major; under twenty-one years of age he is a minor.[14] A minor may be considered as either *pubes* or *impubes*. A minor boy is presumed to have reached the age of puberty when he completes his fourteenth year; a girl, however, after her twelfth year.[15] Below these years of fourteen and twelve a minor is considered *impubes*.[16] And a person below the age of seven years is given the special name of infant, and is presumed to lack the use of reason.[17]

Thus the present law of the Church approximates to a great extent the division of persons by reason of age as found in the Roman Law. However, there is this one great difference. Church law considers as an adult one who has completed his twenty-first year of age.[18]

---

[12] C. 9, X, *de desponsatione impuberum,* IV, 2; this decretal is also found as c. 12, Compilatio I, *de desponsatione impuberum,* IV, 2; JL, n. 13969; c. 10, X, *de desponsatione impuberum,* IV, 2; this decretal is also found as c. 13, Compilatio I, *de desponsatione impuberum,* IV, 2; JL, n. 15730; c. 14, X, *de desponsatione impuberum,* IV, 2; this decretal is also found as c. 2, Compilatio III, *de desponsatione impuberum,* IV, 2; Potthast, n. 2775.

[13] Wernz-Vidal, *Ius Canonicum,* II, 5.

[14] Canon 88, § 1.

[15] Canon 88, § 2.

[16] Canon 88, § 3.

[17] *Loc. cit.*

[18] Vermeersch-Creusen (*Epitome Iuris Canonici cum Commentariis ad Scholas et ad Usum Privatum* [3 vols., Mechliniae-Romae: H. Dessain,

A minor boy after his fourteenth year and a minor girl on completion of her twelfth year are considered to be *pubes*. This puberty, of which the canon treats, is juridical or legal puberty and not physiological puberty. Natural or physiological puberty is reached at different times in different individuals depending on race, climate, environment, and a host of other conditions. Hence, it is impossible for the legislator to determine a fixed age at which all persons attain natural puberty. But since a definite and uniform age of puberty is necessary for society, and since this judgment cannot be left to individuals to decide, for innumerable difficulties and differences of opinions would arise, the ecclesiastical lawgiver, guided by the principles of Roman Law, has declared that the legal age of puberty is fourteen years complete for boys and twelve years complete for girls. Therefore puberty is presumed to be present when such an age is reached. This is a presumption of law, as is clear from the words of the canon *censetur pubes,* and hence yields to contrary proof. Michiels, however, maintains that this presumption is a *praesumptio iuris et de iure,* so that whenever the law treats of those who are *pubes* one must never take cognizance of the actual power to procreate but only the age as declared by the canon.[19] Coronata, on the other hand, teaches that this presumption is one of law only, so that if one is actually proven to be *pubes* before this canonical age he may be considered such in all matters that are favorable to him. However, this should not be done in matters that are unfavorable to him, since all restrictions placed on a minor are to benefit and not to penalize him.[20]

Vol. I, 6. ed., 1937; Vol. II, 5. ed., 1934; Vol. III, 5. ed., 1936], I, n. 208) (hereafter cited as *Epitome*) state that this is the first time that any general canonical legislation is available concerning the age of majority. Furthermore, they maintain that the definition of this age is canonical, even though many civil codes have now adapted this age of majority for many acts. Cf. also Baumer, "De iure poenali pro delinquentibus minoris aetatis in Codice iuris canonici et novissimo schemate Codicis poenalis helvetici"—*Apollinaris* (Romae: 1928–), VI (1933), 469, nota 74.

[19] *De Personis,* p. 29.

[20] *Institutiones Iuris Canonici ad Usum Utriusque Clerici et Scholarum* (5 vols., Taurini: Marietti, 1928–1936), I, 120, nota 3; this work will hereafter be cited as *Institutiones Iuris Canonici.* Cf. also Beste, *Introductio in*

Another presumption of law is given in canon 88, § 3, for it states that an infant is presumed to lack the use of reason, while a child over seven years is considered to possess the use of reason. However, Maroto declares that the law considers all persons who have not completed their seventh year of age as lacking the use of reason, and this law, he maintains, does not admit proof to the contrary.[21] This opinion of Maroto cannot be sustained, since Canon law does admit and recognize proof for the use of reason before the completion of the seventh year of age. Thus, for example, infants, even before they have finished their seventh year of age, provided they have the use of reason, are to be admitted to receive Holy Communion.[22] This is also supported by a private response of the Pontifical Commission for the Authentic Interpretation of the Code given on January 3, 1918. The Pontifical Commission declared that children who had been admitted to Holy Communion before the completion of their seventh year of age were also bound by the two precepts of annual confession and communion.[23] Thus the presumptions stated in canon 88 are all merely presumptions of law and must cede to proven facts.[24]

The manner of computing the time for these various periods of age is ruled by canon 34, § 3, n. 3. This law states that if the starting point does not coincide with the beginning of the day, then the first day is not counted and the time expires with the end of the last day of the same number. Thus, if a boy was born on August 22, 1920 at four o'clock in the afternoon he is

---

Codicem (2. ed., Collegeville, Minn.: St. John's Abbey Press, 1944), pp. 133–134.

[21] *Institutiones Iuris Canonici ad Normam Novi Codicis* (3. ed., 2 vols., Madrid, 1919), I, n. 426; this work will hereafter be cited *Institutiones Iuris Canonici.*

[22] Canon 859.

[23] This reply of the Pontifical Commission is reported in Bouscaren, *The Canon Law Digest* (2 vols., Milwaukee: Bruce, 1934–1943), I, 54–55, under canon 12.

[24] Beste, *Introductio in Codicem*, pp. 133–134; Oesterle, *Praelectiones Iuris Canonici* (2 vols., Romae: in Collegio S. Anselmi, 1931), I, 51; Claeys Bouuaert-Simenon, *Manuale Iuris Canonici ad Usum Seminariorum* (Vol. I, 3. ed., 1930; Vol. II, 1931; Vol. III, 3. ed., 1931, Gandae et Loedii: Apud Auctores in Seminariis Gandavensi et Loediensi), I, n. 238; this work will hereafter be cited as *Manuale Iuris Canonici.*

presumed to have reached the age of puberty on August 23, 1934, and is an adult on August 23, 1941. Thus the time is computed mathematically and not morally, and each period of age must be completed and not merely begun. In the pre-Code law the computation of age was not fixed as it is in the present law of the Church. The majority of pre-Code canonists considered a moral completion of the age period to be sufficient, but were not agreed as to what constituted this moral completion. A few among them held that an age period was morally completed even though one or two days were lacking. They followed the principle *minimum pro nihilo reputatur.* The more common opinion, however, held a moral completion to mean that if the last day was begun then it could be considered as if it were already completed. Thus, for example, a boy born on August 22, 1900 at four o'clock in the afternoon could validly contract marriage on August 22, 1914 at any hour of the day.[25] A final opinion demanded that the time be computed mathematically and rejected all moral computation as insufficient. The time was to be counted from moment to moment, and hence the last day could not be considered complete when begun.[26]

Article 2. The Juridical Effect of Age Concerning the Acquisition and Exercise of Rights

Through the Sacrament of Baptism man becomes a subject of rights in the Church of Christ. This juridical personality resulting from valid baptism is essentially and basically the same in all baptized persons. However, the actual capacity to acquire rights and the capability to exercise those rights once they are attained depend on various circumstances marked out and determined by the positive will of the legislator. Hence the actual juridical capacity varies in different individuals. Thus some possess more rights than others and enjoy greater liberty in the

[25] Sanchez, *De Matrimonio,* lib. VII, disp. 104, nn. 1–3; lib. I, disp. 16, n. 4; Schmalzgrueber, *Jus Ecclesiasticum Universum,* lib. IV, tit. II, n. 60; Wernz, *Ius Decretalium,* IV, n. 321.

[26] Reiffenstuel, *Jus Canonicum Universum,* lib. IV, tit. II, n. 12; Leurenius, *Forum Ecclesiasticum in quo Ius Canonicum Universum Explicatur* (5 vols. in 3, Venetiis, 1729), lib. IV, q. 137, n. 2.

exercise of their rights. One of the determining factors,[27] and it may be said to be the most important, regulating the acquisition and exercise of rights is that of age.[28]

That age should play such an important rôle in determining the actual juridical status of persons is not surprising. For it is an undeniable fact that the development and evolution of the mind is generally dependent in great part on the physical development of the body which comes only with the passing of years. Maturity of mind and judgment usually follows closely the advance in years. Hence, it is only right that the acquisition and exercise of rights be in proportion to the person's age.

As a basis for the acquisition of rights a human act is very often required. Consequently the person must have the use of reason, which is not presumed to be present before the completion of the seventh year of age.[29] Again, the importance of the right and its consequences both to the individual and to society may move the legislator to concede it only to those who have attained a certain age. The reason is that, when the person reaches that age, it may be presumed that he will be mature in mind and will, and be thus fit to possess that right. Thus, for example, the right to vote in ecclesiastical elections is given only to those who have reached the age of puberty,[30] and the right to marry is not granted before a certain age is completed, namely the sixteenth year for the boy and the fourteenth year for the girl.[31] The right to be eligible to receive the order of priesthood is conceded only to those candidates who have finished their twenty-fourth

[27] Examples of other qualities and circumstances which affect the juridical status of persons are the following: place of origin (canon 90), domicile and quasi-domicile (canons 92–95), relationship either by blood or affinity (canons 97–98), and rite (canon 98).

[28] Wernz-Vidal, *Ius Canonicum,* II, n. 2; Michiels, *De Personis,* pp. 18–19; Ojetti, *Commentarium in Codicem,* II, 13; Cappello, *Summa Iuris Canonici* (3 vols., Vol. I, 3. ed., 1938; Vol. II, 3. ed., 1939; Vol. III, 1936, Romae: Apud Aedes Universitatis Gregorianae), I, n. 186; this work will hereafter be cited *Summa.*

[29] Canon 88, § 3.

[30] Canon 167, § 1, 2°.

[31] Canon 1067, § 1. For examples of other rights which the lawgiver concedes to minors when they attain a definite age, confer canons 542, 1°; 555, § 1, 1°; 573; 766, n. 1; 796, n. 3; 1223, n. 2; 1757, § 1; 1795, § 2.

year of age,[32] and eligibility for the office of bishop is restricted to those who are at least thirty years old.[33]

Besides the rights which majors and minors have in common the law concedes a number of rights which are proper to minors. These rights are given to minors precisely because of their age, and they serve to guard the minor against fraud, and also grant special legal protection to his person. Thus, for example, whenever a minor is involved in a contentious trial, he enjoys the right to have an advocate who is to be appointed by the judge.[34] When a minor is gravely injured, he may, in addition to the ordinary means of getting redress, apply to the court for the extraordinary relief of the *restitutio in integrum*.[35] When certain crimes are committed against a minor the lawgiver punishes the offender with special penalties.[36] And if the minor himself is guilty of the crime, then the law presumes that the imputability of the delict is to be lessened in proportion to the minor's age.[37]

In the acquisition of rights minors enjoy with few exceptions the same status as adults. However, in the exercise of these acquired rights there is a vast difference between the two age groups. According to the law of the Church an adult enjoys the full exercise of his rights,[38] and may dispose of them as he wills, providing, of course, he observes the order of nature and the rights of others. The legislator concedes this complete autonomy to those who have attained their majority, because he judges them to be sufficiently mature to exercise their rights sanely and sensibly. In other words, the lawgiver considers majors as able to care for themselves. Minors, on the other hand, in the exercise of their rights remain dependent upon the

---

[32] Canon 975.

[33] Canon 331, § 1, 2°. For examples of other rights for which the legislator requires an age above twenty-one years, confer canons 504; 524, § 1; 559, § 1; 975; 367, § 1; 372, § 1; 399, § 1; 423; 446; 479; 1573, § 4; 1574, § 1; 1589; 1598, n. 2; 2004, § 3; 2017.

[34] Canon 1655, § 2.

[35] Canon 1687, § 1.

[36] Canons 2353; 2354; 2357, § 1; 2358; 2359, § 2.

[37] Canon 2204; cf. also canons 2218, § 2; 2230.

[38] Canon 89: "Persona maior plenum habet suorum iurium exercitium; . . ."

authority of their parents or guardians except in those matters in which the law exempts them.[39] The purpose of the legislator in so restricting minors in the use of their rights is not to punish but to help them. It is not a penalty inflicted upon them, but rather it is a privilege conceded to them. For the restriction serves to prevent minors from injuring themselves by their own acts, and also to protect them against the plots and schemes of unscrupulous persons who would take advantage of their immature judgment to defraud them.[40] In enacting this limitation concerning minors the legislator has also in mind the common good of society, for the free and complete exercise of some rights by irresponsible and immature minors might serve at times to jeopardize and even harm the public good.[41] For example, a minor possessing the right of patronage may not exercise it except through the agency of his parents or Catholic tutors,[42] because if such a right were abused it would bring great harm to the Church.

The Code of Canon Law, therefore, subjects minors in the use of their rights to their parents or legal guardians. The minor is subject primarily to his father,[43] but if the father is dead or if he is impeded because of moral or legal reasons from exercising his authority, then the minor is responsible to his mother, and in the exercise of his rights he remains subject to her. However, if both parents are dead or are prevented from exercis-

[39] Canon 89: ". . . minor in exercitio suorum iurium potestati parentum vel tutorum obnoxia manet, iis exceptis in quibus ius minores a patria potestate exemptos habet."

[40] Claeys Bouuaert-Simenon, *Manuale Iuris Canonici,* I, n. 239, III; Wernz-Vidal, *Ius Canonicum,* II, 4; Augustine, *A Commentary on the New Code of Canon Law* (8 vols., Vol. II, 6. ed., St. Louis: Herder, 1936), II, 11; this work will hereafter be cited *Commentary;* Coronata, *Institutiones Iuris Canonici,* I, 122, nota 1; Cappello, *Summa,* I, 213–214.

[41] Ojetti, *Commentarium in Codicem,* II, n. 2; Michiels, *De Personis,* p. 39; Maroto, *Institutiones Iuris Canonici,* I, n. 428.

[42] Canon 1456: ". . . ius patronatus exercet minores per parentes aut per tutores; quod si parentes vel tutores acatholici sint, ius patronatus interim suspensum manet."

[43] Canon 1648, § 3: "Sed in causis spiritualibus et cum spiritualibus connexis, si minores usum rationis assecuti sint, agere et respondere queunt sine *patris* vel tutoris consensu; . . ."

ing their natural authority, the minor is then placed under a guardian.[44] This tutor or curator is appointed by competent authority which may either be ecclesiastical or civil. When there is question of the minor exercising his ecclesiastical rights the Ordinary usually makes the appointment.[45] But even in this case it suffices if the Ordinary approves the guardian appointed by the civil authority.[46] The Code of Canon Law, however, is silent concerning the manner of designating a curator or tutor. Therefore it may be said that persons who have been designated for these offices by civil law are recognized by Canon law. Nevertheless, the Church reserves to herself the right to appoint another guardian to represent the minor in the ecclesiastical court, if the Ordinary should deem such action necessary.[47]

Thus canon 89 states that a minor in the use of his rights is subject to the authority of his parents or guardians unless the law exempts him from the paternal power. The presumption in this canon favors the subjection of minors to their parents; hence, any exception removing them from the parental authority must be clearly proved. If, therefore, a doubt would arise in a particular case as to whether the minor may exercise a right which he possesses independently of parental authority, such a doubt must be solved in favor of the authority of the parents. The doubt may not be resolved for liberty of action on the part of the children, since the presumption, which governs the case, is for subjection.

The last section of canon 89 does not mention tutors or curators but only the parents.[48] The reason for such an omission is evident, because if the law exempts the minor from the authority of the parents then for a much greater reason should it also remove him from the authority of the guardian. For if the law

[44] Canon 1648, § 1: "Pro minoribus . . . agere et respondere tenentur eorum parentes aut tutores vel curatores."

[45] Canon 1648, § 3.

[46] Canon 1651, § 1.

[47] Canon 1651, § 2: "Ordinarius potest quoque alium curatorem constituere pro foro ecclesiastico, si, omnibus mature perpensis, id statuendum esse prudenter censuerit."

[48] ". . . iis exceptis in quibus ius minores a patria potestate exemptos habet."

denies this authority even to parents, who from the natural law are constituted guardians of their children, then it would not be right to expect a legal guardian to possess such power, since the power of parents over their children is far more extensive than the authority enjoyed by tutors or curators.

Authors do not agree concerning the extension of the term, "law," as found in canon 89.[49] Blat[50] maintains that not only ecclesiastical law but also divine law both natural and positive is to be understood, for this canon makes no distinction and places no restriction. Gillet,[51] agreeing with Blat, states that the word, "law," in this canon means also the natural and divine law, because the subject matter, with which the canon deals, does not demand any restriction to purely ecclesiastical law. Gillet concedes that in other canons in the Code of Canon Law[52] where the term, "law," appears without any qualification the meaning is obviously ecclesiastical law, for the subject matter with which these canons deal demands such an interpretation. But he teaches that this is not the case in canon 89.

However, the more common opinion is that the natural and the divine law are not included, for this canon considers only a canonical limitation which is of no concern to the divine law, since the divine law belongs to a higher order of law and transcends these positive prescriptions.[53] Thus, for example, the right of a child, who has the use of reason, to enter the true religion irrespective of the wishes of his parents is not an exception

---

[49] ". . . iis exceptis in quibus *ius* minores a patria potestate exemptos habet."

[50] *Commentarium Textus Codicis Iuris Canonici* (5 vols. in 7, Vol. II, *De Personis*, 2. ed.; Romae: Ex Typographia Pontificia in Instituto Pii IX, 1923), II, n. 7; this work will hereafter be cited *Commentarium*.

[51] "De Exemptione a Patria Potestate"—*Ephemerides Theologicae Lovanienses* (Brugis: 1924–), XI (1934), 787; this periodical will hereafter be cited with the abbreviation *ETL*.

[52] Canons 5; 27, § 2; 117, 1o.

[53] Coronata, *Institutiones Iuris Canonici*, I, 122; Beste, *Introductio in Codicem*, p. 134; Michiels, *De Personis*, p. 45; Claeys Bouuaert-Simenon, *Manuale Iuris Canonici*, I, n. 239, III; Vermeersch-Creusen, *Epitome*, I, n. 209.

to this canon 89, for this right flows directly from the divine law.[54]

Moreover, the writer maintains that the term, "law," in this canon means ecclesiastical law, for the very reason that it is in the Code of Canon Law. For the Code of Church Law is primarily and principally a code of disciplinary law, and its prescripts are those of a human lawgiver.[55] It is true, however, that in many places in the Code the divine law both natural and positive is stated, but from the matter dealt with it is always clear that the law is the divine law.[56] But this is not the case in canon 89, for from the mere use of the term, "law," one cannot immediately conclude that the natural and divine law are also included. For it is not clear from the subject matter, namely the exercise of minor's rights, that this canon considers also the natural and divine law. Hence, from the general presumption that the Code of Canon Law is foremost a collection of disciplinary law it follows that the law to which canon 89 refers is only canonical.

The reason advanced by Blat,[57] that the legislator in canon 89 makes no distinction between the divine and the ecclesiastical law, and that, therefore, the one who interprets this canon should place no distinction, is not valid. The general rule of interpretation, which declares that if the law does not distinguish then no distinction should be made is, of course, true. But Blat does not apply this rule correctly in the present case. For this very rule of interpretation, which Blat uses as his argument for the in-

---

[54] However the following authors consider this right of the child to be an exception to canon 89: Blat, *Commentarium,* II, n. 7; Oesterle, *Praelectiones Iuris Canonici,* I, 51; Gillet, "De Exemptione a Patria Potestate"—*ETL,* XI (1934), 787.

[55] This appears from the law of Pope Pius X governing the codification of the Code of Canon Law: "Ut Codex eas tantummodo leges complecteretur, quae disciplinam spectant. Nihil tamen prohibebat, quominus in Codice principia quaedam attingi possent aut deberent, quae ad ius naturae vel ad ipsam Fidem referrentur."—Cited from the Preface to the Code of Canon Law.

[56] Cf. canons 27; 100, § 1; 107; 108, § 3; 109; 218; 219; 329, § 1; 339, § 1; 1060; 1068; 1069, § 1; 1076; 1556.

[57] *Commentarium,* II, n. 7.

clusion of the natural and the divine law, may be rightly used to prove the contrary, namely, the exclusion of both these laws. For the presumption is that, when the term, "law," is used in the Code of Canon Law, it means only ecclesiastical law and not the divine law or civil law unless reasons to the contrary are present. The basis for such a presumption is that the Code is mainly a body of human ecclesiastical laws. From a consideration of canon 89 no such reason is present to overthrow this presumption. Since, then, the legislator does not distinguish the term, "law," in this canon it follows that its meaning must be restricted to ecclesiastical law. Therefore canon 89 enacts that minors in the exercise of their rights are exempt from parental authority only in those matters in which the ecclesiastical law considers them to be exempt. It is true that in virtue of the divine law minors in the exercise of their rights are often exempted from the authority of their parents, as, for example, in their right to enter the Catholic Church. But such exemptions are not considered in the principle given in canon 89.

A second argument for the exclusion of the natural and the divine law may be derived from the position canon 89 occupies in the Code of Canon Law. This canon is found among the preliminary canons which treat about Persons in general. The first canon in the Second Book of the Code [58] considers the juridical constitution of a person in the Church of Christ and mentions the effects thereof. The second canon immediately classifies persons into various age groups,[59] while the next canon determines the influence age has concerning the exercise of rights.[60] Thus it may be argued from the parallel passages of the previous canons that in canon 89 consideration is given only to those rights which are due a person by reason of his membership in the Church, for only about this does canon 87 treat. Therefore, it is not the intention of the legislator to consider those natural and divine rights which belong to all persons because of the natural and the divine law irrespective of their membership

---

[58] Canon 87.

[59] Canon 88.

[60] Canon 89.

in the Church. Rather consideration is given only to those rights which are due to a person as a consequence of baptism.[61]

Thus minors are exempt from parental authority in those matters in which the Canon law expressly exempts them. What, then, if the civil law exempts minors in the exercise of certain rights? Must attention be given to this civil law? Yes, the civil law is also understood, but only for those matters in which the Code of Canon Law adopts the civil law. In other words, after the promulgation of the Code of Canon Law the modern civil law of the various nations ceased to be considered a valid suppletory source of Canon law. For in canon 20 [62] the ecclesiastical lawgiver declares what the supplementary sources of Canon law are, and the civil law is not listed among these sources. Hence civil law is no longer a valid supplementary source for the lacunae found in Canon law.[63] However, in certain instances the Code of Canon Law expressly canonizes the prescriptions of the civil law. For example, the Church adopts the civil law concerning the time for determining the obligations arising from contracts,[64] in regard to adoption as a matrimonial impediment,[65] and in regard to contracts in general.[66] Thus in the matter, for example, of contracts the civil law of the respective nation is to be followed.

---

[61] Damen, "De Irritatione et Suspensione Votorum Spectato Iure Naturali atque Iure Ecclesiastico Antiquo et Novo"—*Apollinaris,* III (1930), 110–111.

[62] "Si certa de re desit expressum praescriptum legis sive generalis sive particularis, norma sumenda est, nisi agatur de poenis applicandis, a legibus latis in similibus; a generalibus iuris principiis cum aequitate canonica servatis; a stylo et praxi Curiae Romanae; a communi constantique sententia doctorum."

[63] Vermeersch-Creusen, *Epitome,* I, n. 128; Chelodi, *Ius de Personis iuxta Codicem Iuris Canonici* (ed. altera a Soc. Ernesto Bertagnolli recognita et aucta, Tridenti: Libr. Edit. Tridentum, 1927), n. 68; this work will hereafter be cited *Ius de Personis;* Maroto, *Institutiones Iuris Canonici,* I, nn. 383–385; Michiels, *Normae Generales Iuris Canonici* (2 vols., Lublin-Polonia: Universitas Catholica, 1929), I, 477–481; this work will hereafter be cited *Normae Generales;* Beste, *Introductio in Codicem,* pp. 18, 85; Sipos, *Enchiridion Iuris Canonici* (Pécs: Ex Typographia "Haladás R.T.," 1926), pp. 43–44.

[64] Canon 33, § 2.

[65] Canons 1059, 1080.

[66] Canon 1529. For other examples where the Church adopts the civil law confer canons 1508; 1513, § 2; 1519, § 2; 1520, § 1; 1523, § 2; 1526; 1527.

Therefore, if the civil law concedes to minors the capacity to enter into a valid contract, such capacity is also recognized by the Church; and if minors in making such a contract are considered by the civil law as independent of parental authority, then such exemption is also conceded to them by Church law. For the Code of Canon Law canonizes the civil prescripts in these matters providing they do not contradict the divine law or go counter to the rulings of the Canon law.

However, concerning many matters, especially about temporal goods and the rights of persons, either no canonical legislation exists, or that which does exist is altogether inadequate to solve the various questions that often arise. For instance, the Canon law states nothing regarding the emancipation of a minor, yet at the same time certain canons presuppose that the minor is not emancipated. Thus the law of the Church assigns to a minor the domicile of the person to whom he is subject;[67] and regarding the marriage of minors who are not emancipated the canons prescribe that parents should be consulted and their permission for the marriage should be received.[68] These two canons, then, affect only minors who are not emancipated. But how will emancipation be recognized? What standard or rule can be used to determine whether or not the minor is emancipated? The Code of Canon Law is silent concerning this question. Similar difficulties exist concerning the appointment of tutors and curators, and in attempting to measure just what power such guardians possess. It is necessary, however, to have a norm which will regulate these questions and provide an answer to these difficulties. Where, then, shall such a rule be found?

According to Mothon,[69] when the Code of Canon Law is silent concerning some matter or when it does not offer a clear and

[67] Canon 93, § 1: ". . . necessario retinet . . . minor, domicilium illius cuius potestati subiicitur."

[68] Canon 1034: "Parochus graviter *filiosfamilias* minores hortetur ne nuptias ineant, insciis aut rationabiliter invitis parentibus; quod si abnuerint, eorum matrimonio ne assistat, nisi consulto prius loci Ordinario." The canon uses the technical term, "*filiusfamilias*," in order to designate a minor who is still under the *patriapotestas*.

[69] *Institutions Canoniques* (3 vols., Vol. I, *Des Personnes,* Paris: Société Saint-Augustin, Desclée, De Brouwer & Cie, 1922), I, Art. 52, 3.

certain rule, the norm should then be taken from the laws of the Church prior to the promulgation of the Code. He maintains that the pre-Code law, which was in actual use in the Church up to May 19, 1918 and which has not been explicitly abrogated, is now implicitly contained in the Code. He considers this to be true even though the present Code does not expressly mention these laws. Such an opinion, however, is contrary to the rules which govern the relationship of pre-Code law to the present law of the Church. Canon 6, 6° prescribes that all other disciplinary laws of the old law which were in force until now, and which are neither explicitly nor implicitly contained in the Code have lost all force of law. Exception is made only for those laws which are either contained in the approved liturgical books or derived from the natural and the positive divine law. Thus the Code does not implicitly retain all those laws which it does not expressly abrogate, but rather it abrogates all laws which are not explicitly or implicitly contained in it. All general laws, then, about which there is no mention in the Code are abrogated. Moreover, if the opinion of Mothon were true, it would lead to great confusion and doubt in Canon law, and so would defeat the very purpose the Church had in mind when she undertook to codify her law.[70]

Maroto[71] proposes the use of pre-Code law to supply a norm for those cases not provided for by the Code. He teaches that even though the old law, which is not expressly contained in the Code, is abrogated, it may nevertheless still be used to supply a norm which is lacking in the present legislation. Therefore, Maroto holds that, if in pre-Code law there is available a norm concerning, for example, the emancipation of minors, then this must be used in order to supply for the defect of a similar law in the Code. If pre-Code law offers such a norm then recourse to any other source is forbidden. The reason Maroto gives to

---

[70] Vermeersch-Creusen, *Epitome,* I, n. 77; Beste, *Introductio in Codicem,* p. 59; Michiels, *Normae Generales,* I, 106; Crnica, "De Lacunis Legis Supplendis ad Normam Codicis J. C."—*Jus Pontificium* (Romae: 1921–), XVI (1936), 191–192; this periodical will hereafter be cited with the abbreviation *JP.*

[71] *Institutiones Iuris Canonici,* I, 160.

support his opinion is that the legislator intended to include such a law in the present Code but through inadvertence failed to do so. But such reasoning contradicts the rule of canon 6, 6°, for, if the legislator does not mention either explicitly or implicitly the pre-Code law, then it is abrogated and cannot be used as a supplementary source for the present Canon law. The lacunae existing in the present legislation must be filled by having recourse to canon 20 and using the principles found therein.

Blat[72] teaches that the pre-Code law, even though it has been abrogated by the Code, may still be used in particular cases in order to supply a norm. He argues that the Code does not include such a law precisely because the cases that are governed by this norm occur infrequently. For this reason, then, the legislator has omitted it from the present law. But if in a particular instance need for such a norm should arise, then Blat states that the pre-Code law could be used to supply the rule. Again such an interpretation is not consonant with the law of canon 6, 6°, for the old law of the Church has no force unless it is contained implicitly or explicitly in the present Code of Canon Law, nor can it be used as a source to remedy the deficiencies found in the present legislation.

Nor is it permissible to appeal to the Roman Law in order to supply the lacunae which exist in the Code of Canon Law. Even though the Roman Law treated at great length, for example, the appointment of tutors and curators,[73] and clearly outlined their rights and duties,[74] and accurately determined the extent of their power,[75] it cannot serve as a supplementary source in this matter for Canon law, for the lawgiver in canon 20 does not mention Roman Law. Moreover, since the Church even refuses to recognize as a subsidiary source her own former law which is not expressly contained in the Code, then for a greater reason should she refuse to concede such honor to the Roman Law. Thus authors

---

[72] *Commentarium Textus Codicis Iuris Canonici* (5 vols. in 7, vol. I, *Normae Generales,* Romae: Ex Typographia Pontificia in Instituto Pii IX, 1921), I, 103–104.

[73] I. (1. 13) 4; I. (1. 15); I. (1. 17) pr.; I. (1. 20); I. (1. 22) pr.; I. (1. 23) 2; C. (1. 3) 52; C (5. 31) 7; D. (26. 7) 5.

[74] D. (26. 7) 33; D. (27. 2); D. (27. 3) 1; C. (5. 49).

[75] I. (1. 21) pr.; D. (26. 7) 10; D. (26. 8) 1; D. (45. 1) 101.

agree that the Roman Law cannot serve as a supplementary source of the present Canon law.[76]

Therefore the norms which govern the emancipation of minors, the appointment of tutors and curators, and the like, concerning which nothing is stated in the Code, must be taken from the civil law of the respective nation. But how is this possible since the modern civil law is not a supplementary source of Canon law? Granting that the Code of Canon Law does not recognize the civil law as such a source, nevertheless the common teaching of authors, who explicitly consider the question of the emancipation of minors and the appointment of tutors or guardians, is that the civil law of the respective nation is to be followed in these matters.[77] Hence according to canon 20 the common teaching of approved authors may be used to supply a norm in the Church's law. Therefore it is clear that the civil law of the respective country is to be followed in matters concerning the emancipation of minors.

This teaching of the authors supports a decision of the Sacred Roman Rota.[78] In this case the Rota treats at great length the

---

[76] Chelodi, *Ius de Personis,* p. 121; Sipos, *Enchiridion Iuris Canonici,* p. 44; Michiels, *Normae Generales,* I, 478–479; Vermeersch-Creusen, *Epitome,* n. 128; De Meester, *Juris Canonici et Juris Canonico-Civilis Compendium* (3 vols. in 4, Brugis: Desclée, 1921–1928), I, n. 27; this work will hereafter be cited as *Compendium Juris Canonici;* Claeys Bouuaert-Simenon, *Manuale Iuris Canonici,* I, n. 13; Crnica, "De Lacunis Legis Supplendis ad Normam Codicis J. C."—*JP,* XVI (1936), 193–196.

[77] Vermeersch-Creusen, *Epitome,* I, n. 128; Michiels, *De Personis,* pp. 44, 138; Michiels, *Normae Generales,* I, 467; Cappello, *Summa,* I, n. 188, 3°; De Meester, *Compendium Juris Canonici,* I, 213, nota 4; Genicot-Salsmans, *Institutiones Theologiae Moralis* (14. ed., 2 vols., Buenos Aires: Dedebec, 1939), I, n. 469; Crnica, "De Lacunis Legis Supplendis ad Normam Codicis J. C."—*JP,* XVI (1936), 198: "Omnes quaestiones circa iura et obligationes quae personis sive ecclesiasticis sive saecularibus competunt et iure civili propriae nationis, sive oriantur ex lege positiva sive ex contractibus innominatis, et non sunt contraria iuri divino vel *ecclesiastico,* solvi debent, si exsurgant in foro ecclesiastico, secundum ius civile respectivae nationis. Ita, ex. gr. quaestiones circa adoptionem, tutelam, potestatem patriam vel maritalem, circa domicilium in concreto determinandum . . . regulantur et solvuntur per praescripta iuris civilis."

[78] S. R. R., *Bogoten., Nullitatis matrimonii,* 8 aprilis 1930, *Coram R. P. D. Arcturo Wynen,* dec. XVIII—*Decisiones,* XXII (1930), 214–228.

question of emancipation of minors, and therein it explicitly teaches that emancipation is a civil and not a canonical institute. Even after the publication of the Code of Canon Law this institute of emancipation remains a civil institute. Furthermore, the Rota concedes that the present discipline of the Church admits emancipation of minor children. Moreover, the Rota declares that the norms governing emancipation are to be taken from the civil law of the respective nation.[79] The Rota rules out the possibility of appealing to the Roman Law in order to decide the manner of emancipation, and it gives as its reasons that much of the Roman Law regarding emancipation is no longer practical and the fact that many nations never accepted this institute as given in the Roman Law.[80] Therefore the Rota concludes that the only possible way to judge emancipation is to follow the norms established by the civil law which is in force in each country.[81] It may be remarked that in this same decision the Rota, in affirming that a minor child retains as a necessary domicile the domicile of his parents, declares that this is true only as long as the child is under the parental authority. The Rota then proceeds to declare the manner in which this authority ceases, and teaches that one of the ways the cessation occurs is by means of emancipation.[82]

The civil law, then, may be canonized by the Church either

---

[79] "Emancipatio neque ante neque post Codicem Iuris Canonici est institutio canonica, sed est institutum exclusive iuris civilis, quo cum primum locum habuit, fatentibus Doctoribus nostri iuris, cessat patria potestas etiam in foro ecclesiastico et cum ea finitur filiorum minorum domicilium legale qua tale. Iamvero nostris temporibus aliquis emancipatus fit non iuxta dispositiones iuris romani, sed secundum dispositiones hodierni iuris civilis, et post eiusmodi emancipationem filius consideratur et est independens a patris potestate."—*ibid.*, n. 12, p. 220.

[80] *Ibid.*, n. 8, p. 218; n. 12, p. 220.

[81] "Quare dicendum est ex ipsa natura rei sequi, iudices ecclesiasticos ad statutendam validitatem vel invaliditatem emancipationis recurrere debere ad modernum ius civile, . . ."—*ibid.*, n. 12, p. 220.

[82] "*Filii familias* proinde aetate *minores*, etsi de facto non habitent apud patrem, domicilium suum legale qua tale conservant, quousque sunt sub potestate paterna, illudque amittunt, ut primum cessat haec potestas. Iamvero paterna potestas, si abstrahatur a morte patris, iuxta unanimem doctrinam canonistarum cessat, quando filius fit sui iuris, quod accidit aut per filii *emancipationem* aut per adeptam *maioritatem*."—*ibid.*, n. 6, p. 217.

explicitly or implicitly. The Church adopts the civil law explicitly when it directly states that the civil law is to be observed in a certain matter, as, for example, in contracts; implicitly, when through the use of canon 20 the Church indirectly canonizes the civil law. But in either case the civil law cannot be called properly and in the strict sense a supplementary source of Canon law, because the Church in these matters actually takes it over and makes it her Canon law.[83] Hence any exemption from parental authority a minor might enjoy under canon 89, for instance in the making of a contract, would radically proceed from the Canon law, since the Church in this matter adopts the civil law and canonizes it. Therefore, though the term, "law," in canon 89 means also the civil law, it extends to the latter only in so far as the Church has directly or indirectly adopted it.

In the exercise of their rights minors are subject to their parents or guardians except in those matters in which the law exempts them. This exemption must be expressed by the lawgiver. His will to exempt minors must be made manifest; otherwise the presumption in favor of their subjection rules. But something may be expressed in law either explicitly or implicitly. Thus, for example, in the Sacrament of Penance the law declares that jurisdiction, which is necessary to hear confessions validly, must be conceded expressly.[84] But this is not the same as to say that jurisdiction must be explicitly given. Thus no explicit grant of jurisdiction is necessary; an implicit concession suffices. For instance, the local Ordinary in appointing a newly ordained priest as an assistant to a parish may state: "I give you the faculties of this diocese so that you may hear confessions." Such a concession of jurisdiction would, of course, be explicit. On the other hand, in assigning the same priest to a parish the local Ordinary may neglect to tell him that he has the faculties to hear confessions in the diocese. Nevertheless, in this case jurisdiction is implicitly given to the assistant for the hearing of

[83] Vermeersch affirms that the civil law, when it is explicitly or implicitly canonized by the Church, becomes in a true and proper sense a supplementary source of Canon law.—*Epitome,* I, n. 128.

[84] Canon 879, § 1: "Ad confessiones valide audiendas opus est iurisdictione scripto vel verbis expresse concessa."

confessions in the parish, for it is contained in and bound up with his appointment to the parish. Hence jurisdiction is expressly given, not explicitly, it is true, but implicitly because it is included in the appointment given to the priest by the Bishop and flows from it.

This same reasoning applies to a minor's exemption from dependence on parental authority in the exercise of his rights, for the legislator may make known either explicitly or implicitly his intention to exempt minors. He does so explicitly, when in conceding a right to the minor he declares in unmistakable terms that the minor may use this right independently of parental control; implicitly, when the exemption may be drawn out or deduced from some rule which he expressly states. In other words, the exemption of minors is contained in that rule, and follows from it as an effect from a cause.

Thus in the exercise of the following rights the law explicitly exempts minors from the parental authority. First, a minor even though he has not attained the age of puberty may acquire his own quasi-domicile.[85] Secondly, after he has reached the age of puberty, he may freely choose the church for his funeral and the cemetery for his burial.[86] Thirdly, in cases which directly involve spiritual matters or which are connected with spiritual affairs minors, after completing their fourteenth year of age, enjoy full procedural capacity. Hence they can sue and defend without the consent of their parents and tutors and can in person plead their case. Those under fourteen years of age, if they enjoy the use of reason, may also respond without the consent of their parents or guardians but they must act through a procurator. They may, however, with the approval of the Ordinary designate their own proxy.[87]

Besides these explicit exemptions there are a number of other rights which minors may exercise independently of parental authority, because the law implicitly exempts them. Concerning this fact of implicit exemption all authors who consider the sub-

---

[85] Canon 93, § 2.

[86] Canon 1223, §§ 1 and 2.

[87] Canon 1648, § 3.

ject agree.[88] Thus a minor may enter a religious institute after he has completed his fifteenth year of age,[89] and after his sixteenth year he may make a valid temporary profession.[90] He also enjoys the right to receive tonsure and the minor orders independently of the wishes of his parents, provided, of course, he is otherwise fit to enter the clerical state.[91] And by the very fact that the law exempts a minor from parental authority concerning the exercise of his right to enter the religious or clerical state, it necessarily follows that he is also exempt in exercising those rights which are proper to his new station in life. Thus, for example, a novice before taking temporary vows may freely dispose by last will of all goods which he actually possesses or may subsequently possess.[92] Finally, the law implicitly exempts a minor in regard to the exercise of his right to marry, for he may validly, and under certain conditions also licitly, contract marriage without the knowledge and even against the wishes of his parents or guardians.[93]

Therefore the legislator explicitly and implicitly withdraws minors in the exercise of certain rights from the authority of their parents or guardians. Concerning those exemptions which he grants explicitly there is no difficulty, for these are able to be easily known. But there is a problem regarding implicit exemptions. For what rule can be used to determine when the legislator implicitly exempts minors? How is such an exemption recognized? There is no agreement among the few authors who consider this question. Vermeersch, in an earlier edition of his work,[94] offers an explanation which is not altogether correct.

---

[88] Coronata, *Institutiones Iuris Canonici,* I, 121–122; Michiels, *De Personis,* p. 46; Vermeersch-Creusen, *Epitome,* I, n. 209; Gillet, "De Exemptione a Patria Potestate"—*ETL,* XI (1934), 789; Piontek, "De Acephalis in Iure Canonico"—*JP,* XVII (1937), 179.

[89] Canon 555, § 1.

[90] Canon 573.

[91] Canons 973–974.

[92] Canon 569, § 3.

[93] Canon 1034.

[94] *Epitome Iuris Canonici cum Commentariis ad Scholas et ad Usum Privatum* (3 vols., Vol. I, 3. ed., Mechlinae-Romae: H. Dessain, 1927), I, n. 180. However in the fourth (1929), fifth (1933), and sixth (1937) editions of his work this explanation does not appear.

He maintains that an implicit exemption is present whenever the canons list certain conditions necessary for the acquisition and exercise of a right, but make no mention about dependence on parental authority. Thus, for example, the law enumerates certain qualities which are necessary before one may be admitted to the novitiate [95] or to the reception of Orders,[96] but consent of parents or guardians is not listed as one of these requisites. Hence Vermeersch concludes that in such cases the law may be said to implicitly exempt minors from the authority of parents and guardians.[97] However, this reason runs counter to the rule which the legislator states in canon 89, for in that canon the general presumption favors the authority of the parents. The minor in the exercise of his rights is presumed to be dependent on his parents and tutors unless the law exempts him. This exemption must be proved. In canon 89 the legislator has once and for all set forth the general rule that parental consent and help are necessary for the minor in the use of his rights. Hence the lawgiver need not in each and every case, which involves the right of a minor, reiterate as a positive condition the necessity of parental consent. The presumption for subjection remains sufficient and operative until the contrary is proved. Because of the omission, then, of the need of parental consent from the list of conditions necessary for the acquisition and exercise of certain rights, it does not follow that therefore the law implicitly exempts a minor from dependence on parental authority.

Nor can it be argued in support of Vermeersch's opinion that the legislator does not acknowledge the presumption in canon 89 as regulating the whole subject of the exercise of a mnior's rights, and that therefore the argument given by the writer is not conclusive. This objection may be expressed in the following manner. If the presumption in canon 89 were operative, then why would the lawgiver in conceding a right to a minor consider it necessary to explicitly mention this subjection to parents?

---

[95] Canon 542.

[96] Canons 973–974.

[97] This same argument is also advanced by Damen. Cf. "De Irritatione et Suspensione Votorum Spectato Iure Naturali atque Iure Ecclesiastico Antiquo et Novo"—*Apollinaris,* III (1930), 117.

Yet the lawgiver does so in various canons. Thus, for instance, he grants to a minor the right of patronage but explicitly states that the minor may not exercise it independently of his parents or guardians.[98] Moreover in ecclesiastical trials dealing with temporal affairs the legislator declares that the parents or guardians must plead and defend the minor's case.[99] Why, then, this explicit mention of subjection to parental authority if canon 89 presumes that minors in the exercise of their rights are always under the parental control unless the law exempts them? The reason is that in those two canons the legislator is specifically determining the degree or measure of dependence. In exercising the right of patronage and in the capability to stand in court the legislator judges minors wholly incapable to act. Hence in these matters it is not sufficient for the parents or guardians merely to give their consent to a mode of action planned by the minor, but they must actually exercise the right for him. They must represent the minor and, as it were, take his place and act in his name. Therefore the general declaration of dependence which canon 89 enunciates does not suffice, for the words "*obnoxia manet*" of this canon are vague and general and do not delineate the extent of this dependence, but simply state that a minor remains subject to his parents or guardians. From only the words "*obnoxia manet*" the most that can be required of a minor is that he may not exercise his rights unless he confers beforehand with his parents or guardians and asks and receives their consent. If the legislator desires a greater dependence, then, he must state that he does so, as he does in the canons concerning patronage and trials, wherein he determines the exact degree of dependence.[100]

---

[98] Canon 1456: ". . . ius patronatus exercet minores per parentes aut per tutores; quod si parentes vel tutores acatholici sint, ius patronatus interim suspensum manet."

[99] Canon 1648, § 1: "Pro minoribus . . . agere et respondere tenentur eorum parentes aut tutores vel curatores."

[100] Michiels (*De Personis,* p. 47) offers canon 1224, 1° as an example of a case in which the minor is absolutely incapable to act. This canon states that parents must choose the funeral church and cemetery for minors who have not attained the age of puberty. He teaches that subjection to parents is explicitly mentioned, because the lawgiver in this case is determining

Michiels [101] maintains that an implicit exemption from dependence on parents or guardians, which minors enjoy in the exercise of certain rights, may be recognized by analyzing the rule which the legislator makes. He teaches that from such a consideration it will be evident whether or not an exemption is intended by the legislator and included in the given law. Thus, for example, the lawgiver in canons 973 and 974 considers the necessary qualities which a candidate must possess in order to receive tonsure and the minor orders, and he does not exclude those of minor age. Moreover, the legislator in canon 971 [102] absolutely forbids anyone either to force a person to become a cleric or to forbid one, who is canonically qualified, from entering the clerical state. Parents also come under this general prohibition, and have no authority over their children in this matter. Consequently a minor may receive tonsure and the minor orders provided he is otherwise fit even though his parents voice their opposition.

Michiels couples this explanation with a second means of discovering implicit exemption. He holds that an implicit exemption can be recognized whenever the lawgiver concedes to minors rights which of their very nature must be exercised personally, that is, by the minor himself. If the parents or guardians could interfere and prevent the minor from using these rights, then such rights would be useless and would no longer be true rights. However this second reason advanced by Michiels does not help to determine just what those rights are which a minor may exercise independently of parental authority because of this implicit exemption conceded to him by law, for Michiels does not clearly determine what is meant by rights which are to be exercised

the exact degree of dependence. But this example is not true, because those below the age of puberty do not possess the right to choose the church for their funeral or the cemetery for their burial. For canon 1223 declares that everyone enjoys such a right unless the law expressly declares otherwise, and canon 1224, 1° excludes those who are below puberty. Therefore, since they do not possess this right, there can be no question about their incapability to exercise it.

101 *De Personis,* pp. 46–47.

102 " Nefas est quemquam, quovis modo, ob quamlibet rationem, ad statum clericalem cogere, vel canonice idoneum ab eodem avertere."

personally. If by a personal exercise of rights he understands those rights which a minor himself exercises independently of parents or guardians, then it is true that a minor is exempt. But it still does not explain what those rights are. On the other hand, if he means those rights which a minor exercises himself and not through the agency of another person, then the conclusion of exemption does not follow for there are many rights which a minor exercises himself but not without the assistance and direction of parents or guardians.[103]

Gillet[104] affirms, and rightly so, that the legislator intends to implicitly exempt minors in those matters wherein the law not only does not require that the right be exercised dependent on parents or guardians, but where it actually excludes the intervention of this authority. He asserts that such is the case when the minor is bound by either the divine or ecclesiastical law to exercise his right, and when the fitness required in exercising the right is dependent entirely on the judgment of Church authority.[105] Therefore, if a minor is obliged by either the divine law or the Canon law to exercise his right and place a certain act, for example, to receive Baptism or to make his Easter duty, then he must do so, and his parents or guardians have no authority whatsoever to hinder him, for their authority is restricted by the operation of a higher authority, namely, the divine law of God or by the law of His Church. Again, a minor is implicitly exempt from dependence on his parents in all matters that depend exclusively on the decision of an ecclesiastical superior. Thus, for instance, concerning admittance into a religious institute or regarding the reception of Orders Church authorities alone are competent to decide whether the candidate possesses the qualities necessary for the religious or clerical life. No such power is conceded to the parents or guardians of the minor. Consequently, if the minor freely wishes to enter this state of life, and the lawful superior considers him a fit candidate, then the parents do not

---

[103] Cf. Gillet, "De Exemptione a Patria Potestate"—*ETL*, XI (1934), 791.

[104] *Ibid.*, p. 790.

[105] Vermeersch-Creusen (*Epitome*, I, n. 209) and Wernz-Vidal (*Ius Canonicum*, II, 6, nota 6) accept this explanation of Gillet.

possess the authority to interfere, for the minor in the exercise of this right is implicitly exempt from their jurisdiction. In other words, ecclesiastical authority supercedes the authority of parents.

Article 3. The Exercise of the Right to Marry by a Minor

After having examined in a general way the exercise of rights by minors there remains to be seen the exercise by a minor of his right to marry. This subject will be considered by the writer in the present article. The main consideration of this article, however, will be the relationship which exists between parents and their minor children in regard to marriage.

The general principle of law, namely, that all persons may contract marriage who are not expressly prohibited by law, was declared by Pope Innocent III in the year 1198.[106] The Code of Canon Law repeats this same provision in canon 1035.[107] Hence it follows from this principle that a minor child may contract a valid marriage, because he is not forbidden to do so either by divine or ecclesiastical law.

While the right to marry is a natural right and therefore proper to each and every human being, it may nevertheless be circumscribed in various ways by legitimate authority. Thus, the divine positive law prohibits a person who is validly married from contracting another marriage during the lifetime of his or her spouse, and the natural law forbids marriages between brothers and sisters. To these different prohibitions which flow from the divine law both natural and positive, the Church, which is the only competent authority for the marriages of baptized persons,[108] has added other restrictions or impediments to marriage for the good of society. Since marriage is a contract and the basis of society the Church must regulate it with a view to the common good. Thus in relation to the marriage of children she limits the exercise of their natural right to marry until they attain a certain age, namely, sixteen years for males and twelve for females. Furthermore the Church in her Code of Law urges the natural

---

[106] C. 23, X, *de sponsalibus et matrimoniis,* IV, 1; Potthast, n. 329.

[107] "Omnes possunt matrimonium contrahere, qui iure non prohibentur."

[108] Canons 1016; 1038.

duty incumbent upon children to inform their parents and seek their advice before contracting marriage.[109] However, as soon as a minor child attains the age required for marriage he may validly marry without the knowledge or consent of his parents. That parental knowledge or permission are not requisite for a valid marriage was, as has been seen, the teaching of the Council of Trent, and this same doctrine is confirmed by the present Code of Canon Law.

If parental knowledge or consent were necessary for the validity of a minor's marriage, this requisite would necessarily be due either to a prescription of the divine law or the ecclesiastical law. But neither divine nor Canon law enact that marriages contracted by minors unknown to their parents or against their will are invalid. Therefore it is certain that parental knowledge or consent are not essential elements for a valid marriage of minors. The divine positive law makes no such requirement, for it cannot be demonstrated that Christ demanded the knowledge and consent of parents for the validity of a child's marriage. Moreover, from the teachings of Christ the very opposite doctrine can be established, namely that in the choice of one's state of life the individual must enjoy complete liberty of action and be independent of the will of another. Nor does the divine natural law require parental knowledge or consent for a valid marriage. The minor child may contract a valid marriage provided he is able to give a true matrimonial consent. If both parties otherwise qualified by law exchange this matrimonial consent a valid marriage exists.[110] Nothing is stated about the need of parental knowledge or consent in order to effect a valid union. Furthermore the Canon law does not demand for a valid marriage the knowledge and consent of the minor's parents, for nowhere in the Code of Canon Law is such a stipulation made. The legislator in listing the diriment impediments to marriage does not include the lack of parental knowledge or consent among these impediments.[111]

The fundamental reason why the lack of parental knowledge or

---

[109] Canon 1034.

[110] Canon 1081.

[111] Canons 1067–1080.

consent is not a diriment impediment to marriage lies in the fact that every person is *sui iuris* in regard to choosing his state of life, and does not depend on the will of another. In certain matters, among which is marriage, every individual is free to dispose of himself, for he owes obedience to no human superiors but only to God. Thus St. Thomas teaches that no inferior must obey his superior when the latter commands something which exceeds his competency as superior, for in such instances the inferior is no longer subject to the authority of the superior. This according to St. Thomas is true in the matter of marriage, for one is not held to obey human superiors but only God, since in those things which pertain to the conservation of the individual and of the species all men by nature are equal. The Angelic Doctor then concludes that " slaves are not bound to obey their masters nor children their parents in the matter of entering marriage or of preserving virginity, or in the other similar matters." [112] Moreover, since marriage is indissoluble and entails life-long obligations, it is important that the individual be absolutely free in his choice to enter the married state. Therefore children must not be made dependent on the will of their parents but they must be left free to contract or not to contract marriage.[113] Thus Pope Leo XIII wrote: " In choosing a state of life, it is indisputable that all are at full liberty either to follow the counsel of Jesus Christ as to virginity, or to enter into the bonds of marriage." [114]

While it is true that children are not bound to obey their parents in contracting marriage, they nevertheless have a filial duty to assist their parents in need. Frequently this duty of assistance clashes with their plans to enter marriage. Hence, for example, a child desires to marry, but if he or she does so, he will no longer be in a position to lend economic support to his needy parents. Is the child then morally free to marry, or must he

---

[112] *Summa Theologica* (ed. Studii Generalis O. Pr., Ottawa, Canada, 1942), IIa–IIae, q. 104, art. 5.

[113] Sanchez, *De Matrimonio,* lib. IV, disp. XXIII, n. 10.

[114] Encycl. *"Rerum Novarum,"* 15 maii 1891, § 9. English translation is from Husslein, *Social Wellsprings* (2 vols., Milwaukee: Bruce Publishing Co., 1940–1942), I, 173, n. 9.

defer his plans to contract marriage? Authors in discussing this problem generally distinguish three degrees of need on the part of the parents, namely ordinary, grave and extreme. The need is said to be ordinary or common, if it compels the parents to live modestly and sparingly; grave, when the very life of the parents cannot be sustained without great difficulty or only with a notable loss of their status; extreme, if the parents are in such circumstances that it is morally certain death will come upon them unless they receive aid.[115] It is clear that the minor child is in no way bound to forego his right to marry in order to help his parents who are in ordinary need. Hence the child in these circumstances is morally free to exercise his right to marry. However, the child is obliged to assist his parents in grave need. Yet the extent of this obligation may be and often is lawfully circumscribed by conditions which affect the child. Thus from the fact that parents are in grave need it does not necessarily follow that the minor child must abstain from exercising his right to marry. All the circumstances of the individual case must be taken into consideration before an obligation can be placed on the child to postpone his intended marriage. His filial duty to assist his parents in their need would cease to bind, if by its observance the child would be exposed to grave temporal or spiritual dangers. Thus, for example, if delaying the marriage would mean an occasion of sin for the minor child, then he may exercise his right to marry even though his parents are in grave need. In this instance the virtue of piety would no longer oblige the child, and thus he may lawfully contract marriage.[116] This same principle is likewise valid and true in de-

---

[115] Appeltern, *Compendium Praelectionum Iuris Regularis* (2. ed., Parisiis-Tornaci: Établissements Casterman, 1913), pp. 26–27; Wernz-Vidal, *Ius Canonicum,* III, n. 257.

[116] Payen, *De Matrimonio in Missionibus ac Potissimum in Sinis, Tractatus Practicus et Casus* (2. ed., 3 vols., Zi-ka-wei: in Typographia T'OU-SÊ-WÊ, 1935–1936), I, n. 526; this work will hereafter be cited *De Matrimonio;* Cappello, *Tractatus Canonico-Moralis de Sacramentis* (3 vols. in 6, Vol. III, *De Matrimonio,* 3. ed., Romae: Marietti, 1933), III, n. 188; this work will hereafter be cited as *De Sacramentis;* Gougnard, *Tractatus de Matrimonio* (7. ed., Mechliniae: H. Dessain, 1931), pp. 28–29.

termining the child's obligation when the parents are in extreme need.

Parents, then, are not permitted to force their children to enter marriage, nor are they able to demand that the child marry a person whom they choose. Parents are, however, able to induce their children to marry, and they may even suggest and urge marriage with a particular person provided in so doing they leave the freedom of their children intact.[117]

Though parental knowledge or consent is not required for the validity of the marriage, nevertheless children have certain duties towards their parents even in this matter of contracting marriage. They owe their parents love and reverence, and these virtues impose upon them the obligation of not proceeding in such a grave matter as marriage without informing their parents and seeking their advice. If children spurn this obligation without cause they are guilty of a grave sin of disrespect towards their parents. Thus, while minor children are free to choose their state of life, they are nevertheless bound to consult their parents and be guided by the parental advice in regard to marriage. Thus Pope Pius XI in his encyclical on Christian Marriage writes: "Lastly, let them (children) not omit to ask the prudent advice of their parents with regard to the partner, and let them regard this advice in no light manner, in order that by their mature knowledge and experience of human affairs they may guard against a disastrous choice, and, on the threshold of matrimony, may receive more abundantly the divine blessing of the

---

[117] S. R. R., *Nullitatis matrim.*, 24 martii 1926, *Coram R. P. D. Francisco Parillo,* dec. XII, nn. 6–7—*Decisiones,* XVIII (1926), 95–97; S. R. R., *Cracovien., Nullitatis matrim.,* 5 aug. 1926, *Coram R. P. D. Iosepho Florczak,* dec. XXXVIII, n. 4—*Decisiones,* XVIII (1926), 307; S. R. R., *Cracovien., Nullitatis matrim.,* 30 maii 1928, *Coram R. P. D. Iulio Grazioli,* dec. XXIII, n. 5—*Decisiones,* XX (1928), 222–223 S. R. R., *Transilvanien., Nullitatis matrim.,* 4 aug. 1928, *Coram R. P. D. Maximo Massimi,* dec. XL, n. 2—*Decisiones,* XX (1928), 364–365; S. R. R., *Brixien., Nullitatis matrim.,* 7 aug. 1928, *Coram R. P. D. Maximo Massimi,* dec. XLII, n. 2—*Decisiones,* XX (1928), 378; S. R. R., *Nullitatis matrim.,* 18 martii 1929, *Coram R. P. D. Iulio Grazioli,* dec. XX, n. 5—*Decisiones,* XXI (1929), 161. Cf. also Cappello, *De Sacramentis,* III, n. 189; Gougnard, *Tractatus de Matrimonio,* p. 29.

Fourth Commandment: 'Honor thy father and thy mother'—such is the first commandment with a promise—'that it may be well with thee and thou mayest be long-lived upon the earth.' (Eph. vi, 2-3; Exod. xx, 21.)" [118] Thus this duty of the child to show affection and respect towards his parents makes it necessary for him to take counsel with them before he contracts marriage. However, in certain instances even his duty of informing parents and seeking their permission for marriage may no longer bind the child, and thus he may marry licitly unknown to his parents or against their will. The writer will consider this point in detail when he comments on canon 1034 in the following chapters.

[118] Encycl. "*Casti Connubii,*" 13 dec. 1930, § 121. English translation is from Husslein, *Social Wellsprings,* II, 168.

CHAPTER VII

THE PASTOR AND THE MARRIAGE OF MINORS

ARTICLE 1. THE TERM "PASTOR" IN THE LAW OF THE CHURCH

The purpose of this article is to indicate those priests who are included under the term "pastor." The Code of Canon Law employs this term both in a strict sense and in a wide sense. In the strict sense of the term a pastor is understood to be an individual priest or moral person to whom a parish [1] has been given *in titulum* with the care of souls to be exercised under the authority of the local Ordinary.[2]

As a general rule a parish is entrusted to an individual physical person as pastor, but, as canon 451, § 1 provides, it can, *servatis servandis,* also be given to a moral person, as for example a college, a monastery, a chapter or religious congregation. When a parish is thus united *pleno iure* to a moral person then the pastor of this parish is the moral person, and is termed in law the habitual pastor. The actual care of souls, however, is entrusted to an individual priest who acts in the capacity of a parochial vicar and is known in law as the actual vicar.[3] He must be a member of the religious organization to whose house the parish is united. The religious superior nominates him but it remains the right of the local Ordinary to approve him and to institute him in office.[4] This actual parochial vicar in his care of souls has all the pastoral rights and obligations according to the common law of the Church and approved diocesan statutes or praiseworthy customs.[5] Hence he has the right to

[1] Cf. canon 216, §§ 1 and 3 for a definition of the term "parish."

[2] Canon 451, § 1.

[3] Canons 452; 472; 1423, § 2. Cf. Vermeersch-Creusen, *Epitome,* I, n. 537; Augustine, *Commentary,* II, 508–510, 514–516.

[4] Cf. canon 1425, § 2.

[5] Canon 471, §§ 1 and 4.

assist at marriages in the parish and to conduct the required pre-nuptial investigation.[6]

Under the term "pastor" the Code of Canon Law[7] also includes certain priests who enjoy the same rights and share the same obligations as parish priests but are not pastors in the strict sense of canon 451, § 1. They have the right to assist at marriages and to institute the pre-nuptial investigation. The Code divides them into two general classes: I. Quasi-pastors, and II. Parochial vicars, if they have full parochial power.

I. Quasi-pastors are those priests who govern quasi-parishes, that is, congregations of the faithful existing in vicariates and prefectures apostolic.[8] These quasi-parishes are distinct territorial parts of a vicariate apostolic or of a prefecture apostolic, and each part has its own church and quasi-pastor and particular congregation. In this way they resemble parishes. Quasi-pastors, since they have the same rights and duties as pastors, also enjoy the right to assist at marriages and to conduct the pre-nuptial investigation.[9]

II. Parochial vicars are those priests who take the place of a pastor or who assist him in the work of caring for souls.[10] The Code mentions five different classes of parochial vicars and clearly outlines their rights and duties.

A. *Vicarii curati* or *actuales* are those priests who exercise the actual care of souls in a parish that is united *pleno iure* to a moral person. They are actual parish priests. The habitual pastor is the moral person.[11]

B. *Vicarii oeconomi* are priests who are appointed by the Ordinary to a vacant parish to govern it during the time of its

---

[6] Cf. Donovan, *The Pastor's Obligation in Pre-nuptial Investigation,* The Catholic University of America Canon Law Studies, n. 115 (Washington, D. C.: The Catholic University of America, 1938), p. 60; Coronata, *Institutiones Iuris Canonici,* I, n. 488.

[7] Canon 451, § 2, 1o, 2o.

[8] Canon 216, § 3.

[9] S. C. de Prop. Fide, instr., 25 iulii 1920—*AAS,* XII (1920), 331–333; also reported in Bouscaren, *The Canon Law Digest,* I, 147–148 under canon 216.

[10] Vermeersch-Creusen, *Epitome,* I, n. 559.

[11] Canons 471; 1425.

vacancy. They are commonly referred to as "administrators" and have in regard to the care of souls the same rights and obligations as a pastor. Hence they are able to grant permission to a particular priest to assist at a particular marriage within the parish.[12] However, since their appointment is a temporary one, canon 473, § 1 enacts that they may not do anything which might work harm to the future pastor. Before the Ordinary appoints the administrator the Code prescribes that the assistant to the former pastor is to assume charge of the parish during the vacancy unless other provisions have been made. If there are several assistants in the parish, the first assistant is to take charge; if they are all equal, then the senior in office; if there are no assistants, then the nearest pastor must govern the parish. In parishes entrusted to religious the superior of the religious house assumes the office of pastor during the interim.[13]

C. *Vicarii substituti* or parochial substitutes are divided by the Code into three different classes. First, the Code mentions the parochial substitute, who with the approval of the local Ordinary assumes charge of a parish whenever the pastor is to be lawfully absent from his parish for more than a week.[14] Secondly, the Code considers the substitute priest who is appointed by the local Ordinary to govern a parish which is vacant because of the removal of the pastor. Such a vicar substitute is appointed only if the pastor who is removed has recourse to Rome in protest of his removal.[15] Thirdly, if the pastor is forced to leave his parish suddenly due to some grave cause and is to be absent for more than one week, then the priest who takes his place is known as a vicar substitute. He is named by the pastor without previously consulting the Ordinary. However, in such a case the pastor must as soon as possible inform the Ordinary by letter of the reason for his sudden departure and

[12] Pontificia Commissio ad Codicis Canones Authentice Interpretandos (hereafter cited PCI), 20 maii 1923, I—*AAS,* XVI (1924), 114–115, reported in Bouscaren, *The Canon Law Digest,* I, 540 under canon 1096. Cf. Brys, "De Vicario Oeconomo"—*Collationes Brugenses* (Bruges, 1896–), XXIX (1929), 399–400.

[13] Canon 472, 1o, 2o.

[14] Canons 465, § 4; 474.

[15] Canons 474; 1923, § 2.

also mention the name of the priest who is caring for the parish during his absence.[16] In these circumstances the vicar substitute may assist at all marriages in the parish even before he receives the approval of the local Ordinary, and he may continue to assist as long as the local Ordinary whom the pastor notified does not provide otherwise.[17]

With regard to the authority enjoyed by these three classes of substitute vicars, canon 474 expressly enacts that they have full parochial power unless the local Ordinary or the pastor has limited it. If no limitation of their powers is expressed concerning assistance at marriage, they may assist at marriages and institute the pre-nuptial investigation. They possess ordinary power.[18]

D. *Vicarii adiutores* or parochial adjutants are those priests who are assigned by the local Ordinary to a pastor who is no longer capable of caring for his parish because of some permanent disability as old age, blindness, incompetence, etc. The local Ordinary may appoint a parochial adjutant even though the pastor is unwilling to accept one. If the parochial adjutant takes the place of the pastor in all the affairs of the parish, he then has all the rights and duties of a pastor with the exception of the application of the Mass *pro populo.* This obligation rests with the pastor. If, however, he has only part of the pastoral duties to attend to and does not supply for the pastor in all things, then his rights and duties must be determined from the letter of his appointment.[19] Thus in this latter case, since the

---

[16] Canon 465, § 5.

[17] PCI, 14 iulii 1922, IV—*AAS,* XIV (1922), 527–528. Cf. Bouscaren, *The Canon Law Digest,* I, 539 under canon 1095.

[18] This is the teaching of canonists who consider the question. Cf. Cappello, *Summa,* II, n. 557; Cappello, "De Vicario Substituto"—*Periodica de Re Canonica et Morali utile praesertim Religiosis et Missionariis* (Brugis: 1905–); ab anno 1927; *Periodica de Re Canonica, Morali, Liturgica,* XIX (1930), 2*. This period will hereafter be cited as *Periodica.* Beste, *Introductio in Codicem,* p. 300; Coronata, *Institutiones Iuris Canonici,* I, 575; Vermeersch-Creusen, *Epitome,* I, n. 566. Claeys Bouuaert, "De Vicarii Substituti Constitutione ac Munere"—*JP,* VII (1927), 79.

[19] Canon 475, §§ 1, 2 and 3. Cf. Bastnagel, *The Appointment of Parochial Adjutants and Assistants,* The Catholic University of America Canon Law Studies, n. 58 (Washington, D. C.: The Catholic University of America, 1930).

parochial adjutant does not have all the rights of a pastor he cannot be included under the term "pastor." Whether or not he has the power to assist at marriages and to conduct the prenuptial investigation depends on his letter of appointment from the local Ordinary or on the delegation he has received from the pastor.

E. *Vicarii Cooperatores,* who are commonly known as assistants or curates, are those priests assigned by the local Ordinary to a pastor who because of the large number of the faithful or on account of the extensive territory of his parish cannot by himself properly fulfill all his pastoral duties.[20] These assistants are considered pastors in law only if they are given full parochial power.[21] Their rights and obligations are not determined by the common law but depend on the statutes of the particular diocese, the bishop's letter of appointment, and the commission of the pastor to whom they are assigned. However, unless the contrary is expressly stated, the assistant must help the pastor in the general ministry of the parish and must aid him in all things that pertain to the pastoral office.[22] It is disputed among authors whether the assistant has ordinary or delegated jurisdiction. The Pontifical Commission for the Authentic Interpretation of the Code in a private response settled the question at least with regard to the power of the assistant to assist at marriage.[23] The Pontifical Commission was asked: "Since according to canon 476, § 6, a *vicarius cooperator* is bound by virtue of his office to take the place of the pastor and to assist him in all the work of the parish, it is sought: Whether he can validly assist at marriages and delegate others to assist at the same, if it does not appear from the diocesan statutes, nor from the letters of the Ordinary, nor from his commission from the pastor, that any limitation of his rights has been imposed." The reply of the president of the Commission was: "In the negative to both." Also the common

[20] Canon 476, §§ 1 and 2.

[21] Canon 451, § 2, 2o.

[22] Canon 476, § 6.

[23] 13 sept., 1933—*Irish Ecclesiastical Record* (Dublin: 1864–), XLVI (1933), 637; cf. Bouscaren, *The Canon Law Digest,* II, 333, under canon 1095.

opinion among canonists is that the assistant possesses only delegated jurisdiction.[24] Even though parochial assistants do not have ordinary power they nevertheless are considered here, because usually they are given general delegation by the local Ordinary or by the pastor of the parish to which they are assigned to assist at all marriages within the parish and to conduct the pre-nuptial investigation.[25] The priest who assists at marriage according to the norms of canon 1098 [26] should also be considered here, for even though he is not a pastor he has from the Code the right to assist at marriage in these extraordinary circumstances. His assistance, however, is not necessary for the validity of the marriage nor is he obliged to ask and receive the matrimonial con-

---

[24] Beste, *Introductio in Codicem,* p. 301; Cappello, *Summa,* II, 123–125; De Smet, "Recentiores Variationes in re matrimoniali"—*ETL,* I (1924), 560; Vermeersch-Creusen, *Epitome,* I, n. 571; McBride, *Incardination and Excardination of Seculars,* The Catholic University of America Canon Law Studies, n. 145 (Washington, D. C.: The Catholic University of America Press, 1941), pp. 447–448; Wernz-Vidal, *Ius Canonicum,* V, 628, 633; Dalpiaz, "Num vicariis cooperatoribus competat ipso iure ex can. 476, § 6 potestas assistendi matrimoniis in paroecia, cui sunt addicti"—*Consultationes Iuris Canonici* (2 vols., Romae: Apud Custodiam Librariam Pontificii Instituti Utriusque Iuris, 1934–1939), I, 67–73. As to those who maintain that the assistant enjoys ordinary power, cf. Augustine, *Commentary,* II, 575–576; Coronata, *Institutiones Iuris Canonici,* I, 578; Stocchiero, "De Jurisdictione Vicariorum Paroecialium"—*JP,* XI (1931), 149–150, 228–231; Stocchiero, "Il matrimonio alla presenza d'un vicario del parroco assente"—*Perfice Munus* (Torino: 1926–), VIII (1933), 220–225; Fanfani, *De Iure Parochorum ad normam Codicis Iuris Canonici* (Turin: Marietti, 1924), n. 308. However Fanfani in the second edition of his work changed his opinion and now teaches that the assistant has only delegated jurisdiction—cf. Fanfani, *De Iure Parochorum* (2. ed., Taurini-Romae: Marietti, 1936), n. 473.

[25] Cf. canon 1096, § 1.

[26] "Si haberi vel adiri nequeat sine gravi incommodo parochus vel Ordinarius vel sacerdos delegatus qui matrimonio assistant ad normam canonum 1095, 1096;

1°. In mortis periculo validum et licitum est matrimonium contractum coram solis testibus; et etiam extra mortis periculum, dummodo prudenter praevideatur eam rerum conditionem esse per mensem duraturam;

2°. In utroque casu, si praesto sit alius sacerdos qui adesse possit, vocari et, una cum testibus, matrimonio assistere debet, salva coniugii validitate coram solis testibus."

sent of the parties. It is his duty to investigate the freedom of the parties to marry and to see that the dignity of the Sacrament of marriage is safeguarded. In fulfilling this obligation he may be considered to act as a pastor.[27]

Concerning military chaplains the Code of Canon Law explicitly enacts that their powers are determined according to the special regulations which emanate directly from the Holy See.[28] Thus whether or not they are to be included under the term "pastor" and so have the right to assist at marriage and make the pre-nuptial investigation must be determined from the prescriptions enacted by the Holy See. No general rule can be given but their faculties must be consulted for each individual case. If full parochial jurisdiction is conceded to them, they will have the status of personal pastors and may assist at the marriages of their Catholic subjects and conduct the pre-nuptial investigation.[29]

Do priests who are appointed chaplains at hospitals, schools, prisons, orphanages and the like come under the term "pastor," and have they the right to assist validly at marriages and institute the pre-nuptial investigation? Such priests do not enjoy the rights of pastors, and hence simply as chaplains they do not have the right to assist at marriages. However, if the local Ordinary would withdraw these institutions from the jurisdiction of the local pastor, as the law permits him in canon 464, § 2, and make them parishes with the chaplain as pastor, then they could assist validly at all marriages within the institution. Or the local Ordinary could appoint the chaplain of the hospital as a parochial assistant in the parish within whose boundaries the hospital is located. The chaplain then could receive either from the local Ordinary or from the pastor of the parish general delegation to assist at all marriages within the territorial limits of the parish. Hence he could assist at marriages in the hos-

---

27 Cf. Ayrinhac-Lydon, *Marriage Legislation,* pp. 265–266; Donovan, *The Pastor's Obligation in Pre-nuptial Investigation,* p. 68.

28 Canon 451, § 3.

29 For the norms enacted by the Sacred Consistorial Congregation for the Military Ordinariate of the United States of America, cf. Bouscaren, *The Canon Law Digest,* II, 586–605.

pital, not it is true by virtue of his appointment as chaplain but in the capacity of an assistant assigned to the local parish.[30]

Article 2. The Pastor in Canon 1034

> **Canon 1034: Parochus graviter filiosfamilias minores hortetur ne nuptias ineant, insciis aut rationabiliter invitis parentibus; quod si abnuerint, eorum matrimonio ne assistat, nisi consulto prius loci Ordinario.**

What pastor in particular has this obligation, which the above canon imposes, of warning children not to enter marriage if their parents are unaware of or reasonably opposed to the proposed union? It is true that all pastors by virtue of their office of caring for souls have a grave obligation to instruct prudently their flock concerning the Sacrament of Matrimony and to point out and explain all obstacles which might impede the valid and licit celebration of this Sacrament.[31] Included, however, in such general instructions is the obligation and duty incumbent on children to consult their parents and to seek their permission before contracting marriage. This has always been the teaching of the Church, and was clearly enunciated in the Catechism of the Council of Trent in these words: ". . . amongst many other matters there is one which demands the zealous exhortation of pastors; it is that children pay it as a tribute of respect due to their parents, or to those under whose guardianship and authority they are placed, not to engage in marriage without their knowledge, still less in defiance of their express wishes." [32]

But canon 1034 does not refer to this general instruction which all pastors must give concerning the Sacrament of Matrimony. The legislator in this canon has in mind a definite and particular situation where the spouses, one or both of whom are minors,

---

[30] Cf. Drumm, *Hospital Chaplains,* The Catholic University of America Canon Law Studies, n. 178 (Washington, D. C.: The Catholic University of America Press, 1943), pp. 131–139; Donovan, *The Pastor's Obligation in Pre-nuptial Investigation,* pp. 67–68.

[31] Canon 1018: "Parochus ne omittat populum prudenter erudire de matrimonii sacramento eiusque impedimentis."

[32] *The Catechism of the Council of Trent,* translated by J. Donovan, p. 339.

actually present themselves to the pastor in order to arrange for their forthcoming marriage. Hence the pastor mentioned in this canon is the pastor whose duty it is to institute the pre-nuptial investigation, which obligation according to canon 1020, § 1 devolves on the pastor who has the right to assist at the marriage.[33]

Proof of this assertion may be had both from the wording of canon 1034 and from the position which this canon occupies in the Code of Canon Law. For from the very words of this canon it is clear that by the term "pastor" is understood the priest who has the right to assist at the marriage, because the canon explicitly enacts that if the children disregard his counsel he is forbidden to assist at their marriage. But such a prohibition presupposes that the pastor has the right to assist at the marriage, for, if he does not possess such a right, it would be impossible to speak of its limitation or restriction. Moreover, this canon is placed by the legislator under the rubric "de iis quae matrimonii celebrationi praemitti debent . . ." and forms part of the pre-nuptial investigation. In fact, the Instruction issued by the Sacred Congregation of the Sacraments on June 29, 1941 [34] concerning the rules to be followed by the pastor in making the canonical inquiries before he permits the parties to enter marriage explicitly mentions in several places the procedure which the pastor is to follow when there is question of assisting at marriages of those who are of minor age.[35]

Therefore the pastor mentioned in canon 1034 is the pastor who has the obligation to conduct the pre-nuptial investigation and who enjoys the right to assist at the marriage. This priest

---

[33] "Parochus cui ius est assistendi matrimonio, opportuno antea tempore, diligenter investiget num matrimonio contrahendo aliquid obstet."

[34] S. C. de Sacr., instr., *De normis a parocho servandis in peragendis canonicis investigationibus antequam nupturientes ad matrimonium ineundum admittat* (*Can. 1020*), 29 iun. 1941—*AAS,* XXXIII (1941), 297. Cf. Bouscaren, *The Canon Law Digest,* II, 253-276, under canon 1020; *The Jurist* (Washington, D. C., 1941-), II (1942), No. 1 (January), *Supplement; The Ecclesiastical Review* (Philadelphia, Pa., 1889-), CV (1941), *Supplement* (hereafter cited as *ER*).

[35] *AAS,* XXXIII (1941), 300; 311, n. 12; 314, n. 9; 315; cf. Bouscaren, *The Canon Law Digest,* II, 257; 268, n. 12; 271, n. 9; 272.

according to canon 1097, § 1, 2°, is the pastor of the place where one or both of the parties have a domicile, quasi-domicile, or month's residence; and in the case of *vagi* and those who have only a diocesan domicile the proper pastor to assist at their marriage is the pastor of the place where the parties are actually living at the time. Canon 1097, § 2 enacts that unless a just cause is present, the marriage should as a rule be celebrated in the presence of the pastor of the bride. Accordingly, it is the latter pastor who should normally institute the investigations and interview the parties concerning their freedom to marry. In case of marriages of mixed rite, unless particular law decrees otherwise, the marriage should be celebrated in the rite of the man and before his pastor.[36] If, however, it happens, as it frequently does, that the man belongs to a different parish or diocese, the examination of him by the pastor of the bride may be difficult and at times even impossible. In such a case the aid of the pastor of the groom should be invoked in order to properly conduct the pre-nuptial investigation. The Code of Canon Law definitely sanctions this procedure,[37] and the Sacred Congregation of the Sacraments in their Instruction of 1941 clearly teaches that the pastor of the groom shall either of his own accord, or at the instance of the groom, or of the bride's pastor conduct the examination concerning the groom.[38] In this case, then, if the groom is of minor age the obligation of canon 1034 is likewise shared by the pastor of the groom.

The right to assist at the marriage, as remarked above, depends on whether one of the parties has a domicile, quasi-domicile, or month's residence in the parish, or actual residence in the parish if the person is a *vagus*. Hence it is necessary to discuss the legislation concerning domicile and quasi-domicile of a minor, for

[36] Particular law decrees otherwise for Greek-Ruthenians. Marriages, both between Greek Ruthenians and between the faithful of different rites, are to be blessed in the rite of the woman, by the woman's pastor—cf. Bouscaren, *The Canon Law Digest*, II, 7.

[37] Canon 1029: "Si alius parochus investigationem aut publicationes peregerit, de harum exitu statim per authenticum documentum certiorem reddat parochum, qui matrinomio assistere debet."

[38] *AAS*, XXXIII (1941), 299, n. 4, a; cf. Bouscaren, *The Canon Law Digest*, II, 255, n. 4, a; *ER*, CV (1941), *Supplement*, p. 3, n. 4, a.

the law on these points is proper to minors and presents some difficulties in practice. It is true that questions of domicile and quasi-domicile in regard to marriage have not under the present law of the Code the importance they once possessed under the *Tametsi* legislation of the Council of Trent, because they no longer determine the validity or invalidity of the marriage. However, the licitness of the marriage depends in great part on the question of domicile or quasi-domicile of the parties, and the pastor before proceeding with the marriage must determine whether at least one of the parties to the marriage is his subject as regards contracting marriage. Therefore the pastor at the outset of the pre-nuptial investigation must interrogate the parties concerning their domicile, quasi-domicile, or month's residence in order to determine whether or not he has a title to assist lawfully at the marriage.[39]

The legislator in canon 93, § 1 assigns to a minor the domicile of the person to whom he is subject. This is termed in law a legal or necessary domicile because it is imposed by law, and is given to the minor regardless of his will in the matter. Thus a minor has a necessary domicile even though the two elements essential for acquiring a voluntary domicile are absent. Neither the intention to dwell in a certain place nor actual residence in that place is necessary. Even without such intention or residence the minor necessarily shares the domicile of the person under whose authority he is placed. And just as the minor child is incapable of refusing a legal domicile, so also he is powerless to free himself from such a domicile as long as he is a minor. Even if he should leave the domicile of his parents or guardians with the intention of never returning, he would nevertheless retain their residence as his necessary domicile. The minor child shares the domicile of his father, but if his father is dead or is impeded from exercising his authority on account of physical, moral, or legal reasons then the child retains the domicile of his mother. In defect of both parents the minor has as his necessary domicile

---

[39] S. C. de Sacr., instr., 29 iun. 1941—*AAS*, XXXIII (1941), 310, n. 3; *ER*, CV (1941), *Supplement*, p. 15, n. 3; Bouscaren, *The Canon Law Digest*, II, 266, n. 3.

the domicile of his guardian who is appointed by the civil law.[40]

A minor child as long as he is a minor is absolutely incapable of ever acquiring his own proper domicile. Why? Because to acquire a voluntary domicile there is needed either actual residence in a parish or quasi-parish or at least in a diocese or vicariate or prefecture apostolic together with the intention of remaining there permanently, unless one is called elsewhere, or by actual residence extended over a period of ten years, independent of the element of intention.[41] Neither of these two ways is possible for a minor who is still under the authority of his parents or guardians. Not the first, namely residence combined with the intention of remaining there permanently, because minors are still subject to the *patriapotestas,* and as long as such dependence or condition exists any intention on their part of remaining independent of this subjection in another place is juridically impossible. Such an intention has no force in law and is entirely inefficacious.[42] Nor can a minor acquire his own domicile by merely going to a place distinct from his parents and by residing there for ten complete years. It seems, however, that all the conditions necessary for attaining a domicile are herein fulfilled. Nevertheless Canon law refuses in such a case to attach to this residence the effect of domicile.[43] The same objection could be urged concerning the impossibility of a wife who is not legitimately separated from her husband to acquire her own domicile. It is surely physically possible for her to reside away from her husband for ten complete years, and thus seemingly fulfill all the requisites for attaining a proper domicile. Yet there is an official response from the Pontifical Commission for the Authentic Interpretation of the Code which declared that the wife is incapable of acquiring her own domicile unless she has obtained from an ecclesiastical judge a decree of separation perpetually

[40] De Meester, *Compendium Iuris Canonici,* I, 213, nota 4; Ojetti, *Commentarium in Codicem,* II, 55, n. 5; Michiels, *De Personis,* p. 138; Claeys Bouuaert-Simenon, *Manuale Iuris Canonici,* I, 143; Maroto, *Institutiones Iuris Canonici,* I, 213, nota 4.

[41] Canon 92, § 1.

[42] Vermeersch-Creusen, *Epitome,* I, n. 214; Coronata, *Institutiones Iuris Canonici,* I, 131.

[43] Kinane, "Domicile in the New Code"—*IER,* XI (1918), 230.

or for an indefinite time.[44] Thus the lawgiver refuses to acknowledge such residence, established by those persons who in law have a necessary domicile, as capable of effecting a proper domicile.

Further proof of the incapability of the minor child to acquire his own domicile may be taken from the pre-Code law. For the law of the Code concerning the legal domicile of a minor is taken entirely from the pre-Code law except for the change with regard to the age at which a person ceases to be a minor. In the present law of the Code a person is a minor until the completion of his twenty-first year, whereas in pre-Code law the age was held to be twenty-five years complete. With this exception, then, the present Code law concerning the impossibility of the acquisition of a domicile by a minor is the same as in pre-Code law. Now in pre-Code legislation it was held that a minor child was altogether incapable of acquiring his own domicile, and he necessarily shared the domicile of his parents or guardians. Proof of this fact is supplied by pre-Code authors,[45] and by the jurisprudence of those times.[46] Hence, according to canon 6, 3º, these canons which agree with the old law in part only, must be interpreted according to the old law in the part in which they agree with it; and thus the interpretations accepted by approved authors are to be followed in the interpretation of these laws of the Code.[47] Post-Code authors, too, are unanimous in their teach-

---

[44] PCI, 14 iulii 1922 ad I—*AAS,* XIV (1922), 526; cf. Bouscaren, *The Canon Law Digest,* I, 83, under canon 93.

[45] Feije, *De Impedimentis et Dispensationibus Matrimonialibus,* p. 123; Wernz, *Ius Decretalium,* IV, 260, nota 190; Bangen, *Instructio Practica de Sponsalibus et Matrimonio,* Tit. II, *de matrimonio contrahendo,* pp. 34–35.

[46] S. R. R., *Ravennaten. Nullitatis matrimonii,* 15 maii 1911, *Coram R. P. D. Friderico Cattani,* dec. XVIII, n. 5—*Decisiones,* III (1911), 191; also reported in *AAS,* III (1911), 487; S. R. R., *Parisien. Nullitatis matrimonii,* 27 ian. 1912, *Coram R. P. D. Seraphino Many,* dec. VI, n. 7—*Decisiones,* IV (1912), 62; also *AAS,* IV (1912), 281; S. R. R., *Baiocen. Nullitatis matrimonii,* 17 martii 1923, *Coram R. P. D. Ubaldo Mannucci,* dec. VII, nn. 2–3—*Decisiones,* XV (1923), 62; S. R. R., *Gratianopolitana, Nullitatis matrimonii,* 8 aprilis 1913, *Coram RMo P. D. Michaele Lega,* dec. XX, n. 4—*Decisiones,* V (1913), 231–232; S. R. R. *Parisien. Nullitatis matrimonii,* 4 martii 1916—*AAS,* VIII (1916), 370.

[47] Canon 6, 3º: "Canones qui ex parte tantum cum veteri iure congruunt, qua congruunt, ex iure antiquo aestimandi sunt; . . ."

ing that a minor is incapable of acquiring a proper domicile of his own.[48] Thus the proper pastor by reason of domicile of minor children is the pastor of the parish where the parents of the children have their domicile.

However, there are two exceptions to this general rule that a person below twenty-one years of age necessarily shares the domicile of his parents and guardians and is incapable of acquiring his own domicile. The first exception is if a minor is legitimately emancipated according to the civil law of the country in which he lives; and secondly, if the minor has the permission of those to whose authority he is subject he may acquire his own domicile. These two exceptions were admitted in pre-Code law, and therefore by reason of canon 6, 2°, 3°, even though the Code does not expressly mention them, they are still retained.

The first exception, namely that an emancipated child may acquire a voluntary domicile of his own choice, was freely admitted in the jurisprudence of pre-Code times,[49] and is confirmed today by many post-Code authors.[50] The Code of Canon Law, too, insinuates that minors can be emancipated even though it nowhere states so directly. As already remarked, the legislator in canon 1034 considers minors who are still *filiifamilias,* that is those who are still under the *patriapotestas.* Hence the lawgiver seems to acknowledge that there are persons who, though they

---

[48] Coronata, *Institutiones Iuris Canonici,* I, 131; Cappello, *Summa,* I, n. 195; Gougnard, *Tractatus de Matrimonio,* p. 203; Vindex, "Domicilium et Quasi-Domicilium Eorumque Effectus in Codice Iuris Canonici"—*JP,* VI (1926), 47, 49; Michiels, *De Personis,* p. 139; Wernz-Vidal, *Ius Canonicum,* II, n. 12; Vermeersch-Creusen, *Epitome,* I, n. 214.

[49] S. R. R., *Baiocen. Nullitatis matrimonii,* 17 martii 1923, *Coram R. P. D. Ubaldo Mannucci,* dec. VII, n. 3—*Decisiones,* XV (1923), 62–63; S. R. R., *Nullitatis matrimonii,* 8 martii 1924, *Coram R. P. D. Iosepho Florczak,* dec. XII, n. 6—*Decisiones,* XVI (1924), 93; S. R. R., *Bogoten. Nullitatis matrimonii,* 8 aprilis 1930, *Coram R. P. D. Arcturo Wynen,* dec. XVIII, nn. 6–13; *Decisiones,* XXII (1930), 217–221.

[50] Ojetti, *Commentarium in Codicem,* II, 55, n. 5; Cappello, *Summa,* I, 227; Wernz-Vidal, *Ius Canonicum,* II, n. 12; Michiels, *De Personis,* p. 138; Browne, "Questions about Domicilio"—*IER,* LXVII (1936), 633; Farrugia, "De Ecclesiastico Domicilio"—*Il Monitore Ecclesiastico* (Romae: 1876–), VII (1935), 317. Cf. Kinane, "Domicile in the New Code"—*IER,* XI (1918), 230, who denies that minors can be emancipated.

have not as yet completed their twenty-first year, are nevertheless free from the authority of their parents or tutors. Otherwise the addition of the term *filiusfamilias* as inserted in canon 1034 would be meaningless. Moreover, in canon 93, § 1 the legislator assigns to a minor the domicile of that person precisely to whom the minor is subject. Though the legislator in this canon neither affirms nor denies the subjection or emancipation of minors, nevertheless the conscious use of such cautious phrasing on the part of the lawgiver leads one to believe that there are instances where persons below twenty-one years complete are subject to no one.

The second exception, namely, that with the consent of their parents or guardians minors may acquire their own domicile, was commonly taught in the pre-Code era. In fact a decision of the Sacred Congregation of the Council of February 21st, 1835 expressly confirmed this teaching,[51] and the Rota admitted this teaching as certain.[52] Moreover, since canon 93 repeats the old law, the rule of interpretation set forth in canon 6, 2°, 3° bids us to interpret this canon from the authority of the old law and to respect the interpretation advanced by the approved authors of that time. Therefore, even after the promulgation of the Code of Canon Law a minor child with the consent of his parents and guardians may acquire his own domicile. This opinion is also upheld by post-Code authors as Wernz-Vidal,[53] Ferreres,[54] Michiels,[55] and Browne.[56]

However, De Meester denies that a minor can acquire his own domicile even though he has the permission of his parents or guardians. De Meester reasons that the private will of the individual is not able to change what is constituted and decreed by the public lawgiver.[57] This reason advanced by De Meester

---

[51] *Thesaurus S. C. Concilii,* XCV (1835), 30–34, 41.

[52] S. R. R., *Nullitatis matrimonii,* 28 augusti 1911, *Coram R. P. D. Aloysio Sincero,* dec. XXIX, n. 35—*Decisiones,* III (1911), 445–446.

[53] *Ius Canonicum,* II, n. 12.

[54] *Compendium Theologiae Moralis ad Normam Codicis Canonici* (14. ed., 3 vols., Barcinone: Eugenius Subirana, 1928), II, 478, nota 1.

[55] *De Personis,* p. 138.

[56] "Questions about Domicile"—*IER,* XLVII (1936), 633.

[57] *Compendium Iuris Canonici,* I, 214, nota 1: "Ita minorennes nec propria

does not seem to be a valid one, for in the case under discussion the private will of the individual does not in any way change the law of canon 93, § 1. This law remains intact even when private permission of parents or guardians is given, but what is changed is the condition or basis on which the application of the law depends. In other words, every minor retains as a necessary domicile the domicile of the person to whom he is subject. That is the law as stated by the legislator in canon 93, § 1. But if the minor is not subject to anyone, then the Code of Canon Law does not enact that he retains a necessary domicile. The law of canon 93, § 1 applies if the minor is not emancipated; if, on the other hand, he is emancipated then the necessary domicile which is given by law to the minor immediately ceases to exist. Hence there is certainly no question in this case of a private individual effecting a change in a law made by the legislator. Moreover, even in the case in which the person under whose authority the minor child is placed permits the minor to establish residence permanently in another place, such a mode of action is equivalent to emancipation, and is recognized in civil law as one way in which emancipation may be effected.[58] Hence, since the bond of subjection between the child and his parents or guardians is thereby severed, it is now possible for the child to acquire his own domicile, because his intention of permanently residing away from his parents or tutors is no longer juridically inefficacious.[59]

When the child attains his majority, or if he is emancipated by proper authority before he completes his twenty-first year, or if

---

nec accedente parentum voluntate possunt amittere hoc domicilium quamdiu minores sunt, quia voluntate privata nequit mutari ius publicum."

[58] Vernier, *American Family Laws* (5 vols., Vol. I, *Introductory Survey and Marriage,* 1931; Vol. 5, *Incompetents and Dependents,* 1938, Stanford University, California: Stanford University Press), V, 240–243; Robinson, *Elementary Law* (2. ed., Boston: Little, Brown and Co., 1910), pp. 207–208. Also for reference to various court decisions on parental emancipation of the child, cf. Bouvier's *Law Dictionary* (Rawle's third revision, 2 vols., Kansas City, Missouri, and St. Paul, Minnesota, 1914), I, 1004; II, 2453.

[59] Cf. Michiels, *De Personis,* pp. 132, 138; Browne, "Questions about Domicile"—*IER,* XLVII (1936), 633; Fallon, "Domicile of a Wife Who Becomes Insane"—*IER,* LVII (1941), 81.

with the consent of his parents or guardians he acquires his own domicile elsewhere, then in these three cases the parental domicile ceases to be for him a necessary domicile. However, it does not cease as a voluntary domicile unless the contrary is expressly proven. The presumption in law is that the necessary domicile passes over into a voluntary domicile and is retained as such by the emancipated child.[60] Since on the one hand the retention of a domicile is a *res favorabilis,* while its loss on the other hand is a *res odiosa,* the loss must be clearly established. Otherwise the presumption for retention of the domicile rules.[61]

In practice it is difficult to learn just when this voluntary domicile is lost. It surely is not lost automatically when the child acquires another proper domicile or quasi-domicile, because the plurality of domiciles, or a domicile together with a quasi-domicile is not contradictory. Nor is it lost if the parents themselves change their domicile and acquire another. For this change of domicile does not in any way sever the family bond between the parents and their children. Therefore a child, who has reached his majority or one who though below twenty-one years is already emancipated, retains the domicile of his parents as a voluntary domicile unless it is proven by competent witnesses or by other means of proof that the child has renounced his parental domicile. If such a child would leave home with the intention of not returning except as a visitor, it may be presumed that he no longer

[60] "Ut autem reipsa amittatur, requiritur renunciatio, secus enim domicilium necessarium censeretur transire in voluntarium et tamdiu retineri praesumeretur, quamdiu non constaret, illi, expresse vel tacite, directe vel indirecte, fuisse renuntiatum. Ita ex. gr. filiifamilias, donec sint aetate minores, patris vel tutoris domicilium et quasi domicilium sortiuntur, illudque retinent quousque, sui iuris effecti, eidem non renuntient. . . ."— S. R. R., *Ravennaten. Nullitatis matrimonii,* 15 maii 1911, *Coram R. P. D. Friderico Cattani,* dec. XVIII, n. 5—*Decisiones,* III (1911), 191; cf. also *AAS,* III (1911), 487. Cf. De Meester, *Compendium Iuris Canonici,* I, 214, nota 2; Cappello, *Summa,* I, 234; Beste, *Introductio in Codicem,* pp. 139, 141; Sipos, *Enchiridion Iuris Canonici,* p. 79, nota 16; Chelodi, *Ius de Personis,* p. 169; Farrugia, "De Ecclesiastico Domicilio"—*Il Monitore Ecclesiastico,* VII (1935), 317.

[61] S. R. R., *Baiocen. Nullitatis matrimonii,* 17 martii 1923, *Coram R. P. D. Ubaldo Mannucci,* dec. VII, n. 2—*Decisiones,* XV (1923), 62. Cf. Vermeersch-Creusen, *Epitome,* I, 181.

retains as his own the parental domicile. However, if the child leaves home due to some temporary cause, as, for example, military service in the armed forces of his country, or for reasons of study, health or temporary employment, the presumption for retention of the parental domicile remains, since in all these cases the child intends to return to the parental domicile as a resident. Even if a girl should leave her parents' home in order to contract marriage and on leaving declares her intention of not returning but of residing with her husband, such departure of itself does not cause the loss of the parental domicile. The reason is that her will in this matter is not absolute but conditional, for it depends on the condition, "if the marriage takes place." Hence she retains the domicile of her parents until the day she is actually married.[62]

Though a minor child, as long as he remains subject to another person, is absolutely incapable of acquiring his own proper domicile, he can, nevertheless, attain his own quasi-domicile after he has completed his seventh year of age. The legislator in canon 93, § 2 expressly concedes this right to the minor child.[63] Thus he may acquire a proper quasi-domicile in either of two ways: (1) by residence together with the intention of remaining in a determined place the greater part of the year, unless he is called elsewhere, or (2) by actual residence in a place for the greater part of the year, irrespective of his intention.[64] According to the first method the minor child acquires his own quasi-domicile from the very first moment of residence, while according to the second way he attains it only after actual residence of more than six months.[65]

In acquiring a quasi-domicile the minor is exempt from the authority of his parents or guardians. However, the element of

---

[62] Cappello, *Summa*, I, 229, 232–234; Beste, *Introductio in Codicem*, p. 141; Michiels, *De Personis*, pp. 155–156; Browne, "Two Cases of Domicile in Relation to Marriage"—*IER*, LXIX (1937), 416.

[63] "Minor infantia egressus potest quasi-domicilium proprium obtinere; . . ."

[64] Canon 92, § 2.

[65] ". . . any period of time extending beyond six months is considered the greater part of the year."—Doheny, *Canonical Procedure in Matrimonial Cases* (Milwaukee: Bruce Publishing Co., 1938), p. 15.

establishing residence away from the parental hearth by means of which a distinct quasi-domicile is obtained comes within the scope of parental authority. The parents, then, are able to forbid the child to reside away from them, and the child must obey provided, of course, the command of the parents is reasonable and just. Nevertheless, if the child should disobey the precept of his parents and leave home and fix his residence in some definite parish or diocese, he would obtain thereby his own quasi-domicile. The parents are competent to forbid the child to leave, but they are not able to frustrate the effects of such illicit residence as far as the obtaining of a quasi-domicile is concerned. Thus, even though the child would establish residence in a place distinct from his parental home and against the just will of his parents or tutors, he, nevertheless, would acquire his proper quasi-domicile provided all the conditions necessary for its attainment are present.[66]

The legislator concedes this right of acquiring a quasi-domicile only to a minor who has ceased to be an infant, because during infancy the minor is not capable of fulfilling the conditions necessary in order to obtain a quasi-domicile. The reason motivating the legislator to concede this right to a minor who is no longer an infant is that frequently a minor child must for various reasons as military service, study, health, and the like, reside away from his parents. Thus in order that the minor during these periods of separation from the family domicile may not be deprived of any spiritual benefits, the legislator concedes to him the right of acquiring a quasi-domicile so that he might have his own proper pastor and Ordinary in the place where he resides. Moreover, a minor is not by reason of his status juridically incapable of acquiring his own quasi-domicile, for the intention to reside for the greater part of a year in a place distinct from that of his necessary domicile is compatible with the element of subjection and dependence which is proper to the minor's state.[67]

---

[66] Cf. Gillet, "De Exemptione a Patria Potestate"—*ETL,* XI (1934), 789, nota 9.

[67] Ojetti, *Commentarium in Codicem,* II, 55, n. 7; Michiels, *De Personis,* pp. 132–133, 139.

There remains to be considered the question of a necessary quasi-domicile, for if such an institute exists, it would supply a title for the pastor to assist lawfully at the marriage of minors. Thus, for example, if the parents have a domicile in parish A in New York and a quasi-domicile in parish B in Washington, the minor child certainly shares their domicile in New York. Does he also share their quasi-domicile in Washington? Thus does a minor necessarily acquire the quasi-domicile of the person to whom he is subject? Canonists, who consider this question, disagree. Some categorically declare that a necessary quasi-domicile does not exist in the present canonical legislation.[68] As proof of their opinion they offer two basic arguments: (1) the silence of the Code concerning the existence of a necessary quasi-domicile, and (2) the lack of necessity or even utility for such an institute in the present discipline of the Church. Vermeersch also denies the existence of a necessary quasi-domicile.[69] However, he admits its existence only in one case, namely when otherwise the minor would be a *vagus*. Thus Vermeersch declares that, if the person to whom the minor is subject does not have a proper domicile but only a quasi-domicile, and, at the same time, the minor himself neglected to acquire his own proper quasi-domicile, then the minor child necessarily shares the quasi-domicile of his parents or guardians. Only in this case, according to Vermeersch, can a necessary quasi-domicile be said to exist. In all other cases he maintains that the existence of a legal quasi-domicile would contradict the legal system of the Code.

However other authors, and rightly so, admit the existence of

---

[68] Kinane, "Legal or Necessary Quasi-Domicile"—*IER*, XXVII (1926), 81–82; De Smet, *Tractatus Theologico-Canonicus de Sponsalibus et Matrimonio* (4. ed., Brugis: Car. Beyaert, 1927), p. 35; this work will hereafter be cited as *De Sponsalibus et Matrimonio;* Ojetti, *Commentarium in Codicem,* II, 50, nota 40; De Meester, *Compendium Juris Canonici,* I, 214, nota 7; Doheny, *Canonical Procedure in Matrimonial Cases,* p. 18; Toso, *Ad Codicem Iuris Canonici Commentaria Minora* (5 vols., Romae: Marietti, 1921–1934), lib. II, tom. II, 21, n. 4; Costello, *Domicile and Quasi-Domicile,* The Catholic University of America Canon Law Studies, n. 60 (Washington, D. C.: The Catholic University of America, 1930), p. 177. However Costello admits the opposite opinion as probable.

[69] *Epitome,* I, n. 214.

a necessary quasi-domicile for minors.[70] They argue that the necessary participation by a minor in the quasi-domicile of his parents or guardians respects and keeps intact the authority which is given by the Code to parents and guardians over those of minor age. It is obvious that the subjection of a minor to those persons under whose authority he is placed demands that the minor retain their domicile. This dependence and subjection of a minor also logically requires that he necessarily retain the quasi-domicile of his protectors. In other words the same basic reason why a minor necessarily retains the domicile of his parents or guardians is likewise operative in the question of quasi-domicile.

Nor is the reason drawn from the silence of the Code a conclusive argument for the non-existence of a legal quasi-domicile. For, as Michiels [71] demonstrates, there is a reason on the part of the legislator for such silence. In canon 92 the lawgiver mentions both a voluntary domicile and quasi-domicile. In the first paragraph of that canon he considers domicile, while in the second paragraph of the same canon he treats of the institute of quasi-domicile. But it is necessary for the legislator to discuss these two institutes separately, since in canon 92 he is considering the different ways in which a voluntary domicile and quasi-domicile can be acquired. Now the mode of attaining a voluntary domicile differs from the manner of acquiring a voluntary quasi-domicile, so the lawgiver is forced to treat these two institutes separately. However, in canon 93 the legislator mentions explicitly only the necessary domicile. He is silent concerning a legal quasi-domicile, but such silence does not mean that it does

---

[70] Maroto, *Institutiones Iuris Canonici,* I, 478–479; Coronata, *Institutiones Iuris Canonici,* I, 132; Wernz-Vidal, *Ius Canonicum,* II, n. 12; Michiels, *De Personis,* pp. 151-152; Cappello, *Summa,* I, n. 195, 2°; Chelodi, *Ius de Personis,* p. 166; Beste, *Introductio in Codicem,* p. 140; Claeys Bouuaert-Simenon, *Manuale Iuris Canonici,* I, 143; Oesterle, *Praelectiones Iuris Canonici,* I, 53; Cocchi, *Commentarium in Codicem Iuris Canonici ad Usum Scholarum* (5 vols. in 8, Taurinorum Augustae, 1922–1930; Lib. II, *De Personis,* Marietti, 1922), II, 22; this work will hereafter be cited as *Commentarium;* Vindex, "Domicilium et Quasi-Domicilium Eorumque Effectus in C. J. C"—*JP,* VI (1926), 49, 51; Ramstein, *The Pastor and Marriage Cases* (2. ed., New York: Benziger Bros., 1938), n. 45.

[71] *De Personis,* p. 152.

not exist. The reason is simply because a necessary quasi-domicile is acquired in the same way and for the same reasons as a necessary domicile. Therefore there is no reason for the legislator to mention explicitly a necessary quasi-domicile, but it suffices if he mentions expressly only the necessary domicile, as he actually does.

The second argument advanced by authors to prove the non-existence of a necessary quasi-domicile is that in the present law of the Church there is no need for such an institute. The writer concedes that a necessary quasi-domicile is not absolutely requisite that the minor have his own proper pastor and Ordinary, and in this respect the argument of the authors who propose it is valid. However, the existence of such an institute is necessary in order that the juridical system of the subjection of minors to parents or guardians, which is intended by the legislator, be kept intact. Hence this argument given by the authors to disprove the existence of a necessary quasi-domicile is not conclusive.

Thus the question concerning the existence of a legal quasi-domicile is disputed among post-Code authors. However the existence of such an institute is affirmed by most authors of great name as is clear from an examination of their teaching regarding this question.[72]

It is the opinion of the writer that a legal quasi-domicile exists in the present law of the Church. Besides the reasons already given as proof of this opinion a further argument can be validly drawn from the old law of the Church. Since the present Canon law on domicile repeats in great part the pre-Code law, there seems to be no good reason for departing from this pre-Code legislation. In the old law a legal quasi-domicile was certainly admitted, and time and time again its existence was affirmed by the jurisprudence of those times.[73] Hence, since no convincing

[72] However McBride (*Incardination and Excardination of Seculars,* p. 323) states: "Most canonists after the Code are agreed that a necessary quasi-domicile does not exist any longer." The only proof McBride offers for such a sweeping statement is a reference to Costello's work on *Domicile and Quasi-Domicile.* It must be said that this assertion of McBride's is false, as is evident from an examination of the works of leading post-Code authors. Furthermore such an assertion is not substantiated by Costello.

[73] "Qui vero tenentur sequi domicilium necessarium, habere possunt etiam

argument can be offered to prove that the pre-Code legislation concerning this institute has been abrogated by the Code, it follows that a minor necessarily shares the quasi-domicile of the person to whom he is subject.

Thus it may frequently happen that by reason of domicile and quasi-domicile a minor girl may have several proper pastors who are entitled to institute the pre-nuptial investigation and to assist at her marriage. Who from among these pastors has preference? The Code of Canon Law gives preference to no one of these pastors in particular. Therefore the pastor whom the bride selects from among these several competent pastors enjoys the right to assist at the marriage, and it becomes his duty to follow out and observe the prescription of canon 1034. In the following article the procedure of the pastor in such marriages will be examined.

Article 3. The Procedure of the Pastor in the Marriage of Minors

In this present article the procedure of the pastor in the marriage of minors will be considered in detail. His duties will vary according to three different possibilities, and so a threefold division within this article logically suggests itself. Thus the writer will discuss the procedure of the pastor in the marriage of minors:

A. When the parents know of the marriage and give their consent;
B. When the parents are uninformed of their children's plan to marry;
C. When the parents know of the marriage but refuse to give their consent.

---

quasi domicilium pariter necessarium, seu legale, si nempe hi, quorum domicilium necessario sequuntur alicubi acquirant quasi domicilium in sensu iuris canonici."—S. R. R., *Ravennaten., Nullitatis matrimonii,* 15 maii 1911, *Coram R. P. D. Friderico Cattani,* dec. XVIII, n. 5—*Decisiones,* III (1911), 191; also given in *AAS,* III (1911), 487. Cf. S. R. R., *Nullitatis matrimonii,* 28 augusti 1911, *Coram R. P. D. Aloysio Sincero,* dec. XXXIX, nn. 34–35, 37—*Decisiones,* III (1911), 445–446; S. R. R., *Parisien., Nullitatis matrimonii,* 27 ian. 1912, *Coram R. P. D. Seraphino Many,* dec. VI, n. 7—*Decisiones,* IV (1912), 62; also given in *AAS,* IV (1912), 281.

These three different possibilities will now be treated separately.

A. WHEN THE PARENTS KNOW OF THE MARRIAGE AND GIVE THEIR CONSENT

In this instance there is no special difficulty for the pastor. He will proceed in very much the same way as he would for any other marriage. However, there are a number of items which assume added importance when there is question of a minor entering marriage, and all of these points deserve the careful attention of the pastor. These particular questions will be considered under this present division, and will be valid for all marriages in which one or both parties are of minor age.

First, the pastor should especially note the age of the parties. Provided that the groom has completed his sixteenth year of age and the bride her fourteenth year,[74] and if they are not hindered by any impediment,[75] a valid and licit marriage can be celebrated. The pastor must be careful to establish proof concerning the exact age of the parties, for if one of them is below the canonical age even by a single day the marriage would be invalid.[76] Necessary and sufficient proof of age can be had from the baptismal certificates of the parties concerned. If such a

[74] Canon 1067, § 1.

[75] Canons 1058–1080.

[76] This is true for marriages between two Catholics, or between two baptized non-Catholics, or between a Catholic and a baptized non-Catholic. However, for a marriage involving a baptized Catholic or non-Catholic and an infidel a distinction must be made. If the baptized party has not the requisite age as set forth in Canon 1067, § 1, then a valid marriage is impossible without a dispensation from the impediment of nonage, and this is true irrespective of the age of the unbaptized party. If, on the other hand, the baptized Catholic or non-Catholic possesses the necessary canonical age, no dispensation is required in order to contract a valid marriage even though the infidel party is under the stated canonical age. It is presupposed, of course, that the requirements of the natural law concerning due discretion are fulfilled. However, canonists are not in agreement concerning the last case mentioned above, namely, when a baptized non-Catholic who has the requisite canonical age marries an infidel who is under age without a proper dispensation from the State, if the infidel is bound by a civil impediment of nonage. Cf. Payen, *De Matrimonio,* I, nn. 955–956; Gasparri, *De Matrimonio,* I, n. 256; Cappello, *De Sacramentis,* III, 410–411; Feije, *De Impedimentis et Dispensationibus Matrimonialibus,* pp. 407–408.

document cannot be obtained, affidavits from their parents, relatives, or close friends testifying to the age of the parties suffice. However, the mere testimony of the parties given in the prenuptial invstigation that they are of age should not always be accepted as sufficient proof. Nor does the age which appears on the civil marriage license, which is required by the civil law in most States,[77] constitute convincing proof, for very often, as experience testifies, such averments of age are not correct. In many cases the parties deceive the clerk in the license bureau either by misrepresenting their age or by obtaining their license to marry through a fraudulent substitution of persons. Therefore in the absence of all other proof the mere statement of the parties or the age as it is stated on the license cannot in every case be accepted as conclusive proof. In such cases, if no other proof is available, the pastor should as a last resort receive a suppletory oath from the party whose age is doubtful.[78]

The age, as already remarked, must be complete. The sixteenth year for the boy and the fourteenth year for the girl must be computed in accordance with canon 34, § 3, 3°. Hence the day of the birth is not counted because the birth does not necessarily coincide with the beginning of the day. The last day in the computation of the necessary age must be completed in its entirety. Thus, for example, a boy born on January 2, 1929, could not validly marry without a dispensation until January 3, 1945; a girl born on the same date could not contract a valid marriage before January 3, 1943. The condition "*nisi malitia suppleat aetatem*," which ruled in pre-Code legislation, is no longer valid under the law of the Code. Hence the age limit in the present discipline of the Church must be physically complete to the day.[79]

Even though the marriage is valid if contracted by a boy immediately after the completion of his sixteenth year and by

---

[77] Alford, *Jus Matrimoniale Comparatum* (Romae: Anonima Libraria Cattolica Italiana, 1938), pp. 199–204; this work will hereafter be cited *Jus Matrimoniale*.

[78] Cf. canons 1829–1830 for rules when the suppletory oath is necessary.

[79] Chelodi, *Ius Matrimoniale Iuxta Codicem Iuris Canonici* (3. ed., Tridenti: Libr. Edit. Tridentum, 1921), pp. 66–67; this work will hereafter be cited *Ius Matrimoniale;* Cappello, *De Sacramentis*, III, n. 337.

a girl immediately after her fourteenth year, nevertheless the Church discourages such early unions. That is to say, in canon 1067, § 2 the legislator urges pastors of souls to dissuade young people from marrying before they have reached the age at which marriage is usually contracted according to the prevailing local customs. This is a wise prescript, and the pastor should observe it faithfully. He should convincingly point out to the parties the social disadvantages of contracting marriage before the age accepted as suitable by the community wherein they reside. Moreover, persons of such youthful age are immature physically, mentally, and morally for marriage, and thus are apt to enter into unwise unions. To marry at too early an age is harmful to both the contracting parties and their future children alike, for the spouses have not the necessary stability of purpose for rearing a family, and very often the youthful husband is in no wise capable of providing financially for a wife and children. Therefore, even though the parents have already given their consent for such a marriage, the pastor should nevertheless discourage the children from executing their plans for marriage. Moreover, he should confer with the parents and explain to them the mind of the Church in this matter, and urge them to exhort their children to defer their intended marriage until they have arrived at a more suitable age. If it should happen, however, that the youthful parties have a grave cause for contracting marriage before the customary age of their respective locality, the pastor would be doing wrong in refusing to assist at their marriage. Thus, if marriage provides the only practical and ready means for the parties to free themselves from a habit of sin, or if the girl is already pregnant, or if the marriage does not take place scandal would result, then in these and similar circumstances the pastor should assist at the marriage. For in such instances there is sufficient cause present for the pastor not only to permit the marriage but even to advise the parties to contract it.[80]

Secondly, when the nupturients, who are of minor age, allege that their parents know of and consent to their forthcoming marriage, the pastor must be morally certain that the parties are

[80] Cappello, *De Sacramentis,* III, 407; Wernz-Vidal, *Ius Canonicum,* V, 232; Gougnard, *Tractatus de Matrimonio,* pp. 375–376.

speaking the truth. Pastoral experience proves that it happens not infrequently that the parties in their impassioned desire to marry deliberately deceive the pastor and enter upon marriage without consulting their parents or obtaining permission from them. Hence, the pastor is in duty bound to investigate this assertion of the minor spouses that they have consulted their parents and have received permission from them. Innumerable difficulties have arisen, and every Chancery is acquainted with the many sad cases which result from the failure of the careless or credulous pastor to observe carefully this norm. If the pastor is not personally acquainted with both the parties and their parents, he must not rest content with the simple assertion of the parties themselves, even though it has been affirmed under oath that their parents or guardians know of and consent to the marriage. Nor is the possession by the parties of a civil license to marry sufficient proof, even though the parties in order to obtain such a license need the written consent of parents or guardians, for fraud is readily practiced in these matters, as has already been mentioned above regarding the proof for age.

Thus, the Sacred Congregation of the Sacraments orders the pastors to consult the parents of the minor spouse if he is uncertain as to whether they know of and consent to the marriage. The Sacred Congregation has, moreover, prepared a special questionnaire which is to be used by the pastor in making this inquiry.[81] According to this questionnaire the pastor is to remind the parents of the sanctity of an oath and the severity of the punishments meted out to perjurers,[82] and he is to impress upon them the solemnity of the act which he is about to perform. The pastor then places the parents under oath and writes down their testimony. The parents are to be interrogated separately, and when the testimony is complete both the parents and the pastor affix their signature to the separate documents. The pastor

---

[81] S. C. de Sacr., instr., 29 iunii 1941, Allegatum III—*ASS,* XXXIII (1941), 315; cf. *ER,* CV (1941), *Supplement,* p. 21; Bouscaren, *The Canon Law Digest,* II, 272, under canon 1020. This questionnaire is included in an appendix to this present work.

[82] Canon 2323: "Qui . . . periurium extra iudicium commiserit, prudenti Ordinarii arbitrio puniatur, . . ."

then adds the place and the date together with the seal of the Church. According to the Instruction both the father and the mother of the minor spouse must testify and their deposition is registered in two separate forms. If the parents are dead, and the minor is under the authority of guardians, it is evident from the Instruction that they are to testify.

It may be mentioned here that according to the Instruction of the Sacred Congregation of the Sacraments, when the pastors are of different dioceses, and the bride's pastor is to assist at the marriage, the matrimonial documents should be transmitted to him through the groom's diocesan Chancery and a testimonial from this Chancery should indorse the groom's freedom to marry. If, on the other hand, the pastor of the groom is to assist at the marriage, the documents are to be sent to him through the Episcopal Curia of the diocese of the bride, and this Curia is likewise to give the testimonial of her freedom to marry. When the pastors of the parties belong to different dioceses, the Sacred Congregation prescribes that the pastor who is to assist at the marriage receive the authorization of his own Curia. This authorization or permission is known as the *nihil obstat.* Even when the parties belong to different parishes within the same diocese, the Instruction of the Sacred Congregation recommends that the pastor before he assists at the marriage receive the *nihil obstat* from the diocesan Curia. However, the Sacred Congregation does not order this to be done but merely states that such procedure is desirable. Therefore in this latter case unless the Ordinary has ordered the *nihil obstat* to be obtained, the pre-nuptial documents need not be referred to the Chancery, but may be exchanged directly between the pastors.[83] However, in many dioceses throughout the United States the Ordinary requires that even when the parties belong to different parishes within the same diocese the pre-nuptial questionnaire together with the other documents must be forwarded to the Chancery

---

[83] Cf. S. C. de Sacr., instr., 29 iunii 1941—*AAS,* XXXIII (1941), 299, n. 4, a; Cloran, *A Guide to the Use of the Instruction of the Sacred Congregation of the Sacraments on the Norms To Be Observed by Pastors in Pre-Nuptial Investigations* (Des Plaines, Illinois: St. Mary's Press, 1942), Sec. II, n. 4, a, 2, 3; Bouscaren, *The Canon Law Digest,* II, 255, n. 4 a.

for the *nihil obstat.* Other dioceses prescribe this practice only when a dispensation is needed before the marriage can be celebrated.

This requirement causes no little trouble for the officials in the Curia, who must carefully examine the submitted documents, and one of their difficulties concerns marriages in which one or both parties are minors. For among those questions which are listed on the pre-nuptial questionnaire there is one which is proper to a marriage in which at least one of the spouses is a minor. The pastor must ask the party who is still a minor if he has consulted his parents or guardians about the marriage and received their consent. The pastor then notes the response of the minor, which is generally in the affirmative, but does not indicate whether he has made an investigation in order to prove the truth of the minor's assertion. Hence, in all these cases the official of the Curia in checking the questionnaire before affixing the *nihil obstat* is doubtful concerning this question. Therefore the official in returning the questionnaire to the pastor usually calls his attention to this point, and states that the *nihil obstat* is granted conditionally depending on whether the pastor has duly investigated the affirmative statement of the minor. Therefore, the pastor should note on the questionnaire itself that he is absolutely certain or enclose with the questionnaire the actual written testimony which he has obtained from the parents or guardians stating that they know of and consent to the marriage.[84]

Thirdly, the pastor must establish beyond doubt the absolute freedom of the parties in contracting marriage. This obligation, of course, binds the pastor for all marriages at which he is to assist, but it has special application and efficacy with regard to the marriage of minors. For it is a well known fact that parents sometimes force their children to contract marriage. Many parents in their desire to see their son or daughter marry into wealth or society do not scruple to reject the spouse chosen by their children and to substitute another party who conforms more to their selfish interests and usually less to the happiness

[84] For a copy of the pre-nuptial questionnaire prepared by the Sacred Congregation of the Sacraments in their instruction of June 29, 1941, cf. *AAS,* XXXIII (1941), 309–313, Allegatum I.

of their children. The minor child, because of his youthful age and immaturity, is afraid to assert himself against the will of his parents, and so consents to the marriage arranged by them. The result is that usually the union is an unhappy one, and the parties later on seek a separation and even a civil divorce. Frequently the marriage contract is invalid due to reverential fear, which under certain circumstances may be sufficiently grave to nullify the matrimonial consent.[85] In fact, the Sacred Congregation of the Sacraments declares, "Let pastors weigh well the fact that one of the chief sources of the nullity of marriages brought before the ecclesiastical tribunal is force and fear."[86] And from an examination of the published cases of the Sacred Roman Rota it is evident that the majority of these cases which were tried on the grounds of force and fear involved marriages of minors, especially where the girl was of minor age, and where the union was arranged and enforced by domineering parents, relatives or guardians.[87]

---

[85] Canon 1087. Cf. Cappello, *De Sacramentis,* III, 687; Wernz-Vidal, *Ius Canonicum,* V, n. 497; Payen, *De Matrimonio,* II, n. 1683.

[86] S. C. de Sacr., instr., 29 iun. 1941—*AAS,* XXXIII (1941), 304, n. 7; cf. *ER,* CV (1941), *Supplement,* p. 9, n. 7; Bouscaren, *The Canon Law Digest,* II, 261, n. 7.

[87] Cf. S. R. R., *Parisien., Nullit. matrim.,* 13 martii 1911, *Coram R. P. D. Seraphino Many,* dec. XII—*Decisiones,* III (1911), 114–121; S. R. R., *Varsavien., Nullit. matrim.,* 10 augusti 1923, *Coram R. P. D. Andrea Jullien,* dec. XXVIII—*Decisiones,* XV (1923), 237–247; S. R. R., *Parisien., Nullit. matrim.,* 21 nov. 1923, *Coram R. P. D. Ubaldo Mannucci,* dec. XXXI—*Decisiones,* XV (1923), 264–273; S. R. R., *Nullit. matrim.,* 28 iulii 1923, *Coram R. P. D. Iosepho Florczak,* dec. XXII—*Decisiones* XV (1923), 190–197; S. R. R., *Nullit. matrim.,* 11 martii 1924, *Coram R. P. D. Ubaldo Mannucci,* dec. XIII—*Decisiones,* XVI (1924), 138–144; S. R. R., *Vicariatus Apost. Tonkini Maritimi, Nullit. matrim.,* 9 aprilis 1924, *Coram R. P. D. Andrea Jullien,* dec. XVII—*Decisiones,* XVI (1924), 138–144; S. R. R., *Colocen., Nullit. matrim.,* 21 iulii 1924, *Coram R. P. D. Maximo Massimi,* dec. XXXIII—*Decisiones,* XVI (1924), 289–293; S. R. R., *Plocen., Nullit. matrim.,* 17 nov. 1926, *Coram R. P. D. Iulio Grazioli,* dec. XLVI—*Decisiones,* XVIII (1926), 374–380; S. R. R., *Vic. Apost. Oceaniae Centralis, Nullit. matrim.,* 23 iulii 1927, *Coram R. P. D. Andrea Jullien,* dec. XXXVII—*Decisiones,* XIX (1927), 315–322; S. R. R., *Brixien., Nullit. matrim.,* 11 augusti, 1927, *Coram R. P. D. Iosepho Florczak,* dec. XLVIII—*Decisiones,* XIX (1927), 426–434; S. R. R., *Mediolanen., Nullit.*

Therefore, the pastor with utmost diligence should investigate the freedom of the parties when they are of minor age. He should interrogate the bride and groom separately concerning their freedom in giving their consent to the marriage.[88] He should especially question the minor bride as to whether she is being compelled by any person or circumstance to contract marriage. A more cautious interrogation of the bride is necessary because she is more liable to be subject to fear than the groom. This observation is implied by the legislator in canon 1020, § 2, and is explicitly stated in the Instruction of the Sacred Congregation of the Sacraments.[89] This Instruction also adds that the pastor should not acquiesce too readily in the replies of the parties which deny that they are under force or fear, but directs him to proceed with further investigations. He should consult their parents or guardians and should seek out their relatives and friends who could testify concerning the freedom or lack of freedom of the parties in contracting marriage. Such further inquiry is all the more necessary if the pastor knows that the girl or boy comes from a home where the parents are known for their exceptional strictness with their children, or where the parents are ambitious and self-seeking even at the expense of their children's welfare. Again, among certain nationalities parental domination is more marked and noticeable than among other peoples.

The pastor should bear in mind that especially among minors the desire to contract a marriage frequently does not stem from motives of mutual love between the parties, but only from a sense of honor or duty coupled with the fear of civil law penalties or parental harm if the marriage is not celebrated. Thus, it may happen that the boy and girl sin together with the result that

---

matrim., 8 augusti 1929, *Coram R. P. D. Francisco Morano,* dec. XLIX—*Decisiones,* XXI (1929), 410-417; S. R. R., *Nullit. matrim.*, 18 martii 1929, *Coram R. P. D. Iulio Grazioli,* dec. XX—*Decisiones,* XXI (1929), 159-170; S. R. R., *Plocen., Nullit. matrim.*, 14 ianuarii 1930, *Coram R. P. D. Francisco Morano,* dec. III—*Decisiones,* XXII (1930), 40-44.

88 The presence at this inquiry of another prudent person, but not the father or mother of either party, is permissible.

89 S. C. de Sacr., instr., 29 iunii 1941—*AAS,* XXXIII (1941), 304, n. 7.

the girl becomes pregnant. Her parents urge her to marry the boy as soon as possible for otherwise she will bring disgrace and shame not only to herself but upon all the members of the family. Often in such a case the parents of the girl will threaten her accomplice with dire consequences unless he marries their daughter. If the pastor learns of this he must refuse to assist at the marriage. He should, moreover, discourage the parties from marrying and explain to them that marriage would not be the proper and wise solution of their difficulty under those circumstances. If the parties are entering marriage out of fear or duress, even though it would be insufficient to cause the invalidity of the contract, the pastor should nevertheless refuse to assist at the marriage. He should explain to them that the Church is loath to solemnize a marriage unless the parties to the contract are acting freely and of their own accord. If, however, the spouses insist on being married, even though the force or fear still persists, the pastor should without assisting at the marriage refer the case to the Ordinary and await his decision.

Fourthly, when minor children plan to be married the pastor should see to it that they are properly instructed according to canon 1033 concerning the sanctity and obligations of marriage. This instruction must be given to all persons about to enter the married state, but special care must be taken by the pastor if minors are involved. Two reasons necessitate this: (1) The youthful age of the parties offers a presumption that they are more in need of such direction than others who are more advanced in years; and (2) the pastor must be careful not to scandalize or shock these young people by the manner in which he imparts this instruction. He should prudently and tactfully instruct them that marriage is a permanent society of a man and a woman for the procreation and education of children, and explain to them the mutual rights and obligations of husband and wife. Possession of this knowledge of what constitutes the essential object of the marriage contract is all important for without it a valid marriage is impossible. Thus, if a person would marry without having any idea whatsoever of the mutual right and obligation to the conjugal act, his marriage would be invalid. The lawgiver in canon 1082, § 2 expressly declares that, in order that matrimonial consent be possible, it is necessary that the contracting parties at least be not lacking in the knowledge that marriage is the permanent union of man and woman for the procreation of children. However, clear and explicit knowledge is not necessary; a general knowledge of the essence of the marriage contract suffices.[90]

Though ignorance of the primary purpose of marriage is not presumed to be present after the age of puberty,[91] nevertheless this presumption does not excuse the pastor from imparting the necessary instruction. For the legislator in stating this presumption, which, of course, admits of proofs to the contrary, has in view the case where later on the validity of a marriage is attacked in an ecclesiastical court on the basis of ignorance of one or both of the contracting parties. He does not intend to exempt the pastor from instructing the parties concerning the nature and use of marriage. In this general instruction the pastor would do well to advise the parties that, if doubts should arise later concerning the morality of actions in their married life, they should not hesitate to speak to their confessor about these difficulties rather than seek such information from their married friends. The pastor should also give to the minor spouses some approved Catholic book or pamphlet which treats the subject of marriage clearly and simply, for this reading matter will supplement the private instructions given to the spouses by the pastor.

The pastor, furthermore, should inquire, unless reasons to the contrary are present, whether the spouses are sufficiently instructed in Christian Doctrine. They should at least know the principal mysteries of their faith, the Apostles' Creed, the Our Father and Hail Mary, the Act of Contrition, the Acts of Faith, Hope, and Charity, together with the Sacraments, the Ten Commandments, and the Precepts of the Church. Authors agree that such knowledge is required and sufficient.[92] If the parties lack this knowledge the pastor should instruct them; but a

[90] Cappello, *De Sacramentis,* III, nn. 581–582; Vlaming, *Praelectiones Iuris Matrimonii,* II, n. 524; Gougnard, *Tractatus de Matrimonio,* pp. 152–153.

[91] Canon 1082, § 2.

[92] Cappello, *De Sacramentis,* III, 182; Payen, *De Matrimonio,* I, n. 412.

refusal on their part to accept this instruction from the pastor is not a sufficient reason to deter them from contracting marriage.[93]

Finally, the pastor must be careful to observe the law concerning the publication of the banns for the marriage of minors. Before the marriage is celebrated the banns must be announced on three successive Sundays or holydays of obligation. The purpose or end of this legislation is to inform the faithful of the forthcoming marriage, so that if any of them would know of an impediment affecting the parties they must reveal this to the pastor or Ordinary before the marriage takes place. This law of the banns also serves as an added safeguard to prevent the celebration of the marriage of minors without the knowledge or consent of parents.

But by whom are the banns to be announced? Canon 1023, § 1 enacts that the proper pastor of the parties has the obligation to publish the banns. Now the proper pastor according to canon 94 is the pastor of the parish in which the parties have their domicile or quasi-domicile, or if it is question of *vagi,* their residence. Since the legislation on domicile and quasi-domicile of a minor, as already remarked, is peculiar to minors, the pastor must be careful to apply these principles to the law of publishing the banns. Thus, if both the bride and groom are of minor age and reside in the same parish with their respective parents, the proper pastor for the publication of the banns is the pastor of the parish wherein the parents reside. If, however, the bride's parents live in parish A and the parents of the groom have residence in parish B, the banns are to be published in both parishes.[94] It may happen that one or both of the minor spouses while necessarily retaining the domicile of their parents or guardians have acquired one or more quasi-domiciles of their own in other

---

[93] PCI, 2—3 iunii 1918, IV, 3—*AAS,* X (1918), 345; cf. Bouscaren, *The Canon Law Digest,* I, 496-497 under canon 1020; S. C. de Sacr., instr., 29 iunii 1941—*AAS,* XXXIII (1941), 304, n. 8.

[94] This is explicitly stated in the Roman Ritual. Cf. *Rituale Romanum Pauli V Pontificis Maximi iussu editum aliorumque Pontificum cura recognitum atque auctoritate Sanctissimi D. N. Pii Papae XI ad normam Codicis Iuris Canonici accommodatum* (Ratisbonae: Sumptibus et Typis Friderici Pustet, 1937), tit. VII, caput I, *de sacramento matrimonii,* n. 7.

parishes or dioceses.[95] In this instance the banns must be published both in the parishes of their quasi-domicile and in the parish where their parents have their domicile. If the parents have more than one domicile the banns must be announced in each and every one of them.

What is to be done if the parents likewise possess a quasi-domicile? Must the banns for the marriage of their minor children also be published in the parental quasi-domicile? According to the opinion of the writer the banns must be announced by the pastor of the parental quasi-domicile, for the writer maintains that minor children who are still under the *patriapotestas* necessarily share the quasi-domicile of their parents. For the institute of a necessary quasi-domicile exists and is possessed by the unemancipated minor.[96] Thus, it follows that the pastor of the parish in which the parents have a quasi-domicile is also the proper pastor of the minor children, and consequently is bound to publish the banns for their marriage.

However, there is, as noted in the preceding article, a dispute among authors as to whether or not in the present discipline of the Church there is such an institute as a legal quasi-domicile. Therefore, because of this difference of opinion among approved authors no certain obligation can be established to announce the banns for a minor's marriage in the parish where his parents have their quasi-domicile.[97] The pastor, however, must be consistent in this matter. He cannot maintain that he has the right to assist lawfully at the marriage of a minor because the parents of the minor spouse have a quasi-domicile in his parish which the minor necessarily shares, and on the other hand to reason that he has no obligation to publish the banns in this parish since the existence of a legal quasi-domicile is disputed among canonists. For his right to assist lawfully at the marriage depends in this case on

[95] It is certain that one can have at the same time more than one quasi-domicile even though some authors as De Meester (*Compendium Iuris Canonici*, I, 216) assert the contrary. Cf. Michiels, *De Personis*, p. 167; Ojetti, *Commentarium in Codicem*, II, 50, nota 46.

[96] Cf. *supra*, pp. 124–127.

[97] Roberts, *The Banns of Marriage*, The Catholic University of America Canon Law Studies, n. 64 (Washington, D. C.: The Catholic University of America, 1931), p. 72, note 5.

the very existence of a legal quasi-domicile. If such an institute exists, and the writer maintains that it does, then the pastor of the parish in which the quasi-domicile is located may lawfully assist at the marriage of the minor, and if he does assist he is obliged to publish the banns.

Therefore, the pastor who is to assist at the marriage of minors must determine the parish or parishes in which the banns are to be published. He must also note that, even though the minor child is emancipated from the parental authority, it does not follow that the child no longer retains the domicile of his parents. It is true that the parental domicile ceases to be for him a necessary domicile, but it still may be retained by him as a voluntary domicile unless it is clear that he has left the parental home with the intention of never returning. These two elements, namely, departure plus the intention of not returning must be present, as canon 95 demands, in order to effect the loss of a domicile or quasi-domicile. If it remains doubtful upon investigation whether the minor child has lost completely the parental domicile, the presumption in favor of its retention rules, and hence the banns must be published in the parental domicile.

It may happen that the parents of the Catholic child are unbaptized. Even in this case the banns of marriage are to be published in the parish of the parental domicile, even though the child since his conversion no longer resides permanently with his parents but has his own quasi-domicile in another parish. The fact that his parents are infidels does not militate against their acquiring a canonical domicile or quasi-domicile. In fact canon 738, § 2 mentions the proper pastor of an unbaptized *peregrinus*. Moreover, the legal domicile or quasi-domicile is given to the baptized child who is surely capable of acquiring one.[98]

There is no obligation to publish the banns in a parish where the parties at one time had a domicile or quasi-domicile but which they now no longer possess, because the pastor of that parish is not their proper pastor. Nor must the banns be an-

[98] S. C. de Sacr. 14 decembris 1915—*AAS,* VIII (1916), 66; Kay, *Competence in Matrimonial Procedure,* The Catholic University of America Canon Law Studies, n. 53 (Washington, D. C.: The Catholic University of America), 1929, pp. 95–96.

nounced in the parish of the place of origin unless the parties still retain a domicile or quasi-domicile there.[99] However, if after attaining the age of puberty either one or both of the contracting parties have lived for six months in some place outside their domicile or quasi-domicile, the pastor must consult the Ordinary. In such a case the local Ordinary may inform the pastor either to have the banns announced in this place, or to acquire affidavits from two trustworthy persons, preferably Catholics, who are able and willing to testify that the parties did not contract any impediment during the time of their residence away from their parish of domicile or quasi-domicile, or to investigate their freedom of status in some other manner.[100] The Ordinary usually will suggest that the use of affidavits be employed in order to establish the free status of the party to marry. If the pastor has grounds for suspicion that the party may have contracted an impediment during his stay outside his proper parish, even though the residence was for a time less than six months, he is bound to refer the matter to the Ordinary. The Ordinary then shall not permit the celebration of the marriage until all suspicion is removed.[101]

If the minor spouse, for example the bride, has residence in a given parish for a month, the pastor of this parish according to canon 1097, § 1, 2° may lawfully assist at the marriage, even though the bride intends to leave the parish immediately after the celebration of the marriage. However, this pastor has no obligation to publish the banns, since in law he is not her proper pastor.[102] However, in this instance and in all other cases in which the parties have several proper pastors, the priest who is to assist at the marriage should notify the pastors of the coming marriage and request them to publish the banns. Before the pastor may solemnize the marriage he must await the response of the

[99] Cappello, *De Sacramentis*, III, 195; Gasparri, *De Matrimonio*, I, n. 158.

[100] Canon 1023, § 2; cf. S. C. de Sacr., instr., 29 iun. 1941, Allegatum II—*AAS*, XXXIII (1941), 314.

[101] Canon 1023, § 3; cf. S. C. de Sacr., instr., 29 iun. 1941—*AAS*, XXXIII (1941), 303, n. 6, b; Bouscaren, *The Canon Law Digest*, II, 260, n. 6, b; *ER*, CV (1941), *Supplement*, p. 8, n. 6, b.

[102] Sipos, *Enchiridion Iuris Canonici*, p. 491, nota 6; Cappello, *De Sacramentis*, III, 195.

different proper pastors concerning the outcome of the publication. What is to be done if this testimony of the various pastors should fail to arrive in time for the marriage? The pastor who is to assist at the marriage should make every effort to acquire the information. If his efforts fail, and there is still time, he must consult his own Ordinary. If consultation with the Ordinary is impossible, the pastor may use epikeia and assist at the marriage without the testimony provided he is morally certain of the freedom of the parties to marry. Such a case frequently arises with regard to the marriage of minors who usually have a number of proper pastors.[103]

If, however, undue delay of the marriage and serious difficulties for the youthful parties would result if the banns were published by all their proper pastors, then the priest who is to assist at the marriage could petition and easily obtain from the Ordinary a dispensation from the banns to be published in a certain place. Since according to the strict letter of the law the banns must be announced by all the proper pastors of the contracting parties, it follows that a dispensation is necessary if the prescript of the law is not to be observed. The fact that the publication of the banns in these parishes may seem useless to the pastor and of little practical worth in helping to establish the free status of the party to marry does not of itself excuse him from the obligation imposed by the law. For the law requiring the publication of the banns of marriage is based on the presumption of a common danger; hence, even though in a particular instance this danger is absent, the law for this reason does not cease to bind. For the purpose of this law of banns is to avoid a common danger; but this danger is not effectively avoided unless the law binds and obliges all.[104] Therefore even in these cases a dispensation from the banns is still necessary.[105]

---

[103] Vlaming, *Praelectiones Iuris Matrimonii,* I, n. 177; Cappello, *De Sacramentis,* III, 216; De Smet, *De Sponsalibus et Matrimonio,* p. 37.

[104] Canon 21: "Leges latae ad praecavendum periculum generale, urgent, etiamsi in casu peculiari periculum non adsit."

[105] Gasparri, *De Matrimonio,* I, n. 158; Ayrinhac-Lydon, *Marriage Legislation,* p. 34; Van Hove, *Commentarium Lovaniense in Codicem Iuris Canonici* (Vol. I, Tom. II [*De Legibus Ecclesiasticis*] Mechliniae-Romae:

The pastor must petition the proper local Ordinary for this dispensation, and the latter is competent to dispense from the publications which need to be made in another diocese.[106] Canon 94 determines this proper Ordinary as the one in whose diocese the contracting parties have their domicile or quasi-domicile. If the parties have a domicile or quasi-domicile in several dioceses, and they intend to contract marriage in one of them, then the pastor must petition the Ordinary in whose diocese the marriage is to be celebrated, for he alone is competent to grant the dispensation. If the parties have several proper Ordinaries but the marriage is to take place outside their jurisdiction, the pastor may seek the dispensation from banns from any one of the proper Ordinaries, for they are all equally able to grant the dispensation.[107] If the minor is a *vagus,* which is possible only if his parents or guardians have no domicile or quasi-domicile and if he himself has failed to acquire at least his own quasi-domicile, then the pastor must petition the local Ordinary in whose diocese the marriage is to be contracted, for he alone may grant the dispensation since he is the only proper Ordinary of the minor.

B. WHEN THE PARENTS ARE UNINFORMED OF THEIR CHILDREN'S PLAN TO MARRY

If the pastor should learn either from the minor parties themselves or from some other source that they have not consulted their parents concerning the forthcoming marriage, he should inquire of them their reasons for so acting. For the procedure of the pastor will be determined by the causes or reasons which the parties allege. If the reasons which the parties advance for not consulting their parents in the judgment of the pastor are not just, he must warn the spouses of their grave obligation to inform their parents. If the spouses refuse to do so, the pastor must instruct them that he cannot assist at their marriage. Rarely will the pastor have a case where the parties have valid and sufficiently grave reasons for marrying without previously consulting their parents.

H. Dessain, 1930), I–II, n. 333; this work will hereafter be cited *De Legibus Ecclesiasticis.*

[106] Canon 1028, § 1.

[107] Canon 1028, § 2.

Usually their reasons are groundless, and are in no wise sufficient to permit the parties their request. Thus, for instance, the parties may state that because of estranged relations between themselves and their parents they will not deign to seek their advice; or the parties may fear that their parents will justly oppose the union. Often the spouses offer as reasons for not consulting their parents their desire to elope, or the wish to marry secretly in order to surprise their parents and friends. The pastor must warn the parties that reasons of this nature are manifestly insufficient to allow the marriage. In such instances the pastor is not obliged to refer the matter to the Ordinary for judgment, but can simply refuse to assist at the marriage. If the nupturients insist on being married and still continue in their obstinacy without cause to consult their parents, it becomes the pastor's duty to inform the parents of the intention of their children to marry. He should do this even though the contracting parties voice their objection.[108]

It may happen, however, that the parties have in the opinion of the pastor a grave and serious reason for desiring to conceal the matter of their forthcoming marriage from their parents. For example, the spouses may have good reasons for contracting marriage, but they know and can prove with certainty that if their parents learn of their plans to marry they will maliciously impede the union. Or it may happen that the girl is pregnant and wishing to safeguard her reputation is anxious to contract marriage as soon as possible. If the parents are consulted, they may as a result learn the reason why their daughter wishes to marry. In order to save themselves this shame and embarrassment and consequent loss of their good name, the nupturients desire to enter marriage without previously consulting their parents. In all such instances, where a grave cause exists for contracting marriage secretly, the pastor must refer the case to the local Ordinary and await his decision. For the pastor is expressly forbidden by the law of canon 1034 to assist at the marriage of minors whose parents know nothing about their intended marriage. This obligation likewise urges even though the parents of one of the parties know of the marriage and give their consent provided the parents of the other minor spouse

[108] Augustine, *Commentary* (8 vols., Vol. V, 5. ed., 1935, St. Louis: B. Herder), V, 80.

remain uninformed. Canon 1034 does not require that both of the contracting parties be of minor age; the prescript of this canon holds as well for a marriage between a person of minor age and one who has attained his majority, because the reasons for the prohibition are also verified in this case and remain equally valid.[109] However, if the marriage in question concerns a person of minor age and one who is an adult, the pastor need not consult the Ordinary, if the parents of the minor spouse know of and consent to the marriage, even though the parents of the adult party remain uninformed; for the law of canon 1034 does not obligate those persons who have attained their majority. Yet the pastor should admonish the unwilling adult to inform his parents of his intentions and to seek their experienced and valuable advice before he makes such an important decision as to enter marriage. The pastor should point out to him that failure to consult his parents regarding his intentions to marry is an evident sign of his contempt and disrespect for them. Moreover, if the civil law should prescribe that the parents be informed beforehand of any marriage to be contracted by their children, even for those who are over the age of twenty-one years, the pastor should take notice of this factor lest he become entangled and embroiled in civil suits and become liable to the severe penalties enacted by the civil law in these cases.[110]

What if the parents of the minor party cannot be reached and the child wishes to marry? In this instance, if the marriage could be deferred without serious inconvenience or harm to the contracting parties until the parents could be informed, the pastor

---

[109] Raus, *Institutiones Canonicae iuxta Novum Codicem Iuris* (2. ed., Lugduni, Parisiis: Vitte, 1931), p. 441; this work will hereafter be cited *Institutiones Canonicae;* Blat, *Commentarium* (Vol. III, Pars I, 2. ed., Romae: Ex Typographia Pontificia in Instituto Pii IX, 1924), III, n. 425; Rossi, *De Matrimonii Celebratione iuxta Codicem Iuris Canonici* (Romae: Fridericus Pustet, 1924), pp. 52–53; this work will hereafter be cited *De Matrimonii Celebratione;* S. C. de Sacr., instr., 29 iun. 1941—*AAS,* XXXIII (1941), 314, n. 9.

[110] Farrugia, *De Matrimonio et Causis Matrimonialibus Tractatus Canonico-Moralis iuxta Codicem Iuris Canonici* (Taurini-Romae: Marietti, 1924), p. 143; this work will hereafter be cited *De Matrimonio;* Cappello, *De Sacramentis,* III, 230; Gougnard, *Tractatus de Matrimonio,* p. 30.

must urge the parties to do so. If, however, it is impossible to contact the parents, and it is foreseen that this condition will continue, then the pastor may assist at the marriage provided he is morally certain of the freedom of the parties to marry. This impossibility of informing the parents may be due to either physical or moral reasons. It is physically impossible if, for example, the parties are separated from their parents by so great a distance that neither the nupturients nor the pastor can inform them in time for the marriage, and the parties have good reasons to marry. In this case authors agree that the pastor is excused from his duty of informing the parents.[111] A moral impossibility of informing the parents is present if the parties in consulting their parents would suffer the loss of their good name because this consultation might lead to the disclosure of secret sins which the nupturients have committed between themselves; or, if the parents were informed of their children's intention to marry they would unjustly but effectively impede the marriage. In these instances it is physically possible for both the parties and the pastor to consult the parents, but it is morally impossible to do so. Nevertheless in these cases the pastor may not assist at the marriage but must refer the case to the Ordinary, since the marriage is to be contracted unknown to the parents.

Donovan,[112] however, simply asserts that there is no necessity to have recourse to the Ordinary when it is impossible to ask parental consent. As proof of this statement he appeals to the canonist Gougnard. But Gougnard [113] does not expressly state that the pastor may assist at the marriage without previously consulting the Ordinary. He only teaches that, in instances where it is physically impossible to inform the parents, the children do not sin against the reverence and respect due to their parents in contracting a marriage without first consulting them. This does not mean that the pastor is therefore free to marry them without having recourse to the local Ordinary. Nor may one reason thus: there is

---

[111] Augustine, *Commentary* V, 80; Gougnard, *Tractatus de Matrimonio,* p. 28; Cappello, *De Sacramentis,* III, 224; O'Donnell, "Consent of Parents in Marriage"—*IER,* VIII (1887), 633–634.

[112] *The Pastor's Obligation in Pre-Nuptial Investigation,* p. 156.

[113] *Tractatus de Matrimonio,* p. 28.

no obligation for the pastor to consult the local Ordinary if the parents are unreasonably opposed to the marriage. But in cases where it is physically or morally impossible to inform the parents, and the parties have good reasons for contracting the marriage, the parents even though they did know of the marriage could not oppose it. If they did express their opposition, they would be acting unreasonably, and hence the pastor would be under no obligation to refer the matter to the Ordinary. Therefore, in such instances, where it is impossible to inform the parents, the pastor may assist lawfully without first consulting the Ordinary. This reasoning runs counter to the ruling of canon 1034 which enacts that the pastor must consult the Ordinary in these two cases: (1) when the parents do not know of the marriage of their minor children, and (2) when they do know of the intended marriage but reasonably refuse to give their consent to it.

In regard to the question of a minor contracting marriage without the knowledge of his parents, authors discuss the possibility of permitting a conditional marriage with the condition, "if my parents will consent to the marriage." This condition is evidently an honest and licit condition, and one that concerns a contingent future happening, namely, the parental permission. It is a suspensive condition, for the commencement of the marriage is suspended until the condition is fulfilled.

Thus, if the contracting parties approach the pastor in order to be married, and the bride informs him that her parents do not know of the marriage, may the pastor assist at a conditional marriage? This case presupposes that the parents of the girl cannot be consulted in time to learn whether or not they would consent to the union. The girl, on the other hand, does not wish to displease her parents, and though desiring to enter marriage as soon as possible will do so, however, only if her parents would give their permission. A situation of this kind could readily arise during time of war when the boy, for example, receives orders that he is to be sent overseas immediately and desires to contract marriage before he departs. The parents of the bride, who is of minor age, do not know of the marriage and cannot be reached. May a conditional marriage be permitted, and if so what are its effects?

The exchange of matrimonial consent under a condition, especially a suspensive one as had in the present case, is contrary to the mind of the Church, for the Church desires that the marital consent be given absolutely and not conditionally. A matrimonial consent which is made subject to a suspensive condition is then something alien to the rite of celebration of marriage as expressed in the Roman Ritual,[114] and is in no way sanctioned by any custom within the Church.[115] The opposition of the Church to such a conditional marriage is based on the fear that the marriage may remain uncertain, and that the spouses may be unduly exposed to the danger of sinning. Moreover, there is present the danger of exposing the very Sacrament of Matrimony to nullity. For these reasons the pastor must discourage the parties from contracting this conditional marriage. If, however, they still insist on entering marriage conditionally, their request can be licitly granted only if there is a grave reason present for contracting the marriage and only after the pastor has consulted the Ordinary and has received his permission. These requirements must be verified even though the Code of Canon Law is silent concerning their necessity.[116] Indeed, some authors demand not only a grave cause for the licit celebration of this conditional marriage, but a cause that is *gravissima* or *urgentissima.*[117]

[114] *Rituale Romanum,* tit. VII, *De Sacramento Matrimonii,* cap. 2, *Ritus Celebrandi Matrimonii Sacramentum.*

[115] Canon 1100; cf. Wernz-Vidal, *Ius Canonicum,* V, n. 515.

[116] Payen, *De Matrimonio,* II, n. 1727; Cappello, *De Sacramentis,* III, 704; Wernz-Vidal, *Ius Canonicum,* V, n. 515; Gasparri, *De Matrimonio,* II, 91–92; De Becker, *De Matrimonio Praelectiones Canonicae* (2. ed., Louvain: Etabliss. Fr. Ceuterick, 1931), 123; this work will hereafter be cited *De Matrimonio;* Chelodi, *Ius Matrimoniale,* p. 134; Claeys Bouuaert-Simenon, *Manuale Iuris Canonici,* II, 297; Ayrinhac-Lydon, *Marriage Legislation,* p. 225; Ramstein, *The Pastor and Marriage Cases,* p. 233; Davis, *Moral and Pastoral Theology* (3. ed., 4 vols., London: Sheed and Ward, 1938), IV, 188.

[117] Raus, *Institutiones Canonicae,* p. 479; Farrugia, *De Matrimonio,* p. 58; Gougnard, *Tractatus de Matrimonio,* p. 142; Cerato, *Matrimonium a Codice I. C. Integre Desumptum* (4. ed., Patavii: Typis Seminarii Patavini, 1929), p. 148; this work will hereafter be cited *Matrimonium;* Noldin-Schmitt, *Summa Theologiae Moralis iuxta Codicem Iuris Canonici* (3 vols., Vol. III, 23. ed., Oeniponte: Typis et Sumptibus F. Rauch, 1935), III, 634; this work will hereafter be cited as *Summa Theologiae Moralis;* Prümmer, *Manuale Theologiae Moralis secundum Principia S. Thomae Aquinatis* (7. ed., 3 vols., Friburgi Brisgoviae: Herder, 1931–1933), III, 533–534; this work will here-

Vlaming,[118] however, holds a singular opinion that it is permissible without any approved reason and without the permission of the Ordinary to place this condition, "if my parents will consent to the marriage," to the contract since it is an honest condition and one that is not opposed to the substance of the marriage contract. He argues that the Code does not require any reason for the placing of such conditions to the marriage. If the legislator would deem it necessary, he would have legislated for it as he clearly does so in canon 1091, wherein he requires a just cause together with the permission of the Ordinary before the pastor may lawfully assist at a marriage which is to be contracted by proxy or for a marriage in which an interpreter plays a part. Therefore the pastor may licitly assist at such conditional marriages even though the parties have no reason for attaching this condition to their consent; nor is the pastor under any obligation to refer the matter to the Ordinary.

This opinion of Vlaming's cannot be held for the reasons already given. Moreover, this opinion expressly contradicts the Instruction of the Sacred Congregation of the Sacraments which decrees, "But as to the legitimate placing of some licit condition concerning the future, the present or the past, let the pastor consult the Ordinary and obey his mandates." [119]

De Smet [120] and Sipos [121] teach that even though the lawgiver has nowhere in the Code of Canon Law enacted a positive prohibition against the pastor assisting at marriages entered conditionally, nevertheless the great difficulties which such marriages give rise to make it necessary that the pastor consult the Ordinary before he assists at the marriage. However, neither DeSmet nor Sipos expressly mention the necessity of a cause, but they seem to imply that a grave cause should be present in order to justify this conditional marriage.

---

after be cited as *Manuale Theologiae Moralis;* Genicot-Salsmans, *Institutiones Theologiae Moralis,* II, n. 458.

[118] *Praelectiones Iuris Matrimonii,* II, n. 551.

[119] S. C. de Sacr., instr. 29 iun. 1941—*AAS,* XXXIII (1941), 304, n. 9; 312-313, n. 17; cf. Bouscaren, *The Canon Law Digest,* II, 262, n. 9; *ER,* CV (1941), *Supplement,* p. 10, n. 9.

[120] *De Sponsalibus et Matrimonio,* p. 132.

[121] *Enchiridion Iuris Canonici,* p. 574.

If the marriage is actually contracted with the condition, "if my parents will give their consent," certain points should be noted. (1) The marriage is valid, if the parents on hearing of the marriage give their consent even though later on the parents withdraw their permission, for a valid and indissoluble marriage exists as soon as the condition, which is the parental consent, is verified. This remains true even though the contracting parties do not know that the condition has been fulfilled.[122] However, if the parents dissent and then only afterwards consent to the marriage, the union is not valid, for the condition is not verified. Though the consent of the contracting parties perdures it is nevertheless juridically inefficacious once the dissent of the parents has taken place. Therefore there is no marriage unless the nupturients renew their consent.[123] (2) If only one of the parents consents, the marriage is not valid, for the condition is not verified. It cannot be maintained that, since the authority to permit the marriage primarily rests with the father, if he alone consents, the condition is fulfilled. For this condition, "if my parents will consent to the marriage," clearly demands the consent of both father and mother. If the condition were, "if my father or mother will consent to the marriage," then of course the consent of either parent would be sufficient to fulfill the condition, and in such a case the marriage would be valid. (3) If the meaning of the condition, "if my parents will consent to the marriage," is merely negative, then as long as the parents do not express their dissent the condition will be fulfilled, and the marriage will be valid. In this instance if the parents on learning of the marriage neither express their consent nor show their disapproval, the marriage is valid. If, on the other hand, the condition, "if my parents will consent to the marriage," is positive in meaning, then a positive consent on the part of the parents is needed in order that the marriage be valid. The presumption is that the condition, "if my parents will consent to the marriage,"

---

[122] Schmalzgrueber, *Jus Ecclesiasticum Universum,* lib. IV, tit. V, n. 40.

[123] Sanchez, *De Matrimonio,* lib. V, disp. VII, n. 8 sq.; Schmalzgrueber, *Jus Ecclesiasticum Universum,* lib. IV, tit. V, nn. 51–53; Gasparri, *De Matrimonio,* II, n. 920; Cappello, *De Sacramentis,* III, n. 641.

is negative in meaning and means, " if my parents will not express their dissent." [124]

This same distinction, namely, whether the condition, " if my parents will consent to the marriage," is negative or positive in meaning, determines the validity of the marriage if the parents should die before the condition is fulfilled. If it is understood in the negative sense, then the condition is verified, for, since the parents are dead, they cannot express their dissent; but if the contracting parties understand the condition in the positive sense so that the condition remains unfulfilled unless the parents express their consent by a positive act of the will, then there is no marriage. For since the parents are dead, it is impossible for them to elicit the required positive act of the will. If at the time the party places the condition, " if my parents will consent to the marriage," the parents are already dead, but this fact remains unknown to the party placing the condition, the marriage seems to be valid at once, because the reason or basis for the condition, namely, the fear of offending the parents by marrying without consulting them, ceases to exist.[125]

It may be said as a general rule that the pastor should discourage the youthful nupturients from contracting marriage under this suspensive condition, " if my parents will consent to the marriage." He should clearly and convincingly explain to them the many difficulties which a conditional marriage of this kind necessarily involves, and since the use of marriage will remain forbidden to the parties until the verification of the condition, none of the rights and privileges which are proper to the married state will accrue to them from the celebration of this conditional marriage. Moreover, the parties are placing themselves in a proximate occasion of sin, and this is the principal reason why the Church dissuades them from contracting a marriage which is made subject to a suspensive condition. However, the advice of the pastor should not be merely negative, but he should attempt to find another solution to

---

124 Sanchez, *De Matrimonio,* lib. V, disp. VII, n. 11; Schmalzgrueber, *Jus Ecclesiasticum Universum,* lib. IV, tit. V, n. 50; Gasparri, *De Matrimonio,* II, n. 920; Cappello, *De Sacramentis,* III, 722; Farrugia, *De Matrimonio,* p. 73.

125 Cappello, *De Sacramentis,* III, 722; Farrugia, *De Matrimonio,* p. 73.

the problem confronting the youthful nupturients. In these circumstances, which the present case contemplates, it would be proper for the pastor to suggest to the parties that they enter into a solemn or formal engagement, as the Code of Canon Law provides in canon 1017, instead of a conditional marriage. In this manner they could pledge to each other their love and later on, if the situation warrants it, they could contract marriage. But if the parties spurn the advice of the pastor and insist on contracting a conditional marriage, then he must consult the local Ordinary and abide by his decision. In the meantime he is forbidden *sub gravi* to assist at the marriage.

If the Ordinary, after a careful consideration of all the circumstances of the case heeding especially the gravity of the cause, in his prudent judgment grants the request of the parties to enter marriage with the condition, "if my parents will consent to the marriage," the pastor must determine the exact sense in which the parties understand this condition before he assists at their marriage. He should interrogate the party who is placing the condition in order to decide whether the consent of both parents is necessary, or whether the consent of either the father or the mother would suffice to fulfill the condition. He should further inquire whether the condition, "if my parents will consent to the marriage," means only that the parents will not dissent, or whether it is to be understood that the parents must positively express their consent. Once the pastor has determined the precise meaning of the condition, he should draw up an authentic document in which he must state in clear terms both the meaning and extent of the condition. Both he and the nupturients should affix their signatures to the document, thereby attesting their agreement to and full understanding of the condition. The document should be dated and sealed with the parish seal. In the actual marriage ceremony the pastor should require that the contracting party, who is entering the union conditionally, express the condition before him and the two witnesses. After the ceremony the pastor must note in the matrimonial register that the marriage was celebrated conditionally, and therein he should express the condition. After receiving authentic information as to whether or not the parents have given their consent, he must indicate this fact in the same register. This procedure on the part of the pastor is, of course, not required for the validity of the marriage, but it is necessary to protect and safeguard the marriage against doubts and attacks in the external forum. For this reason the parties are obliged to inform the pastor immediately concerning the outcome of the condition.[126]

When the parents on learning of the marriage give their consent and so fulfill the condition, the youthful nupturients at that moment become husband and wife and enjoy full use of the marriage rights. No renewal of consent on their part is necessary, for the conditional consent is from the very beginning a true marital consent. With the fulfillment of the condition the conditional consent becomes absolute and a valid marriage exists. Nor is there need of any further ceremony, since the law concerning the form of marriage was observed at the time when the exchange of conditional consent took place.[127] When the condition is verified, the contracting parties at that time must be in the state of grace if they are to receive the Sacrament worthily, for Matrimony is a Sacrament of the Living.[128]

What if the youthful parties in disobedience to the express admonitions of the pastor have carnal intercourse before the verification of the condition? They, of course, commit a grave sin of fornication, but this sin on their part has no effect on the status of the conditional marriage. In the old law of the Church such an action of the parties constituted a *praesumptio iuris et de iure* for the revocation of the condition, and the validity of the marriage in the external forum was immediately presumed.[129] How-

---

126 Sanchez, *De Matrimonio,* lib. V, disp. VIII, nn. 23 sq.; disp. XIII, n. 3; Schmalzgrueber, *Jus Ecclesiasticum Universum,* lib. IV, tit. V, nn. 42–45; Claeys Bouuaert-Simenon, *Manuale Juris Canonici,* II, 297; Gasparri, *De Matrimonio,* II, n. 917; Cappello, *De Sacramentis,* III, 705.

127 Wernz-Vidal, *Ius Canonicum,* V, n. 515; Gougnard, *Tractatus de Matrimonio,* p. 145; Payen, *De Matrimonio,* III, 296, nota 1; Schmalzgrueber, *Jus Ecclesiasticum Universum,* lib. IV, tit. V, nn. 33–38; Prümmer, *Manuale Theologiae Moralis,* III, n. 738.

128 Noldin-Schmitt, *Summa Theologiae Moralis,* III, 635; Cappello, *De Sacramentis,* III, 718.

129 C. 6, X, *de conditionibus appositis in desponsatione vel in aliis contractibus,* IV, 5; this decretal is found also as c. 4, Compilatio, I, h.t., IV, 5. Potthast, n. 1968.

ever, in the present discipline of the Church, this presumption no longer exists, and consequently has no juridical effect on the conditional marriage. The fact that a carnal union of the parties has taken place may indicate a tacit revocation of the condition. In this broad sense, then, it may be said to constitute a presumption. It is surely not a *praesumptio iuris* in the strict sense, for it is not stated in the Code of Canon Law.[130]

The parties may reject the condition, "if my parents will consent to the marriage," before its fulfillment, and if they do so, no renewal of consent nor any new ceremony is necessary for a valid marriage. The absence of the parental consent, since it is no longer a condition for the marriage, and since it is not a canonical impediment to marriage, can in no way impede the validity of the marriage. The spouses, however, should inform the pastor, so that he may record the change in the matrimonial records. Moreover, before the condition is verified the contracting parties may by mutual agreement abandon their plans to marry and withdraw entirely their consent. In such a case it is evident that no marriage exists, even though the parents would on learning of the marriage have given their consent. This is also true, even if only one of the nupturients recalls his consent before the fulfillment of the condition. In these instances, where one or both of the parties withdraw their matrimonial consent, they should immediately notify the pastor of their action, so that there will be in the external forum a valid proof of this revocation of consent. Otherwise the marriage will be presumed a valid one in the external forum when the condition of parental consent is verified.

Thus canon 1034 forbids the pastor to assist at the marriage of a minor without previously consulting the Ordinary, if the parents of the minor do not know of the intended marriage. What must the pastor do if the parents, having been informed of the marriage, refuse to give their consent? The procedure of the pastor in this instance will now be considered.

C. WHEN THE PARENTS KNOW OF THE MARRIAGE BUT REFUSE TO GIVE THEIR CONSENT

If the pastor learns that the parties have consulted their parents

130 Chelodi, *Ius Matrimoniale*, p. 137.

but have not received their consent for the marriage, he must establish the reason for this refusal of permission on the part of the parents, for the procedure of the pastor will differ according to the reasonableness or unreasonableness of the parental refusal. He must diligently inquire of the contracting parties their reasons for desiring to enter marriage, and also the reasons why, in their estimation, their parents object to the union. He must not rest content with the mere testimony of the nupturients, for oftentimes they exaggerate the injustice of the parents' refusal and magnify the importance of their own reasons for marrying. In order to pass judgment on the case the pastor must hear both sides. Consequently, he must consult the parents and ask them their reasons for opposing the marriage of their minor son or daughter. The pastor in making this inquiry must use the form given by the Sacred Congregation of the Sacraments in their Instruction of June 29, 1941.[131] Both the pastor and the parents must sign this document, and a separate form is to be used for the testimony of each parent. The pastor is obligated to use this form, for in case the parents are in his judgment reasonable in their opposition to the marriage, he must submit this document together with his added remarks to the Ordinary. Moreover, in those instances in which the authorization of the Chancery, known as the *nihil obstat*, is needed before the pastor may assist at the marriage, this document together with the other pre-nuptial papers must be sent to the diocesan Chancery.

How is the pastor to determine the reasonableness or unreasonableness of the parent's refusal to consent to the marriage? What norms may he use to aid him in formulating an equitable judgment? It is not sufficient for the pastor merely to determine that the parents have just and grave reasons for opposing the marriage. But these reasons of the parents must be considered in relation to those which their child has for wishing to enter the

[131] Allegatum III—Quaestiones seorsum proponendae parentibus (tutoribus) nupturientis aetate minoris (can. 1034), quando parocho certe non constet de absentia cuiusvis obstaculi ex parte ipsorum—*AAS*, XXXIII (1941), 315; Bouscaren, *The Canon Law Digest*, II, 272; *ER*, CV (1941), *Supplement*, p. 21. For a specimen copy of this form confer Appendix of this dissertation.

marriage. This is the fundamental and basic norm which must guide the pastor in making his decision. Hence the causes for the parental opposition must be just and grave not only objectively, that is, considered in themselves, but also relatively to the marriage in question. The pastor must also keep in mind the reasons of the child. Therefore the pastor would be acting wrongly if he would deem the dissent of the parents reasonable, simply because they have a grave cause to prohibit the marriage. Thus the parents may have grave reasons for refusing their permission, if, for example, the marriage would cause scandal or dissension or would lead to family disgrace, but, on the other hand, the child may have even more serious reasons for contracting the marriage, as, for example, the danger of incontinence. In this instance, then, the parents in refusing their consent would be acting unreasonably.

Hence the pastor before giving his decision must weigh well all the circumstances concerning both the child and the parents. He should consider the age of the parties and also the customary age at which marriage is contracted in their particular locality. Is the child marrying a Catholic or non-Catholic? If a Catholic, is he faithful in the practice of his religion? Is there a vast age difference between the nupturients? What is the family status of the other party? Does he suffer from any physical or moral defects? How long have they known each other? What are their reasons for marrying? Among these reasons, which the parties allege for desiring to contract the marriage, the pastor should especially note whether there is pregnancy involved or any danger of incontinence, concubinage, habitual sin between the parties, loss of reputation or other grave spiritual dangers if the marriage is not permitted. Reasons of this nature are usually sufficient to allow the marriage to be celebrated even against the will of the parents. The pastor must then weigh the specific parental objections. A few of the causes, which are commonly given by the parents to support their objections but which are insufficient to prohibit the marriage, are the following: (1) simple opposition to the marriage supported by no reasonable cause; (2) they desire their child to marry a person of their own choice; (3) opposition to the partner whom their child selects based on reasons of avarice, ambition, social position, personal dislike, and political differences. However, reasonable objections on the part of the parents for refusal of their permission for the marriage would be: (1) the marriage would cause scandal, and dissension would arise within the family; (2) the parents would suffer disgrace or a great material loss; (3) the other party to the contract is a drunkard, a gangster, a convict, an atheist or a member of a non-Catholic sect, a person of inferior status, a person of no education, one who is lazy and incompetent and incapable of supporting a wife and children, or one who is shiftless or in poor health.[132]

If, after a careful consideration of the reasons advanced both by the contracting parties and by the unwilling parents, the pastor prudently judges that in this instance the parents are unreasonable in their dissent, he should with great tact urge the parents to give their permission for the marriage. He should inform them that as Christian parents they are obliged to do so. He should instruct them that their child has a right to contract marriage in this case, and that this right is upheld by the law of the Church. If, however, the parents reject the promptings of the pastor and remain adamant in their refusal, then the pastor may assist at the marriage without previously consulting the Ordinary.[133] The pastor may so act because this right is indirectly conceded to him in canon 1034. For this canon enacts that the pastor must consult the Ordinary only if the parents, while knowing of the marriage, reasonably refuse to give their consent. Therefore, if the parents are unreasonable in their opposition to the marriage, there is no obligation to refer the case to the Ordinary. However, even if the refusal of the parents is manifestly unreasonable, the pastor would do well to consult the Ordinary, especially if the civil law of the locality demands parental consent for the marriage. Moreover, if the parents would threaten civil suit if the pastor assists at the marriage, then the most sensible thing the pastor could do would be to inform the Ordinary of these circumstances. In this in-

---

[132] Gougnard, *Tractatus de Matrimonio,* p. 28; Augustine, *Commentary,* V, 80; Cappello, *De Sacramentis,* III, 226; Rossi, *De Matrimonii Celebratione,* p. 53.

[133] Benedict XIV, ep. encycl. "*Nimiam Licentiam,*" 18 maii 1743, n. 10—*Fontes,* n. 337; Rossi, *De Matrimonii Celebratione,* p. 54; Claeys Bouuaert-Simenon, *Manuale Iuris Canonici,* II, 226.

stance Cerato maintains that the pastor is obliged to consult the Ordinary and abide by his decision.[134] When the parents oppose the marriage without cause, the pastor should still advise the nupturients to yield to their parents' desire and to forego their marriage, if this can be conveniently done without any great hardship. The right of the children to enter the marriage, however, remains intact.[135]

The pastor must never urge the parties to marry against the unreasonable opposition of the parents,[136] for in this matter the parents are jealous of their authority and greatly resent any and all outside interference. An imprudent move on the part of the pastor in this most difficult of all human relations may occasion the defection of the parents from the Church and lead to irreparable harm. If the parties insist on marrying even though their parents remain unreasonable, the pastor should apply for a dispensation from the banns of marriage in order not to antagonize the parents or to embarrass them with the three successive announcements from the pulpit in their parish Church concerning the forthcoming marriage. This would be a sufficiently just and reasonable cause for the pastor to apply to the proper Ordinary for a dispensation from the banns.

If, after investigating the reasons of the nupturients and their parents, the pastor remains doubtful as to the reasonableness of the parental refusal, he is forbidden to assist at the marriage before consulting the Ordinary. For in case of doubt the presumption favors the parents. The basis for this presumption is the reverence due to parental authority.[137] Moreover, the parents because of their age and experience are presumed to be wiser and more prudent than the youthful parties; hence they are more apt to be right in their refusal to consent to the marriage. Furthermore, parents are the natural guardians of their children and as such are deeply interested in their welfare. Therefore a pre-

---

[134] *Matrimonium*, p. 25.

[135] Payen, *De Matrimonio,* I, n. 528.

[136] De Smet, *De Sponsalibus et Matrimonio,* p. 454; Farrugia, *De Matrimonio,* pp. 142–143.

[137] Rossi, *De Matrimonii Celebratione,* p. 53; Cerato, *Matrimonium,* p. 42.

sumption is present that they would do nothing to harm the future happiness of their children.[138]

If the pastor deems that the refusal of the parents is reasonable and just, he is bound by canon 1034 to warn the parties to desist from their intention to enter marriage. This canon places the primary obligation upon the pastor, who must seriously, prudently, and in a fatherly manner exhort the parties to respect the just wishes of their parents. If it so happens that the parochial assistant is the priest who is conducting the pre-nuptial investigation, and he judges that the parents are reasonably unwilling in withholding their consent, he should refer the matter to the pastor, for the authority of the pastor is greater and more respected by the youthful parties. Hence the pastor is likely to be more successful in deterring the parties from going through with their plans to marry. The secondary obligation, which canon 1034 imposes, binds the nupturients who are to accept and obey this grave admonition of the pastor. If, however, the parties reject this pastoral plea, he is obliged by the prescripts of this same canon to consult the Ordinary, and in the meantime he is forbidden to assist at the marriage. This obligation of the pastor to consult the Ordinary and abide by his decision is a serious one and ordinarily binds *sub gravi*.[139] Necessity, urgency, or moral impossibility may at times arise, and these factors, if sufficiently grave, may excuse the pastor from his obligation of referring such cases to the Ordinary. This obligation of the pastor to consult the Ordinary is merely preceptive as is clear from the words of canon 1034.[140] Consequently, this consultation with the Ordinary is not required for the validity of the marriage but only for its licit celebration. Even though the pastor would intentionally and without cause fail to refer the matter to the Ordinary, the marriage would nevertheless be valid. However, the pastor would be guilty of grave sin in so acting.

If the pastor consults the parents of the party who is of minor

[138] Sanchez, *De Matrimonio,* lib. I, disp. XXIII, n. 3.

[139] Gougnard, *Tractatus de Matrimonio,* p. 30; Cappello, *De Sacramentis,* III, n. 192; Rossi, *De Matrimonii Celebratione,* p. 54.

[140] ". . . quod si abnuerint, eorum matrimonio ne assistat, nisi consulto prius loci Ordinario."

age and finds that one parent consents to the marriage while the other dissents, what procedure must he follow? If the father gives his permission for the marriage this consent generally suffices. This is true for two reasons: (1) the power and authority over the family primarily vests with the father, for he is the acting head of the domestic household;[141] and, (2) the father's permission alone is sufficient to obviate any difficulties which otherwise might arise from the standpoint of the civil law. Therefore, if the father of the minor child refuses to consent, while the mother freely gives her permission, this consent of the mother is not sufficient for the reasons already given. Hence, if the mother alone consents the pastor cannot assist at the marriage without consulting the local Ordinary. This procedure is also true if the father, who refuses his consent, happens to be a non-Catholic, while the mother, who grants her permission, is a Catholic. It is equally valid in a mixed marriage where the father of the non-Catholic dissents even though the father of the Catholic minor consents. Gasparri[142] and Petrovits[143] fail to distinguish between the two parents, and so they explicitly teach that, if one of the parents consents and the other dissents, the pastor may lawfully assist at the marriage without consulting the Ordinary. Hence, according to their opinion the consent of the mother would be sufficient even though the father had refused to give his permission. This teaching cannot be maintained for the reasons given above.

If the father is dead, the consent of the mother is necessary and sufficient. If the parents are separated, the consent of the parent who has been awarded the custody of the minor child is necessary. There is no need to consult the other parent. Thus, if the civil court has entrusted the child to the mother, her consent alone is sufficient to obviate any difficulty arising from the civil law. If the ecclesiastical court has given the cus-

---

[141] Vermeersch, *Theologiae Moralis Principia, Responsa, Consilia* (3. ed., 4 vols., Romae: Università Gregoriana, 1937), II, 255; Cappello, *De Sacramentis,* III, n. 191.

[142] *De Matrimonio,* I, 115.

[143] *The New Church Law on Matrimony* (Philadelphia: John Joseph McVey, 1919), n. 123.

tody of the child to the mother, even though no civil court has sanctioned the separation, then in Church law only the mother's consent is required. In this instance, however, the pastor must be careful, for the permission of the father for the marriage may still be demanded by the civil law.

If the parents are dead or are impeded from exercising their authority over the child, must the pastor seek the permission of the guardians before he may assist at the minor's marriage? Authors agree that those who exercise authority over the child in place of the parents should be informed of the marriage, and that their consent to the marriage should be sought. But at the same time they are one in teaching that this is in no way demanded by Canon law.[144] Gougnard[145] simply suggests that it would be a good thing to inform the guardians about the forthcoming marriage. However, there is no canonical obligation to do even this; nor does he mention that the guardians of the child should give their consent.

The argument given by these authors is that canon 1034 mentions only the parents and states nothing regarding tutors or guardians. Moreover, they point out that the reason for the prescription of this canon is that the children owe this as a sign of respect and reverence which is due parents. Consequently, the law of the Church obliges neither the parties nor the pastor to consult the guardians or adoptive parents with regard to the intended marriage.

Conceding the validity of this argument the writer nevertheless maintains that in practice the guardians or adoptive parents must be consulted regarding their knowledge of and consent to the marriage of their minor ward or foster child. The principal reasons for the writer's opinion are the following: (1) The Instruction of the Sacred Congregation of the Sacraments concerning the rules which the pastor must follow in conducting the pre-nuptial investigation is quite definite on this point of the necessity of consulting the guardians. For each time the

---

[144] Cappello, *De Sacramentis,* III, n. 191; Rossi, *De Matrimonii Celebratione,* pp. 53–54; Petrovits, *The New Church Law on Matrimony,* p. 66; Alford, *Jus Matrimoniale,* pp. 206–207.

[145] *Tractatus de Matrimonio,* p. 30.

Instruction mentions the pastor's obligation to consult the parents when he is doubtful as to their knowledge of and their consent to the marriage of their minor ward, it always includes in a parenthesis the word *tutores* immediately after the word *parentes*.[146] Hence, the pastor is to consult the guardians of the child according to this new Instruction of the Holy See if the parents no longer exercise authority over the child.

(2) That the pastor must consult the guardians of the minor child seems to be entirely reasonable and praiseworthy and what one would naturally expect. It is in keeping with the spirit of the Code of Canon Law to consult the guardians of the child and thereby acknowledge the authority of the guardians, for throughout the Code of Canon Law various canons expressly recognize and admit the importance, authority, and position of the tutor in relation to the minor ward.[147] Why, then, should the nupturients, who are of minor age, and the pastor disregard the office and authority of the guardians in the all important question of marriage?

(3) Moreover, the legislator in canon 2353 decrees a penalty against one who would elope with a minor girl, even though she freely gives her consent, unknown to her parents or guardians or against their will.[148] Thus, the Church is desirous to have the guardians know of and consent to the marriage of their minor ward. It would be incongruous, then, in view of this penal canon that the pastor in canon 1034, who is to assist at the marriage of the minor child, should not be obliged by Canon law to exhort him not to enter marriage without the knowledge of his guardians or against their reasonable will. It is the opinion of the writer that the pastor would be obliged to deter the parties from entering such a marriage if for no other reason than to safeguard the groom from contracting the penalties of canon 2353. This

[146] S. C. de Sacr., instr., 29 iun. 1941—*ASS,* XXXIII (1941), 311, 315; cf. Bouscaren, *The Canon Law Digest,* II, 268, 272; *ER,* CV (1941), *Supplement,* pp. 17, 21.

[147] Cf. canons 89; 750, §2, 1°, 2°; 751; 765, 4°; 795, 4°; 860; 1224, 2°; 1456; 1648, §§ 1 and 2; 2353.

[148] "Qui intuitu matrimonii . . . rapuerit . . . mulierem minoris aetatis consentientem quidem, sed insciis vel contradicentibus parentibus aut tutoribus. . . ." Cf. Chapter IX for a complete explanation of this canon.

canon surely presupposes that the guardians of the minor have rights in this matter of their ward's marriage, for it seems that one of the reasons for this penalty against the groom is because he has violated the guardians' rights of vigilance and protection of their minor ward. Hence, the pastor, who is to assist at the marriage, must take cognizance of the rights of the guardians and must respect their rights even in the matter of the marriage of their ward. But a pastor who would knowingly assist at the marriage of a minor who has not consulted her guardians would surely not be respecting the rights of the guardian.

(4) Furthermore, the reason for the prescription of canon 1034 is not based solely and exclusively on the reverence due to parents, as the authors maintain. The legislator has also in mind the welfare of the contracting parties themselves, and he wishes to safeguard them from contracting an unhappy marriage. By way of an aside, it may be noted here that the fundamental reason for every restriction which the Code of Canon Law imposes upon the minor in the exercise of his rights is for the benefit of the minor, and is in no way intended as a penalty or a burden for him. This is also true of the mild restriction in the matter of marriage, namely, that the minor must inform his parents and seek their advice before he enters the contract. Thus the legislator bids him to consult his parents, who will aid him in the selection of a partner. But all minors need this experienced advice of elders, even those minors who have been deprived in one way or another of their natural parents. Therefore the guardians are to substitute, and, as it were, to take the place of parents in advising the minor concerning marriage. The Catechism of the Council of Trent in this connection made mention not only of the parents but also of guardians, and added that they should advise the child and aid him in regard to the entering of marriage. In this way the youthful nupturients would be safeguarded against contracting a hasty and ill-advised marriage.[149] Therefore the reverence due to parents is only one of the reasons why there is in the law of the Church such a canon as 1034.

[149] *The Catechism of the Council of Trent,* translated into English by J. Donovan, pp. 338–339.

(5) Again, the civil law of the various countries prohibits the celebration of marriages for those of minor age without the consent of their guardians, in the event that the parents are dead or have been deprived of their authority over the minor child. Thus, if the pastor proceeds to assist at a marriage in which one or both of the contracting parties are minors without regard for the authority or rights of the guardians, he may be liable to fine and punishment by the law of the State.

Thus, even though canon 1034 expressly requires only that the parents' consent be had, since the canon mentions only the parents of the minor, nevertheless in practice the pastor is obligated to see to it that in the absence or default of the parents the guardians of the minor know of and consent to the marriage. Hence, if the pastor learns that the guardians do not know of the forthcoming marriage or that, having been informed, they remain reasonably opposed to it, the pastor must not assist at the marriage without previously consulting the Ordinary. The five reasons for this opinion of the writer have been expressed above.

If the parents or guardians know of the marriage but neither express their consent nor dissent, the pastor must determine in what sense their silence is to be understood. If, from the circumstances, he judges that the parents or guardians remain silent because they actually disapprove of the marriage, then he must interpret this silence as an expression of their dissent. Consequently, if their refusal is reasonable he must consult the Ordinary. On the other hand, if the pastor judges that the parents remain silent either because they consent to the marriage,[150] or because they are indifferent towards it and thus neither approve nor disapprove of the marriage,[151] he may licitly assist without consulting the Ordinary.

It should be noted that a person under twenty-one years of age, who is about to contract marriage for a second time, is not bound by the prescript of canon 1034. In this instance the minor is already emancipated from parental authority, and therefore is

[150] "Qui tacet consentire videtur"—Reg. 43, R. J. in VI°.

[151] "Is, qui tacet non fatetur; sed nec utique negare videtur"—Reg. 44, R. J. in VI°.

no longer a minor in the sense of canon 1034 which obliges only unemancipated children. After the child's first marriage he is emancipated. This is true since the Church follows the laws of the State regarding emancipation, and the State acknowledges marriage as one of the ways by which the emancipation of a minor is effected.[152]

In the following Chapter the rights and duties of the Ordinary in regard to the marriage of minors wiil be considered.

---

[152] Cf. *infra*, p. 234.

CHAPTER VIII

THE ORDINARY AND THE MARRIAGE OF MINORS

ARTICLE 1. THE RIGHT OF THE ORDINARY TO BE CONSULTED BY THE PASTOR

In the preceding chapter it was pointed out that the pastor has both the right and the duty to determine the reasonableness or unreasonableness of the parental dissent in regard to the marriage of their children of minor age. Furthermore, it was explained if the pastor learns that the parents have not been consulted about the forthcoming marriage, or if after having been informed they reasonably refuse to give their permission, then he must refer the matter to the Ordinary and await his decision. In the meantime he is forbidden *sub gravi* to assist at the marriage.

Why must the pastor in these two instances consult the Ordinary? In other words what is the basis for the right of the Ordinary to be consulted? The principal juridical reason is that canon 1034 explicitly obligates the pastor to seek the advice of the Ordinary. The reasons for this regulation are manifold. Thus, (1) the Bishop is the ordinary and immediate pastor of the diocese entrusted to him,[1] and he has the right and the duty to govern this diocese in all spiritual and temporal matters.[2] He is the divinely appointed custodian and judge of faith and morals. Moreover, the Bishop is better qualified to render this final decision as to whether the pastor should assist at the marriage, for in his position as Bishop he has a wider knowledge of the effects which this permission or refusal will have on the diocese at large. (2) In demanding that the pastor consult the local Ordinary in these cases the Church demonstrates in a practical

[1] Canon 334, §1: "Episcopi residentiales sunt ordinarii et immediati pastores in dioecesibus sibi commissis."

[2] Canon 335, §1: "Ius ipsis et officium est gubernandi dioecesim tum in spiritualibus tum in temporalibus cum potestate legislativa, iudiciaria, coactiva ad normam sacrorum canonum exercenda."

and tangible way her high regard and great esteem for the God-given authority of parents. For before the Church is willing to acknowledge as lawful an action contrary to the will of the parents, she deems it necessary that the higher authority of the local Ordinary be consulted. (3) Since both the nupturients and their parents will usually be unknown to the local Ordinary, impartiality of judgment is ensured by this regulation. (4) The authority and dignity which the local Ordinary enjoys may move the youthful contracting parties to postpone their intended marriage until a more opportune time. (5) This ruling makes for uniformity of discipline within the diocese, since the local Ordinary is the one who is to concede or refuse the permission for all such marriages within his jurisdiction. (6) To judge these cases is a difficult problem and one that is fraught with great danger. Hence, since a more prudent and diligent consideration of all circumstances is necessary, the legislator places the additional legal safeguard of consulting the local Ordinary. These are the manifest reasons which motivate the legislator to enact the law of canon 1034. In two instances, then, the local Ordinary has the right to be consulted by the pastor before a marriage involving a minor can be celebrated.

It has already been explained [3] that the pastor is under no obligation to consult the local Ordinary, if the refusal of the parents is unreasonable. May the local Ordinary, however, demand such consultation even in this instance? Thus, may the Bishop of the diocese either in or out of synod legislate to the effect that no pastor within his jurisdiction may lawfully assist at the marriage of a minor even though the parents are unreasonable in their opposition? The Code of Canon Law expressly acknowledges the legislative power of the Bishop.[4] He may enact laws both territorial and personal, and these laws are binding provided they are in accordance with the prescripts of the general law of the Code. Thus a Bishop could not make a law which would contradict the general law of the Church. He could not prohibit by law what is explicitly and indubitably conceded by the superior

---

[3] Cf. *supra*, 157–158.

[4] Canon 335, § 1.

legislator; nor could he permit by his own law what is expressly prohibited by higher authority. For the Bishop is incompetent to legislate in this manner, and any attempt would be utterly invalid. The Bishop, however, may rule regarding matters which lie outside the general law of the Church; he may also enact laws which adapt and particularize the general law to the local conditions existing within his diocese. Hence his laws must be either in accord with (*secundum ius*) or beyond (*praeter ius*) the general law. Any regulation which is *contra ius* is by that very fact devoid of all force and need not be observed.[5] Moreover, the Bishop cannot legislate against the spirit of the general law of the Church, for canon 335, §1 bids him to exercise his legislative power *ad normam sacrorum canonum.* This phrase evidently includes not merely the actual text of the general law but also its spirit. Consequently, if he attempts to legislate contrary to either element, he would be exceeding his legislative competency and his laws would be invalid.[6]

Though these principles which govern the extent of the legislative power of the Bishop are clear and certain in themselves, nevertheless the application of them to a determinate case frequently causes difficulty. Thus, in the present matter would the Bishop be overstepping the bounds of his power if he would decree that a pastor must consult him before assisting at a marriage which involves a minor whose parents are unreasonably opposed to the marriage? The writer maintains that the Bishop is competent to make this regulation, and if he does so legislate his law is just and valid and must be observed by the pastor. Such a law surely contradicts no explicit ruling of the Code of Canon Law, because the superior legislator does not explicitly declare therein that the pastor may assist at the marriage in these circumstances. At best the legislator remains silent concerning this case. The right of the pastor to assist at the mar-

---

[5] Coronata, *Institutiones Iuris Canonici,* I, 459; Beste, *Introductio in Codicem,* p. 267; Sipos, *Enchiridion Iuris Canonici,* p. 238; Wernz-Vidal, *Ius Canonicum,* II, n. 599; Genicot-Salsmans, *Institutiones Theologiae Moralis,* I, n. 96; Roelker, "The Power to Enact Invalidating Laws"—*The Jurist,* III (1943), 239.

[6] Cf. Roelker, *art. cit.,* 241–242.

riage without previously consulting the Ordinary becomes evident only through the process of juridical reasoning from the actual wording of canon 1034, for in this canon the legislator explicitly demands consultation with the local Ordinary only in the case where the parents do not know of the marriage or are reasonably unwilling. Thus as Ryan states: "Given the regulation of a particular matter by the higher law, the bishop acting in accordance with it not only cannot prescribe what is opposed thereto, or permit what is prohibited thereby, but neither can he prohibit what is explicitly permitted therein, unless the law itself or the superior legislator concedes him this right. He may, however, prohibit what is doubtfully or only implicitly permitted, although he may not permit what is even merely implicitly prohibited by the higher law." [7] Applying this teaching of Ryan to the subject under consideration, it becomes clear that the Bishop may demand that the pastor refer the matter to him before assisting at the marriage of a minor whose parents are unreasonably opposed to the marriage. For the supreme legislator neither in canon 1034 nor in any other canon of the Code of Canon Law explicitly concedes to the pastor the right to assist at the marriage in these circumstances without previously consulting the Ordinary. This right is only implicitly given to the pastor. Therefore, since the right is only implicitly permitted by the superior legislator, the Bishop may forbid the pastor by diocesan law to assist at the marriage. That the Bishop is able to forbid by his own law what is implicitly permitted by the general law of the Church is likewise the teaching of Genicot-Salsmans.[8]

Furthermore, the particular needs of the diocese may demand such an episcopal statute, for frequently the civil law of the locality upholds the parents in their opposition to the marriage even though canonically speaking their refusal is unjust. Hence, if pastors of these places wherein such a civil prescript is opera-

---

[7] *Principles of Episcopal Jurisdiction,* The Catholic University of America Canon Law Studies, n. 120 (Washington, D. C.: The Catholic University of America Press, 1939), p. 134.

[8] ". . . Episcopi possunt per leges dioecesanas, *vetare res Iure communi non nisi implicite permissas,* eo quod non interdicuntur."—*Institutiones Theologiae Moralis,* I, n. 96.

tive would indiscriminately and injudiciously assist at the marriages of minors, great harm would result not only to the pastors themselves but also to the diocese and Church at large. To forestall this danger or to stamp out an existing abuse in this matter the Bishop could reserve to himself by diocesan law the right to determine under what conditions a marriage of this kind can be celebrated. For in so legislating the Bishop would not be acting contrary to the general law of the Church, but would be simply providing for the necessity and utility of his diocese.[9] In fact, a few Bishops of the United States in recent synods and provincial councils have enacted that the pastor must consult the Ordinary when the parents refuse to give their consent. Their laws do not distinguish between reasonable and unreasonable opposition on the part of the parents, and hence likewise bind even though the parents in the judgment of the pastor are unreasonable in their dissent. For these laws have mainly in view the avoidance of a conflict in this matter with the civil law of the territory, and in order to achieve this end they must bind even in cases where the parental refusal is canonically unjust.[10] Since all decrees of the provincial councils must meet with the approval of the Holy See before promulgation,[11]

[9] "Ob hanc potestatem licet Episcopis per leges ac decreta ea omnia statuere quae ipsi in dioecesis regimine opportuniora censeant. . . . Dum Episcopi potestate non pollent condendi leges aut decreta contra ius, scilicet contra generales Ecclesiae leges, ipsi plena praediti sunt potestate condendi leges ac decreta praeter ius, scilicet quae iuri communi non adversenter."—Signatura Apostolica, 15 decembris 1923—*AAS*, XVI (1924), 106–107.

[10] Cf. *Synodus Archidioecesis Sancti Francisci Secunda,* 14 oct. 1936 (San Francisco: Monitor Publishing Co., 1936), cap. VII, n. 228: "Inconsulto Ordinario ne assistat ullus sacerdos matrimonio in sequentibus casibus: . . . 3. Si minores, juxta jus civile, scilicet qui sunt infra annos 21 et 18 respective completos, accedant, quorum parentes matrimonio obsistunt; praesertim si, tamquam minores, prius matrimonium attentassent coram magistratu civili vel ministello acatholico." Cf. *Synodus Dioecesana Fargensis Prima,* 29–30 sept. 1941 (Milwauchiae: Ex Typographia Bruce, 1941), art. XIX, statutum, 350, pp. 68–69. Cf. also *Acta et Decreta Concilii Provincialis Portlandensis in Oregon Quarti,* 10 sept. 1932, cap. II, art. VII, n. 298: "§ 1. Parochus ne umquam matrimoniis minorum assistat absque consensu parentum, etiam partis acatholicae.' § 2. Quodsi parentes maneant inviti, parochus rem deferat ad loci Ordinarium."

[11] Canon 291, § 1.

it may be argued that in this instance, if the council were exceeding its legislative power in enacting this ruling, Rome would have deleted the regulation. Since Rome did not do so, it follows that the decree of the council in this matter is in harmony with the general law of the Church.

Nor does the regulation of the Bishop, in reserving to himself the right to decide when the pastor may assist at the marriage of minors in the event the parents are unwilling without cause, contradict the spirit of the Code of Canon Law. Such a statute is in complete agreement with the mind of the superior legislator. For even though the primary and fundamental reason motivating the lawgiver to formulate canon 1034 is to promote and safeguard the respect and reverence due to parents, nevertheless there are other reasons, as have been indicated, for this law. It is true that if the pastor assists at the marriage against the unreasonable will of the parents there is no violation of rightful parental authority, and no disrespect or irreverence is shown. Hence the basic reason for the law is no longer present. However, the secondary reasons for the law, for example, to prevent scandal, to avoid conflict with the civil law, etc., remain. Where the Bishop, then, actually forbids the pastor to assist at the marriage of a minor whose parents unreasonably refuse their permission and demands that he be consulted in the matter, it cannot be said that he is legislating contrary to the spirit of the Code and the mind of the superior legislator, for the very reasons which impel the Bishop to enact the regulation coincide with the secondary reasons of the superior legislator and are in agreement with them.[12]

Moreover, canon 1034, which concerns the pastoral duties in the marriage of minors, pertains to and forms an integral part of the pre-nuptial investigation. Now the legislator in canon 1020, § 3 obliges and directs the local Ordinary to draw up and prescribe according to his prudent judgment special regulations

---

[12] "In accommodating the higher law to the specific territorial characteristics of his diocese, the bishop must take cognizance of both the mind of the superior legislator and the purpose which the superior legislator intends, since both of these must be substantially respected and preserved intact."—Ryan, *Principles of Episcopal Jurisdiction*, p. 133.

concerning this investigation, and to adapt these rules to meet the particular needs and circumstances of his diocese.[13] Hence, if the necessity or utility of his diocese would in the judgment of the Bishop require that he should be consulted about a minor intending to marry contrary to the unreasonable will of the parents, then the Bishop should enact a law to this effect. A law of this kind would be valid, and the pastor would be obliged to observe it.[14]

Article 2. The Manner and Consequences of the Ordinary's Adjudication

As has been seen,[15] if the pastor learns that the parents do not know of the intended marriage or if knowing of it they reasonably refuse to give their permission, he must consult the Ordinary. Canon 1034 explicitly designates the local Ordinary as the one to be consulted. According to canon 198 it is evident that this term, "*Ordinarius loci,*" includes a number of persons and is in no way restricted to the residential Bishop of the diocese. Besides the Roman Pontiff, it includes within their respective territories the residential Bishop, the Abbot or Prelate *nullius* and their Vicar General, the Apostolic Administrator, the Vicar Apostolic and Prefect Apostolic. Furthermore, those persons are local Ordinaries who in case of vacancy of the above offices succeed to the office during the vacancy either by provisions of law or by reason of approved constitutions. Thus, for example, the diocesan administrator, who is elected by the diocesan consultors upon the death of the Bishop, is a local Ordinary.[16] Major superiors, however, in exempt clerical organizations are not local Ordinaries, and hence are not included under canon 1034.[17]

This right, which the local Ordinary has by virtue of canon

[13] Cf. S. C. de Sacr., instr., 29 iun. 1941—*AAS,* XXXIII (1941), 298–299, nn. 2–3; *ER,* CV (1941), *Supplement,* pp. 2–3, nn. 2–3; Bouscaren, *The Canon Law Digest,* II, 253–254, nn. 2–3.

[14] Cappello, *De Sacramentis,* III, n. 153, 3; Gougnard, *Tractatus de Matrimonio,* p. 30.

[15] Cf. *supra,* pp. 143–165.

[16] Canon 432.

[17] Canon 198, § 2.

1034 to review the case of a minor intending to marry without the knowledge or against the reasonable will of his parents, is ordinary power. Hence by reason of canon 199 he may delegate it to some other priest, preferably the Chancellor of the diocese, who because of the nature of his work is usually present at the diocesan Curia.[18] Moreover, the adjudication of these cases concerning the marriage of minors frequently occasions bitter disputes and resentment. For if the permission to celebrate the marriage is given, the parents feel as though their rightful authority over their children has been violated, while, on the other hand, if the objections of the parents are sustained and the marriage is prohibited the nupturients are offended. Therefore it seems fitting that the Bishop should not personally adjudicate cases of this nature, especially if the parties and their parents are present at the Curia. However the Bishop may, if he so desires, adjudicate the reasons both of the youthful nupturients for wishing to contract marriage and the parental objections to their intended union.

Whenever it is conveniently possible the pastor should direct the interested parties to go directly to the Curia and there explain their case, for then the local Ordinary or preferably his delegate may interview them personally and learn at first hand all the reasons and circumstances of the particular matter. Moreover, as already mentioned, the authority of the local Ordinary or his delegate may help to settle amicably the dispute between the children and their parents. Even though they do appear in person at the Curia, the pastor should nevertheless communicate to the Ordinary his opinion concerning the merits of the case and the effect which the permission or denial of the marriage will have in his parish. If, however, the parties do not go directly to the Curia, the local Ordinary should see to it that he receives from the pastor all the reasons for and against the marriage together with all the circumstances concerning the matter, so that he may be able to decide the case reasonably and justly.

---

[18] Cf. Prince, *The Diocesan Chancellor,* The Catholic University of America Canon Law Studies, n. 167 (Washington, D. C.: The Catholic University of America Press, 1942), pp. 92-93; Prince, "The Chancellor as Delegate of the Bishop"—*The Jurist,* III (1943), 569, 575-576.

The local Ordinary will apply the same basic principles which the pastor employed in order to determine whether the parental dissent is reasonable and just. It is true that the legislator commits to the individual pastor the right to decide this question, and only if the parents are reasonably unwilling must he consult the local Ordinary. Consequently, the local Ordinary is to estimate the gravity of the reasons not in relation to the permission of the parties to contract marriage, but rather with a view to permitting the pastor to assist at the marriage in these circumstances. But in order to determine whether he should grant or refuse this permission to the pastor, it is necessary for him to readjudicate the reasons of the parents in opposing the marriage in the light of the child's reasons to contract this particular marriage. Hence the local Ordinary is to reconsider the judgment of the pastor as to whether the unwillingness on the part of the parents is reasonable and just not only absolutely but also relatively to the marriage in question.

If the local Ordinary judges that the parental dissent is unreasonable, then he must permit the pastor to assist at the marriage. This permission of the local Ordinary suffices to suppress or overrule juridically the objections of the parents, and hence both the pastor and the nupturients may proceed with the marriage. If, however, the local Ordinary, after considering all the circumstances of the case, deems the parental refusal to be reasonable, he must then prohibit the marriage. In this instance he forbids the marriage not precisely on account of the lack of parental consent, as if want of parental permission were a prohibitive impediment, but because of the reasons upon which the parental objections are based. In other words, the local Ordinary judges that the reasons of the parents are founded on a just and canonical cause and outweigh the reasons which the child may have for desiring to enter the marriage.[19] Thus, for example, if the parents oppose the marriage because their minor daughter intends to marry a non-Catholic who is by far her senior in age and whose moral life is questionable, these reasons considered

---

[19] Wernz-Vidal, *Ius Canonicum,* V, n. 140; Gougnard, *Tractatus de Matrimonio,* p. 30.

absolutely and in themselves must be said to be reasonable and valid grounds for objecting to the marriage. Consequently, if their daughter has no cogent reasons for entering this marriage, as she would have if there was present the danger of incontinence or if there was question of validating a civil marriage, then the dissent of the parents is also relatively reasonable and the local Ordinary is able to prohibit the marriage. For as Ayrinhac-Lydon well state: "The Church is simply enforcing here a precept of the natural law, the duty of prudence and reverence to parents; and she considers it important enough to require the intervention of the Bishop for deciding when it ceases to bind or when its violation may be tolerated." [20]

If in such a case as outlined above the local Ordinary would foresee that if he refuses to permit the pastor to assist at the marriage graver evils would arise, then in his prudence he should not prohibit the marriage. Oftentimes the local Ordinary will be forced to permit the marriage even though the refusal of consent on the part of the parents is reasonable and just. Thus, as it frequently happens, the nupturients have no special reasons for desiring to contract this marriage while the parents on the other hand have good and forceful reasons for opposing the marriage. The local Ordinary after reviewing all the circumstances of the case upholds the parental objections and is about to prohibit the pastor from assisting at the marriage. The contracting parties then inform him that if he forbids their marriage they will contract a civil marriage and give up the practice of their Faith. They are set in their plans to be married and will under no consideration heed the remonstrances of their parents, pastor, or even the local Ordinary. In this instance the local Ordinary can permit the marriage as the lesser of the two impending evils. On the one hand there is present the grave sin of disrespect and irreverence towards parents for the virtue of piety is violated in a grave matter,[21] while on the other hand there is the sin of scandal, the celebration of a civil marriage, and concubinage together with its series of grave sins. Since

---

[20] *Marriage Legislation,* p. 51.

[21] Cappello, *De Sacramentis,* III, 225.

both of these evils cannot be effectively prevented, the natural law demands that the lesser of the two evils be permitted. Hence the local Ordinary, notwithstanding the reasonable opposition on the part of the parents, should permit the pastor to assist at the marriage.[22] It cannot be maintained that in this instance the parental dissent is unreasonable, for the malicious will of the contracting parties can have no objective influence on the grave reasons the parents have in withholding their permission. The nupturients through the threat of contracting a civil marriage are forcing the local Ordinary to permit their marriage to be blessed. However, this permission of the local Ordinary is by no means a positive permission or approbation of the marriage, but it is merely a negative permission or a toleration of the evil action of the spouses. The permission to celebrate the marriage is, as it were, extorted from the local Ordinary by the parties, and it does not carry with it a positive approval of their actions.[23] The parents in these circumstances would be unreasonable in their objection to this toleration by the Church of the marriage of their child, since the natural law would obligate them as well as the local Ordinary to permit the lesser evil. However, they are not unreasonable in refusing their permission for and approbation of the marriage.

All authors agree in teaching that the child is guilty of serious sin in contracting marriage against the just opposition of parents, and hence must be treated as a person who does not have the proper disposition for the reception of the Sacrament of Matrimony. Moreover, a confessor must refuse absolution to such a child because he willfully refuses to discharge a grave duty incumbent upon him.[24] However, it is possible with the authoriza-

---

[22] Cappello, *De Sacramentis,* III, n. 192; Gougnard, *Tractatus de Matrimonio,* p. 30; Wernz-Vidal, *Ius Canonicum,* V, n. 140; Genicot-Salsmans, *Institutiones Theologiae Moralis,* I, nn. 13–14; Noldin-Schmitt, *Summa Theologiae Moralis,* I, nn. 83–84.

[23] Cf. Ter Haar, *De Matrimoniis Mixtis Eorumque Remediis* (Taurini-Romae: Marietti, 1931), nn. 65–66; Noldin-Schmitt, *Summa Theologiae Moralis,* III, 568.

[24] Cerato, *Matrimonium,* p. 42; Ayrinhac-Lydon, *Marriage Legislation,* p. 51; Cappello, *De Sacramentis,* III, 225; Wernz-Vidal, *Ius Canonicum,* V, n. 140; Bertolotti, *Casus Conscientiae praesertim de Re Morali et Liturgica*

tion of the local Ordinary for the pastor to assist at the marriage of the minor child even though the parents remain reasonably unwilling, since it is a question of permitting the lesser evil. The child nevertheless is guilty of mortal sin in forcing the celebration of the marriage, and consequently will receive unworthily the Sacrament of Matrimony, since he is bound *sub gravi* to be in the state of grace at the time he contracts marriage, for Matrimony is a Sacrament of the Living. Moreover, since the contracting parties and not the assisting priest are the ministers of this Sacrament, they are likewise obligated to be in the state of grace.[25] However, it is disputed whether this latter obligation binds them *sub gravi* or *sub levi*. The better opinion seems to be that the obligation is not a serious one, since they are not the ordained and consecrated ministers of the Sacrament, and hence the minor child would not sin mortally in his unworthy administration of the Sacrament of Matrimony.[26]

(3 vols., Savonae: Ex Typis Andreae Ricci, 1888), III, 225–227, 404–405, 435; Farrugia, *De Matrimonio,* p. 142; Chelodi, *Ius Matrimoniale,* n. 33; Claeys Bouuaert-Simenon, *Manuale Iuris Canonici,* II, 226; Genicot-Salsmans, *Institutiones Theologiae Moralis,* II, n. 519; Davis, *Moral and Pastoral Theology,* IV, 96.

[25] It was formerly disputed among theologians, but the doctrine is now theologically certain, that the contracting parties are the ministers of the Sacrament of Matrimony. For in the marriages of Christians there is no real distinction between the matrimonial contract and the Sacrament. The one is not able to exist without the other since Christ elevated the very contract to the dignity of a Sacrament. Cf. Gasparri, *De Matrimonio,* I, n. 33; Cappello, *De Sacramentis,* III, nn. 29, 32; Hervê, *Manuale Theologiae Dogmaticae* (4 vols., Vol. IV, 12. ed., Parisiis: apud Berche et Pagis, 1934), IV, nn. 582–583; Farrugia, *De Matrimonio,* pp. 9–11.

[26] "Probabile est *non peccari mortaliter* . . . si is qui sacramentum in lethali conficit, non est ad illud munus *ordinatus,* . . . Hinc probabiliter *a gravi peccato excusantur:* 1º Laici, qui, peccati mortalis rei, . . . comparti *matrimonium* administrant (quamquam hi graviter peccant quatenus idem sacramentum in hoc malo statu *suscipiunt*)—Ita opinantur multi DD. cum S. Thoma, qui rationem gravitatis peccati in indigna confectione sacramentorum constanter . . . repetit ex eo quod peccator agat tamquam minister Ecclesiae vel vi ordinis sibi collati, . . ."—Genicot-Salsmans, *Institutiones Theologiae Moralis,* II, n. 115. Cf. also *Summa Theologica,* III, q. 64, art. 6 ad 2; Cappello, *De Sacramentis,* III, n. 334; Heneghan, *The Marriages of Unworthy Catholics: Canons 1065 and 1066,* The Catholic

Since the priest who is to assist at the marriage is merely the official witness of the Church to the mutual consent of the contracting parties and is not the minister of the Sacrament of Matrimony, his cooperation at a marriage in which one or both of the spouses is in mortal sin can be justified, if a proportionately grave reason is present for him to assist. In the present case there is a sufficiently grave reason to allow his cooperation, for if he does not assist, the nupturients will enter a civil marriage. The assistance of the priest is not intrinsically evil, because it is not a formal cooperation in the sin of the parties but only a material cooperation in the evil.[27] Furthermore, witnesses to a marriage in these circumstances do not cooperate formally in the sin of the contracting parties. For since the marriage is to be celebrated *coram Ecclesia,* the witnesses are not even morally bound to investigate the various circumstances of the marriage, since they may rightly presuppose from the presence of the assisting priest that all the prescripts of the law of the Church have been duly observed. Even if they know that one or both of the nupturients are entering marriage contrary to the reasonable will of their parents, the witnesses, nevertheless, do no wrong by cooperating in the marriage. For since the witnesses are bound only by the virtue of charity to impede the sacrilegious marriage of the parties, any grave inconvenience or loss excuses them from this obligation. Moreover, since it is lawful for the pastor to assist at the marriage in these circumstances, then for a much greater reason is it lawful for the witnesses to cooperate, for the pastor is under a more serious obligation to prevent the unworthy reception of the Sacrament of Matrimony; for the duty of the pastor is not only that of charity but also of justice. Furthermore, the cooperation of the witnesses is necessary in

---

University of America Canon Law Studies, n. 188 (Washington, D. C.: The Catholic University of America Press, 1944), pp. 106–107, 164–165; Prümmer, *Manuale Theologiae Moralis,* III, 46–47; Noldin-Schmitt, *Summa Theologiae Moralis,* III, nn. 29–30; Davis, *Moral and Pastoral Theology,* III, 22; Farrugia, *De Matrimonio,* p. 11.

[27] Cf. Heneghan, *The Marriages of Unworthy Catholics: Canons 1065 and 1066,* p. 165; Gasparri, *De Matrimonio,* I, n. 178; Noldin-Schmitt, *Summa Theologiae Moralis,* III, 34.

order that the lesser of the two evils be achieved, since their assistance at the marriage is required for the validity of the union. Therefore it is altogether lawful for the witnesses to take part in such a marriage.[28]

Article 3. The Prohibition of the Marriage by the Ordinary

In the preceding article it was mentioned that, if the local Ordinary, after diligently considering all the circumstances of the particular marriage and keeping in mind that the supreme law is the salvation of souls, judges that the parental dissent is reasonable and just, he must in ordinary circumstances prohibit the celebration of the marriage. In the present article the writer will discuss the nature and extent of this power of the Ordinary, and will explain the consequences of such a prohibition.

That the local Ordinary possesses the power to forbid the marriage is evident from canon 1039, § 1, for in this canon the legislator concedes to him the right to prevent the celebration of the marriage under certain conditions.[29] Thus the local Ordinary in individual cases may forbid marriage for a time but only for a just cause and only as long as such a cause is present. The prohibition may affect an individual residing in his diocese and binds his subjects even though they are at present outside the territorial limits of the diocese.

The legislator grants this right to all local Ordinaries; hence all those persons who are mentioned in canon 198 possess this faculty to prohibit a marriage. Moreover, since this power which local Ordinaries enjoy is ordinary power, it follows that it may according to the principles of canon 199 be delegated to others. A pastor, however, does not possess the power to forbid the celebration of a marriage since he is not mentioned in canon 1039, §1 as having such power, nor does any other canon in the Code of Canon Law grant him this right. Moreover, the pastor

---

[28] Gougnard, *Tractatus de Matrimonio,* p. 137; Gasparri, *De Matrimonio,* I, n. 477; Cappello, *De Sacramentis,* III, n. 333.

[29] "Ordinarii locorum omnibus in suo territorio actu commorantibus et suis subditis etiam extra fines sui territorii vetare possunt matrimonia in casu peculiari, sed ad tempus tantum, iusta de causa eaque perdurante."

has no power of jurisdiction over his flock in the external forum; nor does he enjoy any judicial or coactive powers in regard to matrimonial matters. Consequently, the pastor could not forbid a minor from contracting marriage against the reasonable opposition of parents by enacting a law or a precept to that effect. Nevertheless, in such instances the pastor has both the right and the duty to stay the marriage until he has consulted the local Ordinary and has received his decision. Therefore in this improper and wide sense it may be said that a pastor is competent to prohibit the celebration of the minor's marriage. But he cannot merely from the authority of his office as pastor refuse to assist at the marriage indefinitely but only for the period of time necessary to consult the Ordinary. He is bound to refer the matter as soon as possible to the local Ordinary. Hence this prohibition by the pastor is not a positive action preventing the celebration of the marriage but only a negative one, since it consists in the refusal to assist at the marriage. The pastor in so acting is simply fulfilling his duty as pastor, and is merely declaring the law and employing the necessary means to insure its observance. For the legislator in canon 1034 demands that the pastor refuse to assist at the marriage in these circumstances and that he consult the local Ordinary. In following out this prescript of the legislator, the pastor indirectly prohibits the celebration of the marriage, for without his presence to ask and receive the consent of the contracting parties the marriage is impossible. But the pastor unlike the local Ordinary does not possess the power to prohibit the marriage by means of a precept.[30]

The pastor could forbid his curate to assist at the marriage of a minor until the local Ordinary had reviewed the case. However, if the curate contrary to the express prohibition of his pastor would assist at the marriage, the validity or invalidity of the marriage is not affected or determined by the mere prohibition of the pastor. If in prohibiting the curate to assist at the marriage the pastor would expressly withdraw his delegation,

[30] Feije, *De Impedimentis et Dispensationibus Matrimonialibus,* n. 549; *Collationes Brugenses,* VI (1901), 594-597; Payen, *De Matrimonio,* I, nn. 591-592; De Smet, *De Sponsalibus et Matrimonio,* nn. 429, 487; Vlaming, *Praelectiones Iuris Matrimonii,* I, n. 189; Augustine, *Commentary,* V, 89.

provided the curate has received his powers to assist at marriage from the pastor and not from the local Ordinary, then the marriage in contravention of the pastoral prohibition would be invalid not on account of the prohibition of the pastor but for reason of the lack of delegation on the part of the curate to assist at the marriage. But if the pastor would merely forbid his curate to assist without expressly withdrawing his delegation, the curate in this instance could validly but not licitly assist at the marriage.

The local Ordinary may prohibit the marriage of a minor, whose parents are reasonably opposed to the marriage, even though the minor child is not his subject by reason of domicile or quasi-domicile. It is necessary, however, and sufficient for the lawful and valid use of this power if the marriage is to be celebrated within the diocese of the local Ordinary, and that the minor is actually present in the diocese at the time of the prohibition. This actual presence within the jurisdiction of the prohibiting Ordinary is a *conditio sine qua non* for the licit and valid prohibition of the marriage if the minor nupturient is a *peregrinus* or a *vagus*. If the minor is not a subject of the local Ordinary and is not actually present within the diocese, then the Ordinary cannot prohibit the marriage. Any prohibition that he could set forth would be illicit and invalid and devoid of all force.[31]

If the minor nupturient is his subject by reason of domicile or quasi-domicile, the local Ordinary may prohibit the marriage even though the contracting parties are not present in his diocese at the time the prohibition is given. He may forbid the marriage even though it is to take place outside his diocese. His power to act so remains as long as one or both of the contracting parties retain a domicile or quasi-domicile within the territorial limits of his diocese. Hence, even though the minor child has his own quasi-domicile in a diocese other than where his parents reside, the local Ordinary of the parental domicile, and probably of their quasi-domicile also, is competent to forbid the celebration of the marriage even though it is to take place outside his diocese, since an unemancipated minor necessarily shares the parental

[31] Cerato, *Matrimonium*, p. 50; Cappello, *De Sacramentis*, III, 61.

domicile and, according to the writer's opinion, also their quasi-domicile. That the local Ordinary possesses the power to act thus is clear from canon 1039, § 1. It also follows from the nature of the episcopal prohibition, for it is imposed as a precept and, hence, being personal attaches to the subject and obligates him even though he is outside the place of his domicile or quasi-domicile. For canon 24 enacts that precepts given to individuals bind them wherever they go.[32]

Moreover, in order that the local Ordinary may forbid the marriage three conditions must be present; otherwise he cannot licitly and validly make use of this power given to him in canon 1039, § 1. In other words, the simultaneous presence of these three following conditions are absolutely necessary that the episcopal prohibition be valid. (1) The prohibition must concern a particular and definite marriage and not merely the marriages of minors in general. Hence the local Ordinary may prohibit the celebration of a particular and determinate marriage, for example, the intended marriage of Bertha and Titius. He may not prohibit by means of a general precept all marriages of minors or any indeterminate marriage. Consequently, he could not issue a general precept whereby he would forbid the marriage of any minor who would attempt to marry without the knowledge or consent of parents. He may not act thus even though the motivating cause would be to eradicate an abuse which is prevalent in his diocese in this matter. Claeys Bouuaert-Simenon, however, teach that in this instance the local Ordinary may prohibit by general precept the celebration of these marriages.[33] However, there is no justification in law for such a mode of action on the part of the local Ordinary, for each and every marriage must be referred to him for judgment, and only after a careful consideration of all the circumstances of the case may he forbid the celebration of the marriage. Moreover, his prohibition of the marriage must be given after the manner of a personal precept.[34] (2) The local Ordinary must have a just cause for

[32] "Praecepta, singulis data, eos quibus dantur, ubique urgent, . . ."

[33] *Manuale Iuris Canonici*, II, n. 246.

[34] Payen, *De Matrimonio*, I, n. 587; Cerato, *Matrimonium*, p. 50; Cappello, *De Sacramentis*, III, 61.

prohibiting the marriage. This cause must be grave both in itself and by reason of the circumstances of the case. Moreover, the nature of the reason for prohibiting the marriage must be in accordance with the general law of the Church, for local Ordinaries are incompetent to introduce some new reason for forbidding the marriage, even though such a cause may in itself be just and not contrary to the general law but merely *praeter jus.* In order that the Bishop may act it is not necessary that the cause be stated as such in the general law. It is sufficient if it is not some reason which is entirely new and clearly and completely *praeter jus* in content.[35] All authors agree in teaching that the reasonable dissent on the part of the parents is a just and grave cause for forbidding a particular marriage which involves a child of minor age.[36] (3) This prohibition of the minor's marriage can be only temporary, and will last as long as the just cause for which it was given continues to exist. The local Ordinary, therefore, cannot forbid the marriage forever or indefinitely. He may forbid the marriage, for example, until the parents are informed or until they give their consent to the union. It is true that in this instance the duration of the prohibition is not certain nor is it explicitly determined. Nevertheless, there is present an implicit determination, for when the minor attains his majority the parental dissent would cease to be a just cause for the prohibition. As soon as the reason for the prohibition ceases, the local Ordinary must withdraw his prohibition. Hence if the parents would give their consent, the celebration of the marriage may take place.

Would the prohibition cease entirely by the very fact that the parents give their consent, or must the pastor and the parties await the decision of the local Ordinary before the marriage could be lawfully celebrated? If indisputable proof is offered that the parents know of the marriage and give their consent, and

[35] Payen, *De Matrimonio,* I, n. 588.

[36] Rossi, *De Matrimonii Celebratione,* p. 54; De Smet, *De Sponsalibus et Matrimonio,* n. 487; Vermeersch-Creusen, *Epitome,* II, n. 299; Payen, *De Matrimonio,* I, n. 588; Cerato, *Matrimonium,* p. 51; Claeys Bouuaert-Simenon, *Manuale Iuris Canonici,* II, n. 246; Cappello, *De Sacramentis,* III, n. 192; Gougnard, *Tractatus de Matrimonio,* p. 30; Blat, *Commentarium,* III, n. 431.

moreover, if it is clear that the only cause of the episcopal prohibition was the lack of this parental knowledge and consent, then the pastor is free to assist at the marriage for the prohibition no longer exists. Proof of this assertion is provided by canon 1039, § 1, which concedes to the local Ordinary the power to forbid a marriage if there is a just cause present but only as long as such a cause continues to exist. Hence by the operation of law the prohibition of the local Ordinary ceases intrinsically and adequately, for the cause or purpose of the prohibition no longer exists. A law, for example, ceases intrinsically when the purpose of the law ceases; in such a case no revocation is necessary on the part of the superior who made the law, for the law ceases of itself. The end or purpose of the law ceases adequately when all its purposes cease and the law becomes useless or harmful. These same principles may apply to the prohibition of the local Ordinary even though it is not a law but only a precept. Therefore, if the sole reason of the local Ordinary in forbidding the celebration of the minor's marriage against the reasonable will of the parents is to uphold and respect rightful parental authority, it would follow that as soon as the parents would give their consent the prohibition of the marriage would cease not only intrinsically but also adequately. Consequently, the contracting parties would be free to marry, and the pastor could lawfully assist at their marriage.[37] Moreover, this prohibition of the local Ordinary is not vindicative but medicinal in nature. It is meant to cure or prevent an evil and not to punish one. Hence when the reason for the imposition of the prohibition ceases to exist, the force and obligation of the prohibition likewise ceases.

This prohibition of the local Ordinary in the present discipline of the Church is not an impediment, even though in pre-Code law it was enumerated among the prohibitive impediments to marriage,[38] for the legislator in canon 1038, § 2 explicitly enacts

---

[37] Cappello, *Summa,* I, nn. 100, 104; Cappello, *De Sacramentis,* III, 62; Payen, *De Matrimonio,* I, n. 589; Blat, *Commentarium,* III, n. 431; Augustine, *Commentary,* V, 88, note 20.

[38] Bernardus Papiensis, *Summa Decretalium,* IV, 1, § 6, p. 131; St. Raymundus a Pennafort, *Summa,* lib. IV, tit. II, *de matrimonio,* § 9, p. 481;

that the right to establish impediments to marriage both prohibitive and invalidating belongs exclusively to the supreme authority of the Church. Since uniformity of discipline in the matter of establishing matrimonial impediments is essential to the welfare of the Church, the Holy See has reserved this right to herself. Hence the local Ordinary possesses no legislative powers in matrimonial matters but merely enjoys judicial and coercive powers. Consequently, he cannot either in or outside of a synod make a law forbidding by way of impediment the celebration of a marriage.[39] Moreover, from an examination of those canons in the Code of Canon Law which enumerate both the prohibitive and diriment impediments to marriage, it is clear that the prohibition of the local Ordinary is not a matrimonial impediment, for the legislator does not mention it in any of these canons.[40]

The prohibition of a marriage by the local Ordinary is not a law but a precept. It is not *a iure* but *ab homine*. He is empowered to forbid marriage only in particular and individual cases; the legislator does not authorize him to do so for all cases. This very concept excludes any idea of a law.[41] Furthermore, the local Ordinary is authorized to forbid a particular marriage only for a time and only while the cause of the prohibition continues to exist. When the cause ceases the prohibition of the local Ordinary also ceases. This temporary factor again excludes the notion of a law for a law connotes stability and perpetuity. Moreover, the prohibition of the local Ordinary is given to an individual and is directed primarily for the welfare of individuals and not in the main for the common good as is law.

In prohibiting the marriage of a minor the local Ordinary may

---

Hostiensis, *Summa Aurea,* lib. IV, tit. *de matrimoniis,* §§ 24-26, p. 291; Cosci, *De Separatione Tori Coniugalis* (Florentina, 1856), lib. II, cap. II, n. 1, p. 272; n. 20, p. 276; n. 17, p. 274; Benedictus XIV, *De Synodo Dioecesana,* lib. VIII, cap. 14, n. 2; Feije, *De Impedimentis et Dispensationibus Matrimonialibus,* n. 548.

[39] Gasparri, *De Matrimonio,* I, n. 230; Payen, *De Matrimonio,* I, nn. 583, 587; Cerato, *Matrimonium,* p. 50.

[40] Cf. canons 1058-1064; 1067-1080.

[41] Cf. Roelker, "The Power to Enact Invalidating Laws"—*The Jurist,* III (1943), 238-239.

give the prohibition either directly to the pastor forbidding him to assist at the marriage, or immediately to the nupturients themselves obligating them to desist from their intentions to enter this particular marriage. However, he may, if he deems it necessary, directly bind both the pastor and the parties by giving a double precept. Even though this prohibition of the local Ordinary is not an impediment, nevertheless it is a grave prohibition. Thus, if the pastor and the parties disregard the prohibition and go through with the celebration of the marriage, their action is gravely illicit but the validity of the marriage is not affected.

The local Ordinary is incompetent to attach an invalidating clause to this prohibition,[42] and if he does so it is devoid of all force. Hence disobedience to the Ordinary's prohibition would not of itself invalidate the marriage. The local Ordinary, however, is able indirectly to impede the valid celebration of the marriage without adding to his prohibition an invalidating clause. Thus if he forbids *sub gravi* all the pastors who are subject to his jurisdiction[43] to assist at this marriage of the minor, and if his prohibition is observed, it follows that a valid marriage cannot take place due to the lack of the proper form for marriage, which requires the presence of an authorized priest to ask and receive the consent of the contracting parties.[44] Nevertheless, if a pastor would disobey this prohibition of the local Ordinary and assist at the marriage in his parish, it would be illicit but valid. The marriage would not be invalid, for the pastor has the power from his office to assist at all marriages within the territorial limits of his parish, and this power is not destroyed or taken away by the prohibiiton of the Ordinary. For the pastor's right to assist at marriages is ordinary power since it is attached by law to the office of pastor and is not dependent on delegation received from the local Ordinary. The marriage would also be valid even though the pastor would delegate another priest to assist. However, in these instances the marriage would be illicit and the pastor

---

[42] Canon 1039, § 2: "Vetito clausulam irritantem una Sedes Apostolica addere potest."

[43] Cannon 111.

[44] Canon 1095, §1, 3o.

would be guilty of grave sin since he contravenes in a serious matter a grave precept of his lawful Superior.[45]

The Bishop would not be exceeding his power if he would annex a penalty to his prohibition. If the precept is given directly either to the pastor or to the minor nupturients, the Bishop may insure its observance by adding a penalty. Furthermore, he could, if he deems it advisable, impose a penal precept even on the witnesses forbidding them to assist at the particular marriage. The Code of Canon Law concedes this power to the Bishop for the legislator in canon 2220, § 1 declares that whoever enjoys the power to make a law or give a precept may also affix to his law or precept a penalty.[46] Since the Bishop from canon 1039, § 1 has the power to forbid by precept a marriage in a particular case, it follows logically that he may annex a penalty to this precept in order to urge its fulfillment.

The Vicar General, however, may forbid by precept the celebration of a marriage, but he cannot add a penalty to his prohibition. That the Vicar General possesses the power to forbid the marriage is evident from canon 1039, § 1, wherein the legislator grants such power to all local Ordinaries, and according to canon 198 the Vicar General is a local Ordinary. Hence he may prohibit a marriage provided he observes the conditions requisite in canon 1039, § 1. It is equally clear that the Vicar General may not compel the pastor, contracting parties, nor witnesses to observe his prohibition by threatening a penalty. For this power of the Vicar General is expressly limited by the prescriptions of canon 2220, § 2,[47] which enacts that the Vicar General acting without a special mandate cannot annex a penalty to any precept that he might give. Since the enacting of penalties is an act of great importance, the legislator prefers that the Bishop exercise his jurisdiction personally rather than permit action in this matter

---

[45] ". . . parochus per se vel per alium paroecianorum nuptiis valide assistit independenter a licentia vel prohibitione Ordinarii (etsi contra Ordinarii prohibitionem illicite) "—Wernz-Vidal, *Ius Canonicum,* V, 628.

[46] "Qui pollent potestate leges ferendi vel praecepta imponendi, possunt quoque legi vel praecepto poenas adnectere; . . ."

[47] "Vicarius Generalis sine mandato speciali non habet potestatem infligendi poenas."

by the Vicar General. Moreover, the Vicar General acting as Vicar General and without a special mandate cannot even subject any delinquent to the penalty which the Bishop may have added to his own precept as a *ferendae sententiae* penalty. Therefore the Vicar General without a special mandate from the Bishop can neither enact nor inflict a penalty on the pastor, minor nupturients or witnesses if the marriage takes place contrary to his own or the Bishop's prohibition. This is the unanimous teaching of all the authors.[48]

Thus the Bishop may impose a precept together with a penalty on the pastor, the contracting parties, and the witnesses. Is he free to annex any type of penalty to this precept, or does the legislator limit him to certain penalties? Canon 2220, § 1 merely concedes him the power to affix a penalty to his precept, but it does not determine what penalties may be inflicted.[49] Hence he may attach any penalty to this precept which is capable of being inflicted *per modum praecepti.* Now the legislator in canon 1933, § 4 states that a canonical penance,[50] a penal remedy,[51] an excommunication, a suspension, and an interdict may be inflicted after the manner of a precept without any judicial procedure.[52]

[48] Cappello, *Tractatus Canonico-Moralis de Censuris iuxta Codicem Iuris Canonici* (3. ed., Romae: Marietti, 1933), nn. 12; 14; this work will hereafter be cited *De Censuris;* Cappello, *Summa,* III, n. 472; Vermeersch-Creusen, *Epitome,* III, n. 411; Chelodi, *Ius Poenale et Ordo Procedendi in Iudiciis Criminalibus iuxta Codicem Iuris Canonici* (Tridenti: Libr. Edit. Tridentum, 1920), n. 24; hereafter this work will be cited *Ius Poenale;* Coronata, *Institutiones Iuris Canonici,* IV, n. 1693; Wernz-Vidal, *Ius Canonicum,* VII, n. 165; Beste, *Introductio in Codicem,* p. 891; Ayrinhac-Lydon, *Penal Legislation in the New Code of Canon Law* (New York: Benziger Brothers, 1936), n. 38; hereafter this work will be cited as *Penal Legislation;* Eichmann, *Das Strafrecht des Codex Iuris Canonici* (Paderborn: Schöningh, 1920), p. 60; hereafter this work will be cited as *Das Strafrecht.*

[49] The phrase "*infligere poenas*" generally signifies both the power to establish penalties and the power to apply them. Cf. Coronata, *Institutiones Iuris Canonici,* IV, 84.

[50] Cf. Canons 2312–2313.

[51] Cf. Canons 2306–2311.

[52] Canon 1933, § 4: "Poenitentia, remedium poenale, excommunicatio, suspensio, interdictum, dummodo delictum certum sit, infligi possunt etiam per modum praecepti extra iudicium."

The excommunication is necessarily a censure, but the suspension and interdict may be established either as a censure or as a vindicative penalty,[53] for canon 1933, § 4 employs the terms without any restriction or distinction. Moreover, since this canon does not determine whether these penalties may be established as *latae* or *ferendae sententiae,* the Bishop is free to constitute them in either manner.[54]

There is a dispute among authors as to whether this canon presents an exhaustive list of penalties which may be inflicted extrajudicially. Noval,[55] Coronata [56] and Esswein [57] maintain that only those penalties enumerated in canon 1933, § 4 may be inflicted by way of precept, and only when the competent superior himself has enacted the penalty *per modum praecepti.*

However, the contrary opinion, namely, that the lawful superior is competent to inflict after the manner of a precept penalties other than those listed in canon 1933, § 4 is upheld by Cappello [58] and Roberti.[59]

Since the opinion of the former group is more in keeping with the canonical rule for interpreting penal legislation,[60] it appears to be the safer and more acceptable doctrine in practice. Moreover, there would have been no need for the legislator to list the penalties as he does in canon 1933, § 4 if the opposite opinion were true, for such an enumeration would be altogether useless, if the other penalties, which are given in the Code of Canon Law, could be inflicted by way of precept.[61] Consequently, the

---

53 Canon 2255, §2.

54 Cf. Coronata, *Institutiones Iuris Canonici,* III, 377.

55 "De Ratione Corrigendi et Puniendi sive in Judicio sive extra Jure Codicis J. C."—*JP,* II (1922), 147-156; III (1923), 36-40; 204-210.

56 *Institutiones Iuris Canonici,* III, 378-379.

57 *The Extrajudicial Coercive Powers of Ecclesiastical Superiors,* The Catholic University of America Canon Law Studies, n. 127 (Washington, D. C.: The Catholic University of America Press, 1941), pp. 112-114.

58 "Irrogatio Poenae per Modum Praecepti extra Iudicium"—*Periodica,* XIX (1930), 37.

59 "Quaenam Poenae Applicari Possint per Modum Praecepti"—*Apollinaris,* IV (1931), 294-300.

60 Canon 2219, §1: "In poenis benignior est interpretatio facienda."

61 Coronata, *Institutiones Iuris Canonici,* III, 378; cf. also Esswein (*The*

Bishop may apply extrajudicially only those penalties given by the legislator in canon 1933, § 4 and which he has determined by his precept to the pastor, the nupturients, or the witnesses.

If the Bishop affixes to his precept a *latae sententiae* penalty, the penalty is incurred as soon as his prohibition is violated.[62] If it is a *ferendae sententiae* penalty, then the pastor or the one to whom the penal precept is given becomes liable for the penalty when he transgresses the precept, but the Bishop must inflict the penalty, for in this instance the penalty is not incurred by the very fact that there is a violation of the precept. Even if the penalty is *ferendae sententiae* and is a censure, it may be inflicted by the Bishop without further admonition or warning once he is certain that the precept has been violated, for the precept threatening the penalty is a sufficient admonition in itself.[63] If, however, the pastor would recede from his contumacy before the application of the penalty, then the Bishop would no longer be able to impose the censure,[64] but he could inflict a vindicative penalty, if such was the nature of the penalty attached for the violation of the precept.

If the Bishop annexes to his precept a *latae sententiae* censure, who may absolve from this penalty if the precept is violated and the penalty is incurred? The answer to this problem depends on the manner in which the precept is given. The Bishop in giving a precept to the pastor forbidding him to assist at the marriage of the minor may say: "If you assist at that marriage you are *ipso facto* suspended, and I reserve to myself the absolution from this penalty." In this instance the Bishop alone may absolve from the penalty. However, if he attaches a *latae sententiae* penalty to his precept but does not mention the fact that the absolution is reserved to himself, then the penalty is not reserved. Hence, in order that the absolution from the censure

---

Extrajudicial Coercive Powers of Ecclesiastical Superiors, pp. 110–114) for a complete discussion of this problem and a critical analysis of the opposite opinion.

[62] Canons 2217, § 1, 2o; 2242, § 2.

[63] PCI, 14 iul. 1922, XV—*AAS,* XIV (1922), 530. Cf. Bouscaren, *The Canon Law Digest,* I, 845–846, under canon 2233.

[64] Canon 2242, §1.

be reserved, the Bishop must expressly state the fact of its reservation. This appears to be the better solution of the difficulty which is inherent in canon 2245. The problem is simply this. In the second paragraph of this canon it is stated that an *ab homine* censure is reserved to the one who inflicted it or who pronounced the sentence, or to his competent superior, successor, or delegate.[65] However, in the fourth paragraph of the same canon it is affirmed that a *latae sententiae* censure is not reserved unless the reservation is expressly mentioned in the law or precept, and in a doubt of law or of fact the reservation does not hold.[66] Hence, when the Bishop forbids a pastor to assist at the marriage by giving him a precept to that effect and annexes to this prohibition a *latae sententiae* censure, the penalty is both *latae sententiae* and *ab homine*. From the second paragraph of canon 2245 it would seem that, in as much as it is an *ab homine* penalty, it would be reserved; while on the other hand, since it is also a *latae sententiae* penalty, it would appear that it is not reserved unless the Bishop mentioned the reservation in his precept.

The writer maintains, as mentioned above, that unless the Bishop expressly mentioned in his precept the reservation of the *latae sententiae* censure the penalty is not reserved. The basis for this assertion rests on the fact that the meaning of canon 2245, §§ 2, 4 is not clear, for it is difficult to reconcile these two paragraphs. The doubt is bound up with the very wording or statement of the law itself. Hence there is present a *dubium juris,* and canon 15 can be applied.[67] Moreover, many authors in discussing this problem maintain that such a *latae sententiae* censure annexed to a particular precept is not reserved.[68] Hence,

---

[65] Canon 2245, §2: "Censura ab homine est reservata ei qui censuram inflixit aut sententiam tulit, eiusve Superiori competenti vel successori aut delegato; . . ."

[66] Canon 2245, § 4: "Censura latae sententiae non est reservata, nisi in lege vel praecepto id expresse dicatur; et in dubio sive iuris sive facti reservatio non urget."

[67] "Leges, etiam irritantes et inhabilitantes, in dubio iuris non urgent; . . ."

[68] Coronata, *Institutiones Iuris Canonici,* IV, n. 1750; Ayrinhac-Lydon, *Penal Legislation,* n. 86; Moriarty, *The Extraordinary Absolution from Censures,* The Catholic University of American Canon Law Studies, n. 113 (Washington, D. C.: The Catholic University of America, 1938), p. 104.

since a reservation, though not a penalty in itself, is nevertheless something odious and involves a restriction of liberty of action, it must according to the principles given by the legislator receive a strict interpretation.[69] Therefore the absolution from the censure attached by the Bishop to his precept is reserved only if he expressly states the reservation.

If the Bishop gives a precept to the pastor not to assist at the particular marriage of the minor, but does not annex a definite penalty to his prohibition, may he proceed to punish the pastor who disobeys his prohibition? Provided scandal is given by the action of the pastor or if the special gravity of the transgression merits punishment, the Bishop may without the previous warning inflict some just penalty on the disobedient pastor. This is an exceptional case, and if neither of the two conditions is verified, the pastor cannot be punished unless he is first warned that a penalty *latae* or *ferendae sententiae* will be incurred or inflicted, and notwithstanding this admonition he violates the precept.[70] This just penalty, moreover, should not be among the graver penalties of the Code of Canon Law. The Bishop should reprimand the pastor, or prescribe a retreat for a time, or inflict some other penalty fitting to the case. However, in practice it would rarely happen that the local Ordinary would be justified in calling forth this power of canon 2222, § 2 in order to punish either the pastor or the delinquent nupturients who acted contrary to his prohibition. For it seems that neither of the two conditions mentioned in the canon and which are requisite for the use of this power would be present.

Since the prohibition of the marriage by the local Ordinary is given after the manner of a precept, it is subject to all the rules which govern precepts. Consequently, this prohibition ceases (1) if the local Ordinary revokes it; (2) if a definite time limit, for

---

[69] Canon 19: "Leges quae . . . liberum iurium exercitium coarctant, strictae subsunt interpretationi."

Canon 2245, § 4: ". . . in dubio sive iuris sive facti reservatio non urget."

Canon 2246, § 2: "Reservatio strictam recipit interpretationem."

[70] Canon 2222, § 2; cf. Coronata, *Institutiones Iuris Canonici,* IV, n. 1695; Chelodi, *Ius Poenale,* n. 25.

example three months, was set and this time has expired; (3) if the cause or reason for the prohibition no longer exists, as has already been explained. Canon 24 explicitly enacts that precepts cease to bind with the expiration of the authority of the one who gave them, and cannot be judicially urged unless they were given in the form of a legal document or before two witnesses. No definite form or wording is necessary for the validity of the precept. In order to fulfill the requirements of a legal document of which canon 24 makes mention, it suffices if there is indicated the name of the party to whom the precept is given together with an exact account of what is forbidden and the penalty for its violation, if there is question of attaching a penalty; the Bishop and the notary add their signatures and the latter must properly note the place, day, month, and year in writing. These requirements, however, are not necessary for the validity of the precept, but are required only to insure its binding force after the death of the person who gave it, and in order that the precept may be urged in a canonical trial. Seldom will the local Ordinary in prohibiting the marriage of a minor embody his prohibition in a legal document. Generally the precept is given orally to the pastor or the contracting parties. This is true because there is really no need to give a formal precept, for if the pastor or nupturients violate his penal prohibition the Bishop will punish them extrajudicially; moreover, the prohibition of the marriage in such cases is usually operative only for a short time.

Van Hove, however, maintains that when the local Ordinary makes use of the power given to him by canon 1039, § 1 to prohibit a particular marriage, he should give his precept according to the solemn form indicated in canon 24. Hence the local Ordinary according to Van Hove should draw up a legal document attesting to his prohibition of the marriage, or he should give the precept only in the presence of two witnesses. This author reasons that, since this prohibition concerns the external forum, and since there is question of imposing a special or additional obligation, the local Ordinary should employ the solemn form in imposing his precept.[71] The writer, however, fails to

[71] *De Legibus Ecclesiasticis*, p. 368, nota 3.

see any particular force in the reasons advanced by Van Hove, and so maintains that the local Ordinary in forbidding the marriage need not employ the solemn form in imposing his precept. It is true that, if the local Ordinary desires to urge judicially his precept or to ensure its binding force after his death, he must impose his precept in the form of a legal document or before two witnesses. Wernz[72] and Payen,[73] however, declare that, if the local Ordinary forbids a marriage by precept, but does not impose his prohibition in the form of a legal document or before witnesses, his precept nevertheless continues to bind even after his death. For these authors state that the reasons for the prohibition, namely, avoidance of scandal and respect for lawful parental authority, remain intact even after the death of the local Ordinary. Hence they assert that a prohibition of this nature comes under the protection and approbation of law, and therefore remains obligatory even though the authority of the one who gave it ceases. This opinion of the above authors, however, appears to the writer to contradict the express teaching of canon 24, and therefore it cannot be sustained. For precepts which are given to individuals and which are not imposed in the form determined by this canon are temporary, and cease to bind with the death of the Bishop who gave them.[74]

Article 4. The Procedure of the Ordinary in Permitting the Marriage

As has been seen, if the local Ordinary after considering all the circumstances of the particular case judges that the parental dissent is unreasonable, he must permit the pastor to assist at the marriage. Moreover, he may permit the celebration of the marriage even though the parental refusal is reasonable and just, provided the prohibition of the marriage would lead to graver evils. In this instance, as has been explained, the local Ordinary

---

[72] *Ius Decretalium,* IV, n. 604, nota 22.

[73] *De Matrimonio,* I, 439 ad 5.

[74] Canon 24: "Praecepta, singulis data, eos quibus dantur, ubique urgent, sed iudicialiter urgeri nequeunt et cessant resoluto iure praecipientis, nisi per legitimum documentum aut coram duobus testibus imposita fuerint." Cf. Coronata, *Institutiones Iuris Canonici,* I, n. 33; Van Hove, *De Legibus Ecclesiasticis,* p. 370.

tolerates the violation of rightful parental authority as the lesser evil.

To permit the marriage of a minor against the wishes of the parents is an action fraught with danger. The local Ordinary in granting this permission will act prudently and reasonably, and will consider carefully all the pertinent circumstances of the case. He will especially note whether the objecting parents are Catholics or non-Catholics, and he will endeavor to determine whether they will respect or oppose his decision. When the parents are unreasonable in withholding their permission, the Ordinary should explain to them that the minor child in these circumstances has a right to enter marriage—a right which the Church respects and upholds; and that therefore the parents have a duty to respect this right of their child, and should cease their unreasonable opposition which in this instance would objectively be sinful. The local Ordinary could impose on the parents a penal precept forbidding them to institute civil action in order to impede the marriage. Authors agree that the parents would not incur the excommunication of canon 2334 if they successfully thwarted the celebration of the marriage by appealing to the civil authorities even after the local Ordinary had permitted the marriage.[75] The reason is that the canon includes only acts of jurisdiction, and the assistance of the priest at marriage is not strictly speaking an exercise of the power of jurisdiction. Since the penal legislation of the Church is to be interpreted strictly, the penalty of canon 2334 is not incurred by the parents in this instance.[76]

The principal difficulty in permitting the celebration of a marriage, which the parents oppose, arises from the civil law, for every State in the United States has statutes dealing with the marriage of minors.[77] The civil law, moreover, is more exact-

---

[75] Canon 2334: "Excommunicatione latae sententiae speciali modo Sedi Apostolicae reservata plectuntur: . . . 2o Qui impediunt directe vel indirecte exercitium iurisdictionis ecclesiasticae sive interni sive externi fori, ad hoc recurrentes ad quamlibet laicalem potestatem."

[76] Vermeersch-Creusen, *Epitome,* III, 276; Cappello, *De Censuris,* n. 261.

[77] Cf. Chapter X, wherein the civil law regulations concerning the marriage of minors is treated.

ing than the Canon law on this point. Thus the problem which the Ordinary will frequently meet may be exemplified in the following case. A child of minor age desires to contract marriage, but the parents oppose the union and refuse to give their permission. Since the parties have cogent reasons for contracting the marriage, the parental dissent canonically considered must be deemed unreasonable. According to the law of the Church, then, the parties are free to marry. However, the civil law forbids a person of minor age from contracting marriage without the consent of the parents. The State enforces this prescript by requiring a civil license or certificate before the marriage may be celebrated, and it makes the issuance of the license in the case of minors dependent on the written consent of the parents or guardians. If one who is authorized to witness marriages according to the law of the State actually officiates at a marriage when the parties have not obtained a license, he is liable to punishment. The officiant is fined a definite sum of money, and, moreover, the State may forbid him to witness marriages in the future.[78] In the case under consideration the parties are incapable of obtaining a civil license, since the parents resolutely refuse to give their permission. In Church law the parties are free to marry and have a right to do so. However, if the pastor assists at the marriage, he is liable to the severe penalties of the civil law, and the non-consenting parents of the minor may bring any transgression of the civil law to the attention of the officials of the State. In this instance, then, what procedure will the local Ordinary follow in permitting the celebration of the marriage? The solution of this problem will be the main consideration of the writer in this present article.

At the outset it is necessary to determine whether or not the local Ordinary, pastor, and contracting parties are obliged in conscience to obey and respect the civil law in these circumstances. When a minor desires to contract marriage contrary to the will of his parents three types of civil law must be considered. (1) There is the civil ruling which requires parental consent for the marriages of persons under a certain age, for example twenty-

[78] Cf. Vernier, *American Family Laws,* I, 60, 62, 120; Alford, *Jus Matrimoniale,* n. 294.

one years. (2) The civil statute demanding a license or certificate before the marriage can be celebrated. (3) The registration of the marriage in the public records of the State. These three types of civil law are interwoven in the present case. Since the nature and obligation of these laws are essentially different, they must be considered separately.

With regard to the first type of law, namely, the civil prescript concerning the necessity of the parental permission, it must be said that it is a just law and objectively considered it is not unreasonable. It is just in the sense that it is not opposed to the divine or to the ecclesiastical law; it is reasonable, for its observance in general will benefit the State and society. However, this civil law in regard to baptized persons is altogether invalid, because it exceeds the competence of the civil legislator. Nevertheless, there is an obligation in conscience for baptized persons to respect and observe this law, since it does not contravene either the divine law of God or the law of His Church. This duty to observe the law derives not from the particular civil law itself, for it is invalid, but from the precept of charity which obligates the contracting parties to protect not only themselves but also their future children from the grave evils which will come upon them if this civil law is imprudently violated. Consequently, the Church teaches that wherever possible such a civil law is to be conscientiously observed, even though the law in itself is invalid as to the baptized. If circumstances render its observance impossible, then legitimate ecclesiastical authority may permit the celebration of the marriage, and any obligation arising from the law of charity to obey this civil law in these circumstances would cease to exist.[79]

The second law concerning the requirement of a civil license or certificate is in itself contrary neither to the divine law nor to the law of the Church. Therefore objectively considered it is a just law. However, the validity or invalidity of this law must be determined from the purpose which the civil legislator intends. If he is merely providing for the civil effects of marriage, the license law is valid even for the marriages of baptized

[79] S. C. S. Off. (Vic. Ap. Iamaicae), 12 ian. 1881—*Collectanea S. C. P. F.*, II, n. 1545, ad 1 et 2; Cappello, *De Sacramentis*, III, n. 74.

persons. Hence under these circumstances it obliges in conscience both the contracting parties and the officiant. If, however, as in some States,[80] the legislator demands a license or certificate for the civil validity of the marriage, such a law is invalid in regard to the marriages of baptized persons, for it exceeds the competence of the civil legislator. If the purpose of the license is to declare that the party who possesses it is bound by no civil impediment to marriage, the license law is valid only for the unbaptized, for a baptized person in contracting marriage is not subject to civil impediments. Hence the baptized parties, the pastor, and the Ordinary are not obliged in conscience to obey this license law in so far as the validity or lawfulness of the marriage is concerned.

The third type of civil law, which has a bearing on the case, concerns the civil registration of the marriage. This is closely connected with the civil law concerning the license, for in most States the civil registration of the marriage is effected by the return of the marriage license to the proper civil official. The officiant signs the marriage license and thereby attests the fact of the celebration of the marriage.[81] The State is competent to legislate concerning the civil registration of the marriage, and, therefore, laws of this nature are valid and just even for the marriages of baptized persons. The officiant is bound to cooperate in order that the marriages at which he assists may be faithfully recorded in the civil records. Failure to do so may cause serious harm to the contracting parties and their children, and wilful neglect in this matter is sinful. This type of civil law, then, is binding in conscience. Moreover, the State may lawfully punish those who disobey this prescription even though the violators are baptized persons.[82]

---

[80] In Arizona, Missouri, Nebraska, Tennessee, Virginia, West Virginia, Wisconsin, statute law requires a license for the validity of the marriage; cf. *Martindale-Hubbell Law Directory* (77th annual edition, 2 vols., Summit, New Jersey: Martindale-Hubbell, Inc., 1945), II; Alford, *Jus Matrimoniale,* n. 287.

[81] Cf. Vernier, *American Family Laws,* I, 145–147.

[82] Gasparri, *De Matrimonio,* I, nn. 238–239; Cappello, *De Sacramentis,* III, nn. 71, 74; Heneghan, "Civil Marriage License"—*The Jurist,* III (1943), 313.

In the present case the minor child is canonically free to contract marriage, but the State indirectly prevents him from doing so by refusing to issue a civil license. Hence the civil law in this instance is unjust, for it is contrary to the law of the Church. Moreover, since the only effective way to register the marriage civilly is rendered impossible due to the lack of a marriage license, the duty of observing this valid civil law of recording the marriage ceases at least for the time being. If later on the parties without serious inconvenience can provide for this registration of their marriage, they would be obligated to do so at least for the protection of their future children. Therefore, it is certain that there is no question of sinful disobedience to the civil laws, if the local Ordinary permits the pastor to assist at the marriage of a minor whose parents are unreasonably unwilling in withholding their consent to the marriage.

Nevertheless, the difficulty remains as to how the marriage can be celebrated, for if the pastor assists at the marriage when the contracting parties have no marriage license, he runs the risk of incurring severe civil penalties. The State in threatening or inflicting this punishment would be acting unjustly, but, nevertheless, the fact remains that the pastor in contravening this civil law would be subject to grave harm. Yet the law of the Church requires for the validity of the marriage the presence of an authorized priest who must ask and receive the consent of the contracting parties.[83] There is no difficulty concerning the two witnesses who would participate in the marriage, for witnesses are not punished by the civil law in this case. Only the officiating minister is subject to the penalties enacted by the civil law. In this instance, then, what procedure is possible for the local Ordinary?

Before the Ordinary advises the pastor to employ the extraordinary remedies permitted by the Canon law, he should attempt to solve the difficulty by either an appeal to the civil courts or by advising marriage outside the jurisdiction of the particular State. In this way the civil effects of the marriage can be safeguarded.

Thus the local Ordinary should carefully examine the civil law

[83] Canons 1094–1095.

of his particular locality in order to see if any redress can be had according to legal norms. In some instances even though the State law may require parental consent for the marriage of minors and also for the obtaining of a license, nevertheless relief can be had by appealing to the Probate Court of the particular County. Thus, for example, in the State of Illinois the Probate Court is empowered to confirm the nomination of a personal guardian for a minor over fourteen years of age. This guardian can then give the consent necessary for a marriage license in spite of the protests of the parents. If the minor child is above the age of fourteen years, he may nominate the guardian of his person, who, if approved by the Court, shall be appointed accordingly.[84] This Probate Court provides that notice of the time and place of the hearing on each petition for the appointment of such a guardian shall be given to the parents,[85] but the Probate Court in extraordinary circumstances may even waive service of this notice to parents.[86] The presiding Judge of the Probate Court then decides whether the Court will uphold the objections of the parents, or whether it will permit the minor to contract the marriage. If the latter, then the Probate Court accepts the consent of the guardian as sufficient to procure a marriage license. The marriage may then be celebrated regardless of the parental dissent. Hence this is the most effective and acceptable solution of the difficulty, and one that should be employed by the Ordinary wherever possible.

If, however, the civil law of the particular State fails to provide the necessary relief, it would be lawful to suggest to the contracting parties marriage in another State where the law regarding parental consent is less severe. If the celebration of the marriage outside the State could be effected without grave inconvenience to the nupturients, the local Ordinary must suggest this solution rather than advise a marriage before witnesses alone.[87] However, in many cases travel to another State would

[84] Cf. *Probate Act and Rules of the Probate Court of Cook County*—Effective January 1, 1940, § 136, p. 36.

[85] *Op. cit.*, Rule 7, p. 91.

[86] *Op. cit.*, Rule 67, p. 113.

[87] Gasparri, *De Matrimonio*, II, n. 1017.

entail a grave inconvenience for the parties, since it would involve, for example, an expenditure greater than that which they can afford. Furthermore, if the civil law of the neighboring State would require for marriage a bona fide residence within its jurisdiction, it would seem that this is a just and valid civil law. Consequently it would seem wrong to advise the parties to go into that State for the purpose of marriage, for this would be encouraging a violation of the civil law of that State. Moreover, many States have what are termed "Marriage Evasion Statutes" which forbid persons to leave the State for the purpose of contracting marriage in order to avoid the marriage laws which are operative in their own State, and violators of this law are subject to punishment.[88]

If the local Ordinary cannot successfully employ either of the two remedies outlined above, he may then turn to the solution offered him by the legislator in canons 1098 and 1104. Canon 1098 considers the celebration of a marriage before witnesses alone, while canon 1104 deals with the marriage of conscience. The writer will now consider these two institutes in relation to the present problem of permitting the celebration of the marriage of a minor against unreasonable parental opposition which is upheld by the civil law.

Canon 1098 enacts an exception to the ordinary form of marriage, for therein the legislator decrees that if the pastor or Ordinary or a priest delegated by either according to canons 1095 and 1096 cannot be had, or if the parties cannot go to him without grave inconvenience, then the marriage even apart from the danger of death may be validly and licitly contracted in the presence only of two witnesses, provided it can be prudently foreseen that the difficulty of having an authorized priest witness the marriage will continue for a month.

Authors discuss at great length whether the grave inconvenience mentioned in canon 1098 would be present in the case where the

---

[88] Marriage Evasion Statutes are in effect in Arizona, Colorado, Connecticut, Delaware, Georgia, Illinois, Indiana, Louisiana, Maine, Massachusetts, Mississippi, Montana, Vermont, Virginia, West Virginia, Wisconsin, Wyoming and the District of Columbia. Cf. Vernier, *American Family Laws,* I, 209–213; *Martindale-Hubbell Law Directory,* II.

competent priest would be forbidden by the civil law under the threat of severe penalties to assist at the marriage. The difficulty centers about the nature of the inconvenience which prevents the pastor from assisting at the marriage. Thus may canon 1098 be validly employed, if the priest is physically present but morally absent, or is it only applicable when the authorized priest is physically absent? In other words, does the legislator limit the valid use of canon 1098 only to cases wherein it is physically impossible for the authorized priest to assist at the marriage?

Before the promulgation of the Code of Canon Law canonists discussed the same problem under the legislation of the Decree *Tametsi* as well as under that of the Decree *Ne temere.* Under the *Tametsi* legislation it is clear from the responses of the Sacred Congregations that the moral absence of the pastor effected by the fear of punishment for violating the civil law was sufficient to permit the celebration of the marriage before witnesses only.[89] Also under the legislation of the Decree *Ne temere* it was the common opinion that a valid marriage could be celebrated before witnesses alone, if it was morally impossible for the authorized priest to assist at the marriage due to the prohibition of the civil law.[90] However, the Sacred Congregation of Sacraments on January 31, 1916 decided that, when the pastor was prevented by the civil law from assisting at the marriage, the case should be referred to the Holy See for decision.[91]

---

[89] S. C. S. Off. (ad Episc. Villespraten.), I, iul. 1863—*Collectanea S. C. P. F.*, I, n. 1240; S. C. de Prop. Fide (ad Praefectum Missionum in Insula Curaçao), 1795—*op. cit.*, I, n. 571.

[90] Cf. Gasparri, *De Matrimonio,* II, n. 1017; De Smet, *De Sponsalibus et Matrimonio,* p. 111; Chelodi, *Ius Matrimoniale,* n. 137; Vlaming, *Praelectiones Iuris Matrimonii,* II, n. 590.

[91] "Quum in nonnullis regionibus, Parochi a civili lege graviter prohibeantur quominus matrimonio assistant, nisi praemisso civili connubio, quod non semper praemitti potest, et tamen ad mala praecavenda et pro bono animarum matrimonium celebrari expediat; quidam horum locorum Antistites a Sacra Congregatione de Disciplina Sacramentorum efflagitarunt: an et quomodo his in adjunctis providendum sit." The Sacred Congregation responded: "Recurratur in singulis casibus, excepto casu periculi mortis, in quo quilibet sacerdos dispensare valeat etiam ab impedimento clandestinitatis, permittendo in relatis adjunctis matrimonium coram solis testibus valide et licite contrahatur."—*AAS,* VIII (1916), 36–37.

When the Code of Canon Law was published, authors were divided on this question. A few of them held that canon 1098 must be interpreted in the light of the response given by the Sacred Congregation of the Sacraments referred to above. Consequently, they required that the priest must be physically absent before canon 1098 can be validly used. Thus they did not permit its use in the case in which the pastor was prevented from assisting at the marriage by the prohibition of the civil law.[92] The majority of canonists, however, interpreted canon 1098 as applicable to the case in which the pastor, although he is physically present in the place where the marriage is to take place, cannot assist at the marriage without the risk of incurring severe civil law penalties. They maintained that in canon 1098 the legislator uses general terms and makes no distinction between physical and moral impossibility in relation to the pastor's assistance at the marriage. Furthermore, these authors held that with the publication of the Code of Canon Law the reply of the Sacred Congregation of the Sacraments of January 31, 1916 ceased to be a guiding principle in this matter.[93]

However, on March 10, 1928 the Pontifical Commission for the Authentic Interpretation of the Code declared that the absence of the priest or Ordinary in canon 1098 is to be understood only in the sense of physical absence.[94] After this authentic response authors began to teach that canon 1098 could not be employed if the pastor is physically present but is impeded by the fear of civil penalties from assisting at the marriage. In such a case there is only a moral impossibility on the part of the priest, and

---

[92] Wernz-Vidal, *Ius Canonicum,* V, n. 547; Oesterle, "Elucubratio Historica circa Declarationem Authenticam Can. 1095"—*JP,* VIII (1928), 174–182; IX (1929), 141–158.

[93] De Smet, *De Sponsalibus et Matrimonio,* pp. 111–112; Chelodi, *Ius Matrimoniale,* n. 137; Vermeersch-Creusen, *Epitome,* II, 405; Cappello, *De Sacramentis,* III, n. 694; Vlaming, *Praelectiones Iuris Matrimonii,* II, n. 590.

[94] An canon 1098 ita intelligendus sit ut referatur tantum ad physicam parochi vel Ordinarii loci absentiam. Responsum est: *Affirmative."—AAS,* XX (1928), 120; cf. Bouscaren, *The Canon Law Digest,* I, 542, under canon 1098.

therefore recourse should be had to the Holy See for instructions on how to proceed in conducting the case.[95]

The authors held this strict opinion until July 19, 1931 at which time the Pontifical Commission for the Authentic Interpretation of the Code, in responding to a doubt concerning their previous response of March 10, 1928, further clarified the meaning of canon 1098. This latest response of the Pontifical Commission declares that the physical absence of the pastor or Ordinary is verified in the case in which they are materially present in the place where the marriage is to be celebrated, but are unable by reason of grave inconvenience to assist at the marriage and ask and receive the consent of the contracting parties.[96] After the above response the vast majority of the authors again returned to the opinion that, if the pastor would be impeded from assisting at the marriage because of the fear of incurring serious civil penalties, the marriage could be celebrated validly before only two witnesses according to the provisions of canon 1098. This today is the more favorable teaching, and it may be held as certain doctrine.[97]

Cardinal Gasparri, who was the President of the Pontifical Commission for the Authentic Interpretation of the Code at the

---

[95] Claeys Bouuaert-Simenon, *Manuale Iuris Canonici,* II, 309; Vermeersch, "Annotationes"—*Periodica,* XVIII (1929), 77–80; Maroto, "Animadversiones"—*Apollinaris,* I (1928), 334–339; Coucke, "Adnotationes"—*Collectiones Brugenses,* XXVIII (1928), 253–255.

[96] "Quaesitum est: An *ad physicam parochi vel Ordinarii absentiam,* de qua in interpretatione die Martii 1928 ad can. 1098, referendus sit etiam casus, quo parochus vel Ordinarius, licet materialiter praesens in loco, ob grave tamen incommodum celebrationi matrimonii assistere nequeat requirens et excipiens contrahentium censensum. Responsum est: *Affirmative.*"—*AAS,* XXIII (1931), 388; cf. Bouscaren, *op. cit.,* I, 542, under canon 1098.

[97] Cappello, *De Sacramentis,* III, 787; Payen, *De Matrimonio,* II, n. 1822; Gasparri, *De Matrimonio,* II, n. 1017; Carberry, *The Juridical Form of Marriage,* The Catholic University of America Canon Law Studies, n. 84 (Washington, D. C.: The Catholic University of America, 1934), p. 147; Ayrinhac-Lydon, *Marriage Legislation,* p. 264; Fallon, "Grave Inconvenience Justifying the Celebration of Marriage Without a Priest"—*IER,* LIX (1942), 470–471; Werts, "The Cessation of Invalidation in Grave Difficulty"—*Theological Studies* (New York: 1942–), IV (1943), 243–244; Creusen, "Célébration du Mariage, Résponse du 25 Juillet, 1931"—*Nouvelle Revue Theólogique* (Tournai: 1869–), LVIII (1931), 827–829; *JP,* XI (1931), 256.

time when both of these responses regarding canon 1098 were given, throws great light on the proper understanding of these two replies. He states that the Pontifical Commission understood this grave inconvenience, which prevented the pastor from assisting at the marriage, to be the fear of incurring the severe penalties threatened by the civil law. He teaches that the response of March 10, 1928 means that the moral presence of the pastor at the marriage is not sufficient, but that it is necessary for him to be present physically, so that he may ask and receive the consent of the contracting parties.[98] Therefore canon 1098 may be employed when the pastor is physically absent so that he is unable to witness the marriage physically and actively by asking and receiving the consent of the parties. It is immaterial whether he is prevented from assisting at the marriage by physical absence from the place or by moral pressure. This explanation of Gasparri's makes it certain that canon 1098 is applicable to the case in which the pastor cannot assist at the marriage due to fear of civil penalties.

However, even after this latest response of the Pontifical Commission some canonists still teach that canon 1098 can be used only if it is physically impossible for the pastor to assist at the marriage. Consequently, they would deny that canon 1098 offers a solution to the difficulty in the case of permitting the marriage of a minor which is forbidden by the civil law. In this instance the presence of the pastor is only morally impossible, for he is physically present in the place where the marriage is to be celebrated. Hence they maintain that the condition for the valid use of canon 1098 is not verified.[99]

The milder opinion, namely, that canon 1098 can be used in the case where the priest cannot assist at the marriage without exposing himself to the danger of incurring severe civil penalties, received explicit approbation in a private response of the Sacred

---

[98] Cf. Gasparri, *De Matrimonio,* II, n. 1017.

[99] Nau, *Manual on the Marriage Laws of the Code of Canon Law* (2. ed., New York: F. Pustet Co., 1934), pp. 159-160; Maroto, "Responsa ad Proposita Dubia 25 Julii 1931"—*Apollinaris,* IV (1931), 381; De Becker, "De Recta Canonis 1098 Codicis Iuris Canonici Interpretatione"—*ETL,* IX (1932), 284-291.

Congregation of the Sacraments to the Bishop of Metz on April 24, 1935.[100] Hence, it is certain that the local Ordinary may use canon 1098, and permit the marriage of the minor to be celebrated before witnesses alone.

Besides the use of canon 1098 the only other canonical solution for the present difficulty is to employ what is known as a "marriage of conscience." A marriage of conscience is a marriage which is celebrated according to the form prescribed by law in canons 1094 and 1095, but in such a manner that it may remain a secret known only to the contracting parties, witnesses, the assisting priest, and the Ordinary. Permission to celebrate a marriage of conscience may be given by the Bishop alone and only for very grave and urgent causes. Even the Vicar General cannot concede this permission unless he receives beforehand a special mandate from the Bishop.[101] The Bishop, moreover, is the sole judge of the necessity for such a marriage. These strict regulations which govern the celebration of a marriage of conscience clearly indicate that it is to be used only as a last resort. Innumerable difficulties are encountered both before and after the celebration of such a marriage. Thus, it is difficult to establish the freedom of the parties to contract marriage, since all the information regarding their status must be gathered secretly. There is always present the danger of scandal, if the parties after the celebration of the marriage would live together as husband and wife in their own locality. Hence it would be imperative that the parties leave their community and seek a new abode.

---

[100] "Ad dubium propositum ab Episcopo Meten. pro opportuna solutione: 'An scilicet, ratione habita responsa dati a Pontificia Commissione ad Codicis Canones authentice interpretandos diei 25 iulii 1931 relate ad can. 1098, ad hunc Canonem referendus sit casus, quo Parochus vel Ordinarius celebrationi matrimonii religiosi assistere nequit, quia lege civili prohibetur, etiam sub poena, matrimonium coram Ecclesia celebrare, nisi praecesserit matrimonium sic dictum civile, et hoc ab auctoritate civili omnino recusatur, v. g. ob defectum instrumentorum quae lex civilis requirit' : Sacra Congregatio de Disciplina Sacramentorum rescribendum censet: '*Affirmative.*'"—Cited from *Periodica,* XXVII (1928), 45-46; cf. also Bouscaren, *The Canon Law Digest,* II, 336, under canon 1098.

[101] Canon 1104.

Moreover, special care must be taken concerning the registration of the marriage.

Thus from these strict rules, which the legislator enacts concerning a marriage of conscience, and because of the difficulties which the celebration of such a marriage necessarily entails, the writer concludes that the Bishop should not employ a marriage of conscience as the solution for the present problem, but that he should rather advise a marriage according to canon 1098. Since there is *per se* no necessity in the present case to keep the fact of the marriage of the minor a secret either from the parents or from the civil officials, there is no particular reason for urging a marriage of conscience as the more favorable solution. Canon 1098 provides an easy and effective answer for the problem, and is preferable for these two reasons: (1) The pastor cannot be punished by the civil law, for he does not assist at the marriage; on the other hand, if a marriage of conscience is used and the secret is divulged, the pastor could be punished by the State, for in this case he actually assists at the marriage. (2) In permitting the celebration of the marriage before witnesses alone all the difficulties which are necessarily connected with a marriage of conscience are avoided; above all, the parties may continue to reside in their present locality.

It may be remarked that in advising the celebration of the marriage before witnesses alone the Ordinary will instruct the parties to go before a priest as soon as possible in order that they may receive the nuptial blessing, and also that the Ritual ceremonies of marriage may be supplied. In the present discipline of the Church it is clear that the obligation to supply these Ritual ceremonies is not a grave one.[102] Gasparri, however, declares that this obligation binds the parties *sub gravi,* and cites as proof of this statement three pre-Code responses of the Sacred Congregation of the Propagation of the Faith and one reply of the Sacred Congregation of the Holy Office. Gasparri admits that merely from a consideration of the Code of Canon Law no grave obligation in this matter can be established.[103] Cappello denies, and rightly so, this opinion of Gasparri. Cappello

[102] Canon 1100.

[103] *De Matrimonio,* II, nn. 1033–1037.

argues that the binding force of these pre-Code responses of the various Congregations has ceased with the publication of the Code of Canon Law, since canon 1098 reconsiders and readjusts the entire subject matter of the former law.[104] The priest, however, in supplying these ceremonies will abstain from asking and receiving the consent of the parties, and he will explain to them that the Ritual ceremonies are in no way necessary for the validity of their marriage.

---

[104] *De Sacramentis,* III, n. 708; cf. also Farrugia, *De Matrimonio,* n. 240; Payen, *De Matrimonio,* II, 253, nota 3.

CHAPTER IX

THE PENALTY OF CANON 2353

Canon 2353: Qui intuitu matrimonii vel explendae libidinis causa rapuerit mulierem nolentem vi aut dolo, vel mulierem minoris aetatis consentientem quidem, sed insciis vel contradicentibus parentibus aut tutoribus, ipso iure exclusus habeatur ab actibus legitimis ecclesiasticis et insuper aliis poenis pro gravitate culpae plectatur.

As has been seen in canon 1034, the legislator demands that before a marriage which involves a minor child may be lawfully celebrated the parents of the minor must know of the intended marriage and be not reasonably unwilling to permit the forthcoming union. This canon then is necessarily connected with canon 2353. For the legislator in canon 2353 inflicts a penalty on any man who abducts a minor girl with a view to marriage or merely for the gratification of his lust even though the child consents to the abduction, provided her parents or guardians are uninformed of or are opposed to her departure. Hence it is evident that in a marriage which involves a minor girl it is easily possible that the delict of canon 2353 may be committed. Indeed this delict may be present even though the marriage actually is not celebrated. All that the canon requires is the abduction with a view to marriage; the intention of the man in abducting the minor girl in view of the marriage is sufficient to bring the man within the scope of canon 2353. Moreover, if he even abducts the minor girl with her own consent but unknown to her parents or guardians or against their will for immoral purposes, he is likewise liable to the penalties of this canon. Since the writer, however, is concerned only with the marriage of minors, he will not consider the carrying off of a minor girl for immoral purposes, but will consider only her abduction with a view to marriage.

Abduction may be considered either as a matrimonial impediment or as a crime. Canon 1074 considers abduction as diriment impediment to marriage,[1] while the crime of abduction is treated in canon 2353. Abduction as an impediment to marriage and abduction considered as a crime are two separate and distinct juridical institutes. Thus it would be false to assert that canon 2353 is merely the penal counterpart of canon 1074. The legislator in canon 2353 is not merely annexing a penal sanction to the matrimonial impediment of abduction. Thus abduction as a crime differs from abduction as a matrimonial impediment in the following manner: (1) The crime of abduction is present if the woman is abducted either for marriage or for immoral purposes. The matrimonial impediment of abduction, however, is had only if the woman is abducted with a view to marriage. (2) The crime of abduction is not committed by violent detention of the woman. To contract the matrimonial impediment, however, it suffices to detain the woman by force in the place of her residence or in a place to which she has freely come. (3) The crime of abduction occurs in the case of a minor girl, even though she consents to the abduction with a view to marriage, whenever her parents or guardians are uninformed of or are opposed to her departure. The matrimonial impediment, on the other hand, is never present when the woman consents to the abduction with a view to marriage. (4) The crime of abduction includes both *raptus violentiae* and *raptus seductionis.* The matrimonial impediment of abduction excludes entirely abduction by seduction. (5) Once the crime of abduction has been committed, the guilty party is powerless to free himself from the penalties of canon 2353 except by the action of a legitimate ecclesiastical superior. However, canon 1074, § 2 provides that the nupturients are able of their own will to escape from the invalidating effect of the matrimonial

---

[1] Canon 1074, § 1: "Inter virum raptorem et mulierem, intuitu matrimonii raptam, quamdiu ipsa in potestate raptoris manserit, nullum potest consistere matrimonium."

§ 2: "Quod si rapta, a raptore separata et in loco tuto ac libero constituta, illum in virum habere consenserit, impedimentum cessat."

§ 3: "Quod ad matrimonii nullitatem attinet, raptui par habetur violenta retentio mulieris, cum nempe vir mulierem in loco ubi ea commoratur vel ad quem libere accessit, violenter intuitu matrimonii detinet."

impediment. Thus from these five considerations it is clear that abduction as a crime does not coincide with the matrimonial impediment of abduction. Under one aspect the crime of abduction is of wider extension than the matrimonial impediment of abduction, while from another viewpoint the very opposite is true. Hence canon 1074 and canon 2353 have reference to separate juridical institutes.

The writer is not concerned with the matrimonial impediment of abduction but only with the crime of abduction. Abduction as a crime is divided by all the authors into abduction by violence (*raptus violentiae*) and abduction by seduction (*raptus seductionis*). Abduction by violence is present whenever a woman is carried off against her will either by means of force or through the use of deceit. Abduction by seduction occurs when a minor girl is taken away with her own consent in view of marriage, but without the knowledge of or against the will of her parents or guardians. Canon 2353 punishes both abduction by violence and abduction by seduction.[2]

The writer will treat the crime of abduction only in the case wherein there is question of the abduction of a minor girl. Nor will the writer consider the crime of violent abduction, that is when the girl is abducted by means of force or deceit. If force or deceit are employed by the man to carry off the minor girl, there is no difficulty in admitting that this action constitutes the crime of abduction which is punished in canon 2353. In this instance it makes no difference if the woman who is abducted is of major or minor age, for if *raptus violentiae* occurs, it is clear from the first part of canon 2353 that the crime of abduction is present regardless of whether the girl abducted is above or below twenty-one years of age. The canon simply uses the generic term "*mulierem*" without any qualification whatsoever,

[2] Wernz-Vidal: "Distinguitur raptus violentiae et raptus seductionis. Primus consistit in abductione mulieris violenta, i.e., vi vel dolo facta contra ipsius puellae raptae voluntatem; et hic est raptus in sensu magis proprio et stricto acceptus; raptus vero seductionis consistit in abductione mulieris minoris aetatis consentientis quidem, sed insciis vel contradicentibus parentibus aut tutoribus. Uterque in ratione delicti et quoad poenas aequiparatur can. 2353."—*Ius Canonicum,* V, n. 308. The divisions of *raptus* given by various authors will be seen in the course of this present chapter.

and therefore includes adults as well as minors.[8] Hence, if force or deceit are the means used to carry off the minor girl, then there is no difficulty, and all authors admit that the man is guilty of the crime of abduction and is subject to the penalties of canon 2353.

The difficulty in this matter arises in the consideration of the case wherein a minor girl with her own consent, but without the knowledge or consent of her parents or guardians, is carried off by a man for the purpose of marriage. In this instance what is necessary to constitute the crime of abduction? The answer to this question is the main concern of the writer in the present chapter.

Canon 2353 in regard to the minor girl uses the term "*rapuerit*" together with the term "*consentientem*." At first blush these words appear to involve a contradiction, for the word "*rapuerit*" seems to connote or imply the carrying off of the minor girl against her will through the use of force or deceit; while, on the other hand, it is clearly stated in the canon that the minor girl consents to the abduction. If *raptus* were understood in the strict and proper sense of the term there would be present here a contradiction. But one must not rely too much on the strict connotation of the term "*rapuerit*," because even in the pre-Code law two types of abduction were recognized, namely, abduction by violence and abduction by seduction. Under this latter type was included the case in which a minor girl of her own accord consented to be abducted or even asked to be taken away without any persuasion or flattery being used by the man, provided her parents or guardians were in ignorance of or opposed to the abduction. This is evident from De Angelis who defines abduction by seduction in the following manner: "Raptus autem seductionis est: 1° cum mulier ipsa cum viro libere consentit in fugam, *imo et eam expetit* ad matrimonium, obstant tamen, utpote inviti vel inscii sunt, parentes aut tutores, sub quorum potestate est constituta: ideo autem licet improprie seducta dicitur, quia hujus criminis raptus censetur principalis auctor vir, qui mulierem depravaverit seductione.—2° cum mulier blanditiis, illecebris,

[8] "Qui intuitu matrimonii vel explendae libidinis causa rapuerit *mulierem* nolentem vi aut dolo, . . ."

dolisque simul illecta consentit in fugam et in matrimonium, et est vel dicitur vere seducta invitis vel insciis parentibus sub quorum potestate est."[4] According to this definition of De Angelis the concept of abduction was present by the mere fact that the parents or guardians of the minor girl were uninformed about her flight with the man or were opposed to it. De Angelis states that in both types of abduction by seduction, namely whether the girl freely asked to go off with the man or was induced to do so by means of promises or flattery and the like, the injury is against her parents or guardians. It is true that De Angelis goes on to state that abduction by seduction is not an impediment to marriage, but this does not detract from his statement that such action is abduction and constitutes an injury to the parents or guardians.[5]

Likewise Wernz in defining abduction by seduction brings out clearly this same point. His definition reads as follows: "Alter (raptus seductionis) habetur, si mulier sive sui iuris sive praesertim puella minor et in fugam et in matrimonium *aut omnino libere aut blanditiis aliisque modis sine vi seducta consentiens* a viro abducatur in alium locum matrimonii contrahendi causa, at insciis et invitis parentibus vel tutoribus, sub quorum potestate forte adhuc constituta est."[6] When speaking of the matrimonial impediment of abduction Wernz definitely excludes abduction by seduction as constituting such an impediment. Nevertheless he clearly states that abduction by seduction constitutes the crime of abduction on account of the very grave injury inflicted on the parents or guardians. The text wherein Wernz makes these conclusions is the following: "Si puella, quae sui iuris nondum est, sed sub potestate parentum vel tutorum adhuc reperitur constituta, *aut libere et sponte aut blanditiis vel similibus modis non violentis seducta* praemissis sponsalibus vel tractatibus consentiat in abductionem matrimonii celebrandi causa per virum factam etiam insciis vel invitis parentibus aut tutoribus, impedimentum

---

[4] *Praelectiones Iuris Canonici ad Methodum Decretalium Gregorii IX Exactae* (5 vols. in 8, Romae–Parisiis, 1877–1894; Vol. V curavit Nazarenus Gentilini, 1887–1891), lib. IV, tit. I, n. 20, p. 59. Italics are the writer's.

[5] *Loc. cit.*

[6] *Ius Decretalium,* IV, n. 277. Italics are the writer's.

raptus ex iure Tridentino non inducitur, *at committitur crimen raptus propter gravissimam iniuriam parentibus* illatam, si sponsalia non praecesserunt. *Quare raptus in parentes* vel raptus, qui dicitur seductionis, neque ex iure Tridentino neque ex legitima quadam consuetudine Ecclesiae Gallicanae constituunt impedimentum dirimens." [7]

From these texts of the pre-Code authors it is evident that the term "*raptus*" is applicable even in the case when the consent of the abducted party is present, especially when the abducted girl was a minor. The fact that abduction by seduction did not constitute a matrimonial impediment did not prevent it from being termed "*raptus*" because of the fact that the knowledge or the consent of the parents or guardians was lacking. Therefore the fact that the legislator in canon 2353 employs the term "*rapuerit*" with reference to the abduction of a minor girl who consents to go off with the man for the purpose of marriage, but whose parents are uninformed of or are unwilling to the abduction, should not cause any great difficulty. However, some of the authors, as will be demonstrated in this chapter, have failed to see or appreciate this possibility.

Thus Vermeersch-Creusen define abduction by seduction as the case when a minor girl is taken away with her own consent but contrary to the wishes of those to whom she is subject. They state that the reason for this is to protect the immaturity of judgment and weakness of will of the minor girl. They then conclude that the delict or crime of abduction is not committed if the minor girl freely and of her own will asks the man to go off with her, so that her departure is not due to persuasions or deceit on the part of the man.[8] Hence they restrict the crime or delict of abduction to the case in which the minor girl is taken away by means of persuasions or deceit on the part of the man.

[7] *Ibid.*, n. 283. Italics are the writer's.

[8] "Raptus violentiae est abductio mulieris cuiuslibet invitae, libidinis explendae vel matrimonii contrahendi causa. Raptus seductionis habetur, si abducatur eodem fine mulier minoris aetatis consentiens, sed invitis iis quibus commissa est. In priore casu protegitur stricte ipsa libertas mulieris, in altero imbecillitas iudicii et voluntatis. Delictum absit, si mulier minor natu sponte petat ut cum amasio proficiscatur, ita ut suasionibus vel *dolo* amasii profectio non debeatur."—*Epitome,* III, n. 555.

The following criticism of the thought of Vermeersch-Creusen on this subject may be offered. In the first place, if deceit (*dolus*) is the means employed by the man in carrying off the minor girl, the abduction, then, is not by seduction, as Vermeersch-Creusen declare, but by violence according to canon 2353. Moreover, if, as they state, the end and purpose of the law of canon 2353 is the protection of the weakness of judgment and will of the minor girl, then why should not this weakness be protected when the child herself suggests to the man the idea of going off to be married? Furthermore, Vermeersch-Creusen fail to contemplate the case in which the man merely proposes the flight and the minor girl immediately consents to the proposition without any need of persuasion. In such a case it cannot be said that the departure is due to persuasion, flattery and the like on the part of the man. Nor can it be maintained that the minor girl freely asked the man that he go off with her to be married. Therefore at least one must admit that Vermeersch-Creusen's treatment of this question concerning the abduction of a minor girl is not complete, if not incorrect. They seem to overlook entirely the importance of the words "*insciis vel contradicentibus parentibus aut tutoribus*" of canon 2353.

Sipos, in considering this subject of the abduction of a minor girl, follows faithfully the opinion of Vermeersch-Creusen and cites them as his sole authority.[9] Hence the same critical analysis which the writer outlined above concerning the opinion of Vermeersch-Creusen likewise holds for the opinion of Sipos. Consequently there is no need to repeat these objections.

Likewise, Payen, referring to Vermeersch-Creusen as his authority, excludes from the delict of abduction what he terms "*simplex fuga.*" He states that in "*simplex fuga*" the man concedes to the wishes of the girl who, although she is a minor, freely and of her own accord wishes to go off with him without ever having been at first unwilling and then later on induced through persuasion and flattery to flee with him. Payen, like

[9] ". . . raptus seductionis ergo tunc tantum habetur, si mulier minoris aetatis abducatur; si ipsa sponte petat discessum cum viro, sine illius suasionibus vel *dolo,* nullum est delictum."—*Enchiridion Iuris Canonici,* p. 550.

Vermeersch-Creusen, declares that the purpose of the penalty is to protect and safeguard the weakness of mind and will of the minor girl.[10] However, a few pages previous when Payen treats of the matrimonial impediment of abduction, he states that in abduction by seduction the whole injury is inflicted on the uninformed or unwilling parents or guardians of the minor girl.[11] If, therefore, this latter statement is true, it is difficult to understand how this injury to the parents or guardians is removed even by the spontaneous consent on the part of the minor girl. If, on the other hand, the immaturity of judgment and weakness of will of the child is what is being protected, it is also difficult to see why this protection is not extended to the case in which the minor girl freely asks the man to go off with her. Moreover Payen, like Vermeersch-Creusen, states that in *simplex fuga* the man accedes to the wishes of the girl who freely desires to go off with him without being at first unwilling and then induced by means of importunate entreaties, promises or flattery to change her mind. Thus Payen also fails to visualize the case wherein the minor girl would willingly accede to the request of the man without any flattery or persuasion or like means being used by him.

It is the opinion of the writer that, when a minor girl is involved, the concept of the crime of abduction is verified whenever her parents or guardians do not know of or are opposed to the child's departure. Whether the minor girl suggests the going off to the man, or whether she freely and spontaneously accedes to his suggestion, or whether she is won over by persuasion, flattery or promises without the use of force or deceit does not alter the case, for in all these instances the delict of abduction is present. The crime in such instances consists in the violation

[10] "Itaque, in hoc canone (2353), punitur raptus violentiae, raptus seductionis, non autem simplex fuga, etiamsi mulier sit aetate minor (can. 88, § 1): raptus violentiae, ut muniatur ipsa mulieris libertas; raptus seductionis, ut imbecillitas judicii et voluntatis directe protegatur; non autem simplex fuga, nam tum vir concedit postulationi mulieris, quae, etsi minor, omnino sponte vult cum amasio fugere, quin prius nolens, fuerit blanditiis et suasionibus ad fugam adducta."—*De Matrimonio,* I, n. 1281.

[11] "Raptus seductionis . . . ita ut tota injuria insciis vel contradicentibus parentibus aut tutoribus inferatur."—*ibid.,* n. 1264.

of the right of parental authority—a right which cannot be forfeited by the mere consent of the minor girl herself. It is immaterial, therefore, whether the minor girl gave her consent spontaneously or only after persuasion and similar means were employed. A sufficient number of authors clearly state that the crime of abduction with regard to a minor girl is committed in any of these instances. Quotations from these authors will serve to substantiate this statement. Because of the importance of the words used by the different authors the writer deems it both helpful and necessary to reproduce in the body of the text or in the footnotes of this dissertation these quotations from the various authors.

Cappello, in treating of the matrimonial impediment of abduction, states: " Si mulier est sui iuris, aut consentientibus parentibus, tutoribus, etc., *aufugit,* omnes admittunt raptum deesse, cum nulla violentia habeatur. Si vero mulier est adhuc sub potestate parentum, tutorum, etc., et iis invitis aut insciis (qui in casu praesumuntur inviti) *aufugit,* item deest impedimentum. Ratio, quia *raptus in parentes vel tutores* puellae aetate minoris commissus, constituit quidem *crimen* non tamen impedimentum matrimoniale." [12] The use of the term *aufugit* by Cappello seems at least to indicate clearly a mutual agreement to the departure so that the abduction is committed solely against the parents or guardians of the minor girl. But this according to Cappello constitutes the crime of *raptus* contemplated by the legislator in the latter section of canon 2353.

Chelodi, in considering abduction as a matrimonial impediment, writes thus: " Raptus, autem, qui dicitur seductionis, cum mulier tum in fugam tum in matrimonium consentit, *aut omnino sponte* aut blanditiis et precibus, nulla vero vi seducta, nullum producit impedimentum. Imo, si puella maior est et tractatus praecesserunt nuptiales, ne contraria quidem praesumptio habetur, quae stat adversus eum qui, nullo praemisso tractatu, mulierem rapit. Quae praesumptio maxima est at semper iuris tantum et non iuris et de iure, si puella in minore aetate insciis vel invitis parentibus *aufugit,* a fortiori si neque sponsalia neque saltem tractatus nup-

[12] *De Sacramentis,* III, 524. Italics are the writer's.

tiales praecesserunt. At, *probato* puellae tum in fugum tum in matrimonium *consensu,* praesumptio dilabitur; nam *raptus in parentes* a iure matrimoniali nostro est alienus. *Adest tamen, in casu, crimen raptus.*" [13] Thus Chelodi considers that abduction by seduction is present regardless of whether the minor girl freely and of her own accord consents to go off with the man, or whether she is induced through persuasion and flattery to give her consent. In either instance, then, abduction by seduction is had. Furthermore, the author states that whenever a girl of minor age goes off with a man there is present a strong presumption against her liberty or freedom in so departing. However he adds that, if it is later proven that the girl consented to the flight, then this presumption against her freedom of action is overthrown and in such a case there occurs *raptus in parentes,* which does not constitute a matrimonial impediment but nevertheless does constitute the crime of *raptus.* Moreover, he does not make any distinction in this connection whether the consent of the minor girl was freely and spontaneously given, or if it was obtained only after persuasion and flattery had been employed, but he simply declares that the crime of abduction exists. This same author is quoted by Coronata as accepting the explanation of abduction given by the civil lawyer Michele Battista, and affirming that this same concept of abduction as given in the Italian Civil Law Code is contained in canon 2353. This explanation reads as follows: " 'La dottrina distingue il ratto proprio, quello cioè commesso con l'impiego della violenza o della frode, dal ratto improprio, il quale richiede il consenso della persona rapita. Di tali due forme il Codice colloca la prima fra i delitti contro la moralità publica e il buon costume (art. 522 e 523) e la seconda fra i delitti contro la famiglia (art 573, 574), poichè nella prima prevale l'offesa alla libertà della vittima, e nell'altra viene offeso il principale attributo della potestà patria o tutoria, che e quello della vigilanza e difesa morale dei figlioli e dei pupilii.'—Michele Battista, *Codice penale, Codice di procedura penale illustrati,* 1931, p. 563, nota 1. Codex noster duas formas delicti raptus utique agnoscit at de ambabus in eadem sede id est hoc c. 2353 agit." [14]

[13] *Ius Matrimoniale,* p. 94. Italics are the writer's.

[14] Cited from Coronata, *Institutiones Iuris Canonici,* IV, 478, nota 10.

Thus Chelodi teaches that the legislator in canon 2353 punishes abduction by violence because of the offense against the liberty of the victim, and abduction by seduction because of the violation of the parent's or guardian's right of vigilance and moral protection of their children or wards. Furthermore, Chelodi in another passage clearly teaches that in abduction by seduction the violence is exercised not on the minor girl but rather on her parents; hence in penal matters the concept of *raptus* is not understood in a strict sense.[15]

Salucci also considers the penalty of canon 2353. When he comments on the first type of abduction mentioned in this canon he insists that it be violent, namely that the abduction be done by force, fear or deceit, and he excludes the delict if the woman consents.[16] On the other hand, when Salucci considers the second part of canon 2353, which deals with the abduction of a minor girl, he clearly and emphatically states that, even if she lets herself be taken away and spontaneously consents to the flight, the crime of abduction is present with all its juridical consequences, because the law does not presume her to be in a position to dispose of herself and, in fact, places her under the *patriapotestas.*[17]

Pistocchi, too, is clear in stating that *raptus* in the case of a

---

[15] "Raptus, qui communiter definitur 'violenta abductio mulieris de loco tuto in locum non tutum,' latissimo sensu in iure criminali sumitur, ita ut complectatur tum raptum violentiae tum seductionis, quo potius in parentes quam in mulierem, consentientem quidem sed minorem violentia exercetur, tum raptum matrimonii causa tum explendae libidinis."—*Ius Poenale,* p. 109.

[16] "È poi necessario che il ratto sia violento, fatto cioè con la forza o col timore oppure con l' inganno. Tutto ciò suppone manifestamente che la donna non sia consenziente: se lo fosse, non avremmo il ratto, ma, caso mai, la fuga."—*Il Diritto Penale secondo il Codice di Diritto Canonico* (2 vols., Subiaco: Tipografia dei Monasteri, 1926–1930), II, n. 263; this work will hereafter be cited as *Il Diritto Penale.*

[17] "Il legislatore, avendo di mira la tutela della libertà individuale, prevede e risolve il caso di una minorenne che si lasci *spontaneamente* rapire *all' insaputa* o contro il consenso dei suoi. Codesta fanciulla, attesa la sua età, non si presume in grado di poter disparre di sè e la legge la pone infatti sotto la patria potesta: *pertanto anche se essa acconsentisse* a farsi rapire avremmo egualmente il ratto con tutte le conseguenze di diritto."—*ibid.,* n. 264. Italics are the writer's.

minor girl is constituted by the fact that the consent of the parents or guardians does not intervene. In such a case the crime of abduction is had, and the man incurs the penalties of canon 2353.[18]

Ayrinhac-Lydon in distinguishing the two types of abduction use as a synonym for abduction by seduction of a minor girl the term "elopement."[19] And in another work these authors in discussing the extent of the matrimonial impediment of abduction exclude elopement as constituting the impediment, and therein they declare that elopement implies or connotes a mutual agreement.[20] Hence it may be stated that according to Ayrinhac-Lydon, if a man and a minor girl agree to go off to be married unknown to her parents or guardians or against their will, while there is no matrimonial impediment of abduction present, there is nevertheless in this instance the crime of abduction according to canon 2353.

Woywod, too, uses the term "elope,"[21] for in translating canon 2353 he writes: "Men who with a view to marriage or for the gratification of lust, carry off a woman by force or deceit against her will, or a woman of minor age who consents to *elope* without the knowledge or against the objection of her parents or

---

[18] ". . . il fatto del consenso della donna minore, tanto per l' uno quanto per l' altro motivo, non toglie la figura del ratto, colpito de le pene, qui indicate, quando non interviene il consenso dei genitori o dei tutori."—*I Canoni Penali del Codice Ecclesiastico Esposti e Commentati* (Torino-Roma: Marietti, 1925), p. 187.

[19] "It is called abduction by violence when the woman is carried off against her will, by force or deceit; and abduction by seduction *or elopement* when a minor is taken away with her own consent, but without the knowledge or against the will of her parents or guardians."—*Penal Legislation,* n. 311. Italics are the writer's.

[20] "Abduction is not to be confused with elopement, for this connotes mutual agreement"—*Marriage Legislation,* p. 161.

[21] The dictionary gives only two definitions of the term "elope." The first and usual meaning is "to run away from home with a lover; originally of a married woman only, now also of an unmarried woman (usually intending to be married to her companion in flight)"; the second meaning is "to abscond or slip away." Cf. *Webster's New International Dictionary of the English Language* (2. ed., unabridged, Springfield, Mass.: G. & C. Merriam Co., 1942).

guardians, . . ."[22] Hence Woywod likewise teaches that, when a minor girl unknown to her parents or guardians or against their will agrees to go off with a man in view of marriage, the crime of abduction, which is punished in canon 2353, is had.

Finally Petrovits, in discussing the matrimonial impediment of abduction, writes as follows: "The authors generally distinguish between *raptus seductionis* et *raptus violentiae.* The former is abduction by seduction, *popularly styled elopement.* The latter implies violence employed by the captor in order to accomplish his end. Abduction by seduction does not give rise to a diriment impediment, for it presupposes that the woman signified her willingness both to the flight and to the marriage, *regardless of the fact whether her consent was spontaneous or the result of flattery, allurement or cajolery.* In this case should the woman be under age an injustice is offered to the non-consenting parents or guardians, but the Tridentine decree on which this law is based does not take their will into consideration; its purpose is merely to safeguard the freedom of the woman in the choice of her consort."[23] Hence it is clear that Petrovits considers as abduction by seduction the case in which a minor girl freely and of her own accord elopes with a man without the need of being induced through flattery or persuasion to give her consent to the flight.

Other authors, while not so clear in describing the manner in which the consent of the minor girl is obtained, nevertheless do state clearly and certainly that in the case of abduction by seduction of a minor girl the injury and violence is directed against the parents or guardians. Hence, according to these authors abduction by seduction is a crime against the parents or guardians of the child, and it is for this reason that the legislator punishes the crime in canon 2353. The writer will now consider in detail the teaching of these authors.

Sole asserts that when a man leaves with a minor girl without the knowledge of her parents or against their will, he is subject

[22] *A Practical Commentary on the Code of Canon Law* (6. ed., 2 vols., New York: Joseph F. Wagner, Inc., 1941), II, n. 2208. Italics are the writer's.

[23] *The New Church Law on Matrimony,* n. 291. Italics are the writer's.

to the penalties of canon 2353 because of the injury done to the parents or guardians of the girl.[24]

Likewise according to Eichmann the crime of abduction exists when a minor girl though consenting goes off with a man provided her parents or tutors are in ignorance of it or are unwilling. He states that the violation of liberty in this instance is against the parents or tutors, for they are deprived of their right of decision.[25]

Wernz-Vidal, as has been seen in their definition of abduction by seduction, do not distinguish as to the manner in which the consent of the minor girl is given, that is, whether she consented spontaneously or only after the man induced her to consent by means of promises, flattery, etc. They simply state that, if the minor girl consents to go off with a man with a view to marry without informing her parents or guardians or against their will, it is *raptus seductionis*.[26] However, they explicitly declare that the violence in this type of abduction is directed not against the minor girl who is abducted but rather against her parents and tutors.[27]

Blat, in commenting on the provision of canon 2353 which concerns the abduction of a minor girl who consents to go off

---

[24] "Hinc si quis rapiat puellam minoris aetatis, . . . consentientem quidem, sed insciis vel contradicentibus parentibus aut tutoribus, incurrit pariter poenam, de qua in canone, aliisque poenis plectandus est, *ob iniuriam illatam parentibus vel tutoribus*."—*De Delictis et Poenis, Praelectiones in Lib. V Codicis Iuris Canonici* (Romae: F. Pustet, 1920), p. 329; hereafter this work will be cited *De Delictis et Poenis*. Italics are the writer's.

[25] Strafbar ist dei Entführung einer minderjährigen Frauensperson (zwischen vollendetem 12. und vollendetem 21. Lebensjahr, can. 88 §§ 1, 2) selbst in dem Falle, das dieselbe in die Entführung einwilligt, wenn die Entführung ohne Wissen oder gegen den ausgesprochenen Willen der Eltern oder Vormünder derselben geschehen ist. Das Freiheitsdelikt richtet sich in diesem Falle gegen die Eltern bzw. Vormünder, deren Bestimmungsrecht verletzt worden ist."—*Das Strafrecht*, p. 182.

[26] *Ius Canonicum*, V, n. 308.

[27] "Iure Codicis, ut apparet ex transcripto canone, delictum raptus, quoad substantiam consistens in violenta abductione mulieris de loco tuto ad locum non tutum, complectitur tum raptum violentiae, cui proprie competit notio data, tum raptum seductionis, *quo potius in parentes violentia exercetur,* dum mulier consentiens equidem sed minor, insciis et contradicentibus parentibus aut tutoribus, abducitur."—*Ius Canonicum,* VII, 530.

with the man for the purpose of marriage, places the very essence of this type of abduction in the fact that the parents or guardians of the child are uninformed of her departure or are opposed to it.[28]

De Smet considers *raptus seductionis* and terms such abduction as *raptus in parentes* thereby indicating that the injury is committed against the parents or guardians of the minor girl.[29]

Coronata is not clear nor is he certain why the abduction of a minor girl, who consents to the abduction, constitutes a delict. He states, on the one hand, that a minor girl, even though she consents to the abduction, is considered to be taken away by means of deceit, and therefore the crime of abduction occurs. On the other hand, he proffers the opinion that perhaps such an abduction is a delict because it does violence to the *patriapotestas* under which the girl is placed.[30] These two reasons advanced by Coronata in order to explain why this type of abduction is a crime are mutually exclusive, for in no way can they be reconciled. Moreover, if deceit is considered to be present this would not be the special type of abduction which is proper to the case of a minor girl, but rather a presumption that it is abduction by deceit which constitutes the crime of abduction in reference to any woman and which is punished in the first part of canon 2353. Furthermore, according to Coronata, if a minor girl consents to go off with a man for the purpose of marriage, the crime of abduction is constituted by the fact that she is considered

---

[28] "Consentientem quidem in abductionem, quae proinde non est nisi apparenter violenta aut dolosa, sed hoc quatenus fit illa insciis vel contradicentibus (ac alterutrum sufficit) parentibus aut tutoribus, queis pro diversitate casuum subiiciatur."—*Commentarium Textus Codicis Iuris Canonici* (6 vols., Romae: Collegio "Angelico," 1920–1927), lib. V, *De Delictis et Poenis* (1924), V, n. 195.

[29] "Habetur 2o raptus seductionis, *seu raptus in parentes,* uti dicitur, consistens in abductione mulieris minoris aetatis, consentientis quidem, sed insciis vel contradicentibus parentibus aut tutoribus."—*De Sponsalibus et Matrimonio,* n. 646.

[30] "Mulier minor etsi consentiens censetur dolo abduci et proinde etsi sine vi abducatur, eius abductio delictum constituit; vel si mavis raptus eius delictum censetur quatenus vim facit patriae potestati sub qua ipsa puella constituta est."—*Institutiones Iuris Canonici,* IV, 479–480.

to have been taken away by deceit. If it is proven, then, that no deceit was employed by the man, the crime would not be had. Therefore the special prescription for a minor girl in canon 2353 would reduce itself to this, namely, that she is always presumed to have been taken away by deceit even though she consents, provided her parents or guardians are uninformed of or are unwilling to her departure. In other words, the lack of knowledge or consent on the part of the parents or tutors of the minor girl would be the foundation only for this presumption, and would not really be an essential and necessary requirement for this type of abduction. However, canon 2353 does not allow such an interpretation nor does it in any way confirm such an explanation. The canon merely enacts that when any woman is taken away unwillingly by the use of force or deceit, and when any minor girl is taken away with her own consent but unknown to her parents or guardians or against their will, the crime of abduction is present. Thus the canon names two specific types of abduction, namely, the abduction by force or deceit of any woman against her will whether she is of major or minor age, and the abduction of a minor girl with her own consent but unknown to her parents or guardians or against their will. On the other hand, if Coronata's second explanation is accepted, the crime of abduction would be present any time the parents of the minor girl were in ignorance of or were opposed to her departure. Since Coronata, then, is uncertain as to the reason why this type of abduction constitutes a delict, it is impossible to determine his requisites for the crime. However, since he considers the possibility that such abduction is a crime because the injury is done to the parents, it may be said that he is at least not expressly contrary to the opinion that any time a minor girl freely goes off with a man for the purpose of marriage unknown to her parents or against their will the crime which is punished in canon 2353 is committed.

Concerning a minor girl there is no doubt that the crime of abduction is present when the child is carried off against her will for the purpose of marriage by means of force or deceit. In this instance the delict is committed regardless of the age of the woman whether she is a major or a minor. The crime of abduction would be present in such a case even though the parents or guardians should know of and consent to the carrying off of the girl, because their knowledge or consent cannot change the nature of abduction by violence or deceit. This type of abduction is considered in the law of canon 2353 with no qualification or restrictions. The authors raise no difficulty in this regard. It is worthy of note that when a woman is carried off by means of deceit she may consent to the material abduction or departure, but be entirely unaware of the purpose the man had in abducting her. Hence she cannot be said to consent to the abduction as such, that is, to the going off in view of marriage. It is for this reason that when deceit is employed the person is still unwilling as regards the abduction considered as a whole, and therefore the legislator in canon 2353 uses the word "*nolentem*" in considering abduction effected by the means of deceit.

With regard to the minor girl the crime of abduction is extended by the canon to include the case in which she is taken away with her own consent for the purpose of marriage, but unknown to her parents or guardians or contrary to their wishes. Hence this second part of canon 2353 deals with the case in which no violence or deceit is used. All authors admit and clearly teach that, if flattery, persuasion, promises or any similar means are employed in order to induce the minor girl to consent to the flight whenever the parents or guardians are in ignorance of or are contrary to the departure, the delict is committed.[31] However, for some reason or other a few authors insist on restricting the crime only to this case, namely, in which the girl is at first unwilling and then without employing force or deceit is won over by means of promises and flattery to go off with the man for the purpose of marriage. Only if the man uses promises, persuasion, flattery and the like to obtain the consent of the girl do these authors admit the crime of abduction.[32] It is not clear

[31] Wernz-Vidal, *Ius Canonicum,* V, n. 308; VII, 530; Vermeersch-Creusen, *Epitome,* III, n. 555; Payen, *De Matrimonio,* I, n. 1281; Chelodi, *Ius Matrimoniale,* n. 89; Farrugia, *De Matrimonio,* p. 323; Salucci, *Il Diritto Penale,* II, n. 264; De Smet, *De Sponsalibus et Matrimonio,* n. 654; Claeys Bouuaert-Simenon, *Manuale Iuris Canonici,* II, 271.

[32] Vermeersch-Creusen, *Epitome,* III, n. 555; Sipos, *Enchiridion Iuris Canonici,* p. 550; Payen, *De Matrimonio,* I, n. 1281.

to the writer why they should make such a distinction. The canon merely states that abduction occurs even if the girl consents to the abduction without the knowledge of or contrary to the wishes of her parents or guardians. It makes no distinction as to whether the girl suggested the abduction, or whether she spontaneously agreed to it, or whether she was at first unwilling and then later won over by means of promises and flattery to give her consent to the flight. The manner in which she gave her consent does not seem to be of importance. The essential requisite is that the minor girl consents to go off without the knowledge of or contrary to the will of her parents or guardians. If a minor girl would consent to go off with a man in view of marriage even though she had been induced through persuasion and flattery to give her consent, there would be no crime of abduction present, if the parents or guardians knew about these persuasions or even suggested them to the man. Hence, in this instance when the minor consents to the abduction the important element appears to be the knowledge or consent of the parents or guardians. This point is brought out clearly by the number of authors already quoted, for, when they consider this type of abduction, they place its complete malice in the fact that a grave injury is done to the authority of the parents and guardians.[33]

Hence the crime of abduction is committed regardless of whether the child asks to go off, or whether she consents spontaneously, or whether she gives her consent only after promises and flattery have been employed by the man, for the consent of the minor girl cannot relinquish or destroy the right of the parents or guardians. If the minor herself suggested the flight to the man and he went off with her, the injury would still be present because he would be taking advantage of the child, since in this case she would not have the watchful protection of her parents or guardians.

The writer holds that canon 2353 applies to any case in which a minor girl consents to go off with a man for the purpose of

---

[33] Chelodi, *Ius Poenale*, p. 109; Pistocchi, *I Canoni Penali del Codice Ecclesiastico Esposti e Commentati*, p. 187; Sole, *De Delictis et Poenis*, p. 329; Eichmann, *Das Strafrecht*, p. 182; Wernz-Vidal, *Ius Canonicum*, VII, 530; Blat, *Commentarium*, V, n. 195.

marriage when her parents or guardians do not know of the departure or are opposed to it. Therefore, he likewise maintains that any time two persons present themselves for marriage and one of them is a minor girl whose parents or guardians do not know of or are opposed to the going away for the purpose of marriage, the man in this case violates canon 2353 and is subject to the penalties stated therein.

Canon 1034 mentions that minors must not contract marriage against the reasonable wishes of their parents. Hence the same must be understood in canon 2353. The term *rationabiliter* could not have been used by the legislator in canon 2353, because this canon treats also of the crime of abduction for the purpose of gratification of lust, and the parents could never be unreasonably unwilling to such action. Therefore the legislator employs the term "*contradicentibus*" in order to include abduction with the intention of marriage and abduction for immoral purposes.

This latter section of canon 2353, which punishes the abduction of a minor girl and which is not an impediment to marriage, since the girl consents to the abduction for the purpose of marriage, is new legislation. Prior to the Code of Canon Law the legislation punished only the contracting of a marriage which was null because of the matrimonial impediment of abduction. This matrimonial impediment of abduction included only abduction by violence, namely the carrying off of a girl by force against her will.[34] Hence, *raptus seductionis,* namely the case in which a minor girl freely and spontaneously gave her consent or consented to the going off only after flattery or promises were used by the man, was not punished by the law of the Council of Trent. Canon 2353, however, does punish this type of abduction, and consequently it must be said that this penalty is new legislation in the

[34] Conc. Trident., sess. XXIV, *de ref. matrim.,* c. 6: "Decernit Sancta Synodus, inter raptorem et raptam, quamdiu ipsa in potestate raptoris manserit, nullum posse consistere matrimonium. Quod si rapta, a raptore separata et in loco tuto et libero constituta, illum in virum habere consenserit, eam raptor in uxorem habeat, et nihilominus raptor ipse ac omnes illi consilium, auxilium et favorem praebentes, sint ipso iure excommunicati ac perpetuo infames, omniumque dignitatum incapaces, et si clerici fuerint, de proprio gradu decidant. Teneatur praeterea raptor mulierem raptam, sive eam uxorem duxerit sive non duxerit, decenter arbitrio iudicis dotare."

discipline of the Church.[35] It may be noted here that pre-Code canonists admitted abduction by seduction of a woman who was of age.[36] However canon 2353 explicitly enacts that in abduction by seduction the penalty is incurred only if the woman abducted is a minor, that is, according to canon 88, § 1, one who is below twenty-one years of age. Sole errs in teaching that the term "*minor*" in canon 2353 signifies a girl who has not as yet completed her twelfth year of age.[37]

The legislator in canon 2353 enacts both a *latae sententiae* and a *ferendae sententiae* penalty as punishment for the crime of abduction.[38] The *latae sententiae* penalty is the exclusion of the abductor from performing legitimate ecclesiastical acts which are listed in canon 2256, 2°.[39] The *ferendae sententiae* penalty consists in other punishments which may be inflicted on him according to the gravity of his crime. Moreover, necessary accomplices incur the penalty of canon 2353 in accordance with the norms of canons 2231 and 2209, §§ 1, 2 and 3. If a pastor violates the prescription of canon 1034 and assists at the marriage of a minor girl who has eloped with a man, he does not incur the penalties of canon 2353. For the pastor in such a case cannot be considered an accomplice to the crime which is punished in canon 2353, since the delict mentioned in this canon does not respect the actual celebration of the marriage.

[35] Ayrinhac-Lydon: "As is clearly seen from the text, the Council deals here exclusively with that form of the crime of abduction which gives rise to an impediment, *i.e.*, abduction by violence with a view to marriage. . . . The present canon is of wider scope but less severe than the Decree of Trent. It punishes abduction whether by violence or by seduction, whether with intent to marry or to gratify lust."—*Penal Legislation,* p. 248.

[36] Wernz, *Ius Decretalium,* IV, n. 277; Feije, *De Impedimentis et Dispensationibus Matrimonialibus,* n. 147.

[37] *De Delictis et Poenis,* p. 329.

[38] ". . . ipso iure exclusus habeatur ab actibus legitimis ecclesiasticis et insuper aliis poenis pro gravitate culpae plectatur."

[39] ". . . Nomine autem actuum legitimorum ecclesiasticorum significantur: munus administratoris gerere bonorum ecclesiasticorum; partes agere iudicis, auditoris et relatoris, defensoris vinculi, promotoris iustitiae et fidei, notarii et cancellarii, cursoris, et apparitoris, advocati et procuratoris in causis ecclesiasticis; munus patrini agere in sacramentis baptismi et confirmationis; suffragium ferre in electionibus ecclesiasticis; ius patronatus exercere."

CHAPTER X

THE AMERICAN CIVIL LAW AND THE MARRIAGE OF MINORS

Just as the Canon law has determined a fixed age below which a valid marriage is impossible, so also the civil law of all the States has fixed a definite age for marriage. Moreover, the civil law has various requirements concerning the age of minority in marriage, and these civil regulations are to a great extent similar to the canonical legislation. Since the writer is not concerned in this dissertation with the diriment impediment of nonage in Canon law neither will he treat this impediment as found in the civil law, but he will consider only the civil legislation of the different States in regard to the contraction of marriage by those who are above the necessary age, but who are still minors in relation to marriage. This period is frequently termed in the civil law as the " age of parental consent." In the present chapter the writer will consider this period.

At common law there was no requirement that parents or guardians consent to the marriage of their children or wards who were under a certain age. If the male child was over fourteen years of age and the female was above twelve years of age, a valid marriage was possible. Even without the consent of their parents or guardians their marriage was valid, and was recognized as such by the civil courts. However in the year 1753 in England the famous "Lord Hardwicke's Marriage Act" was introduced and became law in England. By this Act the marriage of minors was held to be void if entered into without the consent of the parents or guardians. If the father was living, his consent was essential for a valid marriage; if he was dead, the consent of the mother or guardian or the Court of Chancery was necessary in order that the marriage of the minor be valid. Great evils resulted from this Act, and the whole subject concerning the marriage of minors was in a state of confusion during this period. These difficulties caused by the Act necessitated a change in the legislation. Subsequent law, while requiring the consent of the parents or guardians for the marriage of minors, did not make their consent a requisite for the validity of the marriage. The absence of the parental consent in no case rendered the marriage of the minor void.[1]

Thus the common law of England recognized the validity of marriages contracted by minors unknown to their parents or guardians or against their will. When the American Colonies adopted this English common law the same principle of the common law regarding the marriage of minors was accepted in America. Lord Hardwicke's Marriage Act was never in force in America. However, all the States in the United States have changed by statute the requirements of the common law concerning the marriage of minors by ruling that until a certain age has been attained by the minor the consent of his parents or guardians is necessary. The absence of this consent, however, according to the present statutes of all the forty-eight States does not invalidate the marriage. If the civil legislator desires the presence of the consent of parents or guardians for the validity of the minor's marriage, he must expressly state so in the statute; otherwise such a requirement will not be considered essential for the validity of the marriage. In other words, according to the rules of interpretation of the civil law, unless the statute expressly declares a marriage contracted without the necessary consent of the parents or other requirements of the statute to be a nullity, such a statute will be considered to be directory only, so that the marriage will be held valid, although disobedience of the statute may entail penalties for the licensing and officiating authorities.[2]

The age under which parental permission is needed for the

---

[1] Cf. Bishop, *New Commentaries on Marriage, Divorce, and Separation* (2 vols., Chicago: T. H. Flood & Co., 1891), I, nn. 552, 555.

[2] Cf. People vs. Ham, et al, 206 Ill. App. 543; Reifschneider vs. Reifschneider, 241, Ill. 92; Campbell vs. Beck, 50 Ill. 171; Olsen vs. People, 219 Ill. 40; Fisher vs. Bernard, 65 Vt. 663, 27 Atl. 316; Vernier, *American Family Laws,* I, 120; Bishop, *New Commentaries on Marriage, Divorce, and Separation,* I, n. 559.

marriage varies according to the statutes of the different States. However, in this matter there is more uniformity in State legislation than on most points concerning civil marriage legislation. Generally speaking the various States have determined a higher age for males than for females. Of the forty-eight States thirty-one require the consent of parents or guardians for the marriage of any male under twenty-one years of age and for any female who has not completed her eighteenth year. This is required by statute law in the following States: Alabama, Arizona, Arkansas, California, Colorado, Delaware, Illinois, Indiana, Iowa, Kansas, Maine, Maryland, Massachusetts, Minnesota, Mississippi, Missouri, Montana, Nebraska, Nevada, New Jersey, New Mexico, New York, North Dakota, Oklahoma, Oregon, South Dakota, Texas, Utah, Vermont, Washington, and Wisconsin. By statute law the age of parental consent is fixed at twenty-one years for both men and women in the States of Connecticut, Florida, Kentucky, Louisiana, Nebraska, Ohio, Pennsylvania, Rhode Island, Virginia, West Virginia, and Wyoming.[3] The civil law for the States of Idaho, South Carolina, and Tennessee determines this age to be eighteen years for both sexes. Statute law in the State of New Hampshire places this age of parental consent at twenty years for males and eighteen for females. The law for the District of Columbia is in keeping with the requirements of the vast majority of the States and requires the consent of the parents or the guardians for any male under twenty-one years of age and for any female below the age of eighteen.[4] The States of Georgia and Michigan have no statute law which determines a special age for males regarding the necessity of parental consent for marriage. Consequently it is sufficient in these States if the male child has attained marriageable age, which in Georgia is seventeen years and in Michigan eighteen years of age. However, statute laws in both these States require that a girl who has

[3] Cf. *Laws on Domestic Relations in the 48 States, District of Columbia, England, Australia, The Provinces of Canada,* compiled by the Committee on War Work of the American Bar Association, 1943–1944, pp. 16, 24, 44, 47, 76, 94, 101, 104, 120, 127, 133; hereafter this work will be cited as *Laws on Domestic Relations;* Vernier, *American Family Laws,* I, 121–124.

[4] Cf. *Laws on Domestic Relations,* pp. 22, 30, 81, 107, 111.

not yet completed her eighteenth year obtain the consent of her parents or guardians for marriage.[5]

In regard to the details of these various statutes concerning the need of parental consent, there is no uniformity among the States. Thus some States require the consent of both parents, while other States accept the consent of one parent as sufficient. In the laws of a few States it is expressly stated that the parent or other relative having the custody of the child must consent to the minor's marriage.[6] In many States the law demands that the consent of the father is to be obtained; if he is absent or dead the consent of the mother is then needed. This is true in Kansas, Kentucky, Montana, Nevada, Tennessee, Virginia, West Virginia, and Wyoming. The District of Columbia has a similar provision.[7] If the parents of the minor child are dead and no guardian of his person or estate has been appointed, then no consent other than that of the child himself is needed for the marriage. This is true in Maine, Indiana, Massachusetts, Michigan, New Jersey, North Dakota, Vermont and Oregon. In the State of Pennsylvania the presiding judge of the Orphan's Court appoints a guardian for the minor child merely for the purpose of giving consent to the marriage whenever the parents of the minor are dead and when no guardian had previously been appointed. In these same circumstances the States of Colorado, Connecticut, Delaware, Ohio, Texas, Virginia, and Wisconsin demand that the minor obtain the consent of the civil official named in the law before he may contract marriage. In Connecticut, Texas, Virginia, and Wisconsin this civil official is the presiding judge of the Probate Court of the County in which the application for the marriage license is made. In the State of Delaware the judge of the Juvenile Court of Wilmington is the official who is competent to give the needed consent, while in the State of Ohio it is the

---

[5] Cf. *Laws on Domestic Relations,* pp. 27, 59; Vernier, *American Family Laws,* I, 121–122.

[6] The States of New Mexico, North Carolina, South Carolina, Wisconsin, and Wyoming expressly mention that the parent or relative having custody of the minor is the one who is to give consent. Cf. *Martindale-Hubbell Law Directory,* II; Vernier, *American Family Laws,* I, 123–124.

[7] *Ibid.,* pp. 121–124.

judge of the Juvenile Court of the County in which the minor resides. In Colorado the law concedes to the minister the right to decide whether the minor should be permitted to contract the marriage.

The statute law of Arizona, Kansas, Montana, Nevada, Tennessee, Texas, Virginia, West Virginia, and Wyoming expressly enact that the consent of only the father of the minor is necessary. The law of the State of Vermont simply requires the consent of one of the parents or guardian. In other States the law enacts that the consent of the father, mother, or guardian is necessary. Hence in these States it is sufficient if either the father or mother consents to the marriage, and it is immaterial whether the consenting parent is the father or mother of the minor. This is true of the law of Arkansas, Connecticut, Idaho, Illinois, Louisiana, Maryland, Massachusetts, Michigan, Missouri, Nebraska, New Hampshire, North Dakota, Oklahoma, Oregon, Rhode Island, South Dakota, and Washington.[8]

In the State of New Hampshire, if a male under twenty years of age or a female who has not completed her eighteenth year of age contract marriage without the consent of at least one of the parents or guardians, the marriage contract can be declared void. Hence in this State lack of parental approbation may be termed a diriment impediment which renders the marriage voidable at the option of either of the parties, provided they have not lived together after attaining the necessary marriageable age of twenty years and eighteen years respectively. Therefore in New Hampshire this age is properly speaking the age of consent for marriage and not the age of parental consent. The reason, then, why in this State the marriage of a minor below these years is voidable is because he is below the age at which marriage may be contracted, and not, therefore, because parental consent was absent.[9] However, in New Hampshire the Justice of the Superior Court of the State or the Judge of the Probate Court of the County in which the person who is below the legal age for marriage resides may permit a male child between the years of

---

[8] *Ibid.*, pp. 121–124.

[9] Alford, *Jus Matrimoniale*, p. 208; *Laws on Domestic Relations*, pp. 81–82.

fourteen and twenty and a female between the years of thirteen and eighteen to contract marriage.[10]

The statutes of certain States expressly provide that the law concerning the consent of parents or guardians does not oblige a minor who is contracting marriage for a second time. Hence all minors who have been previously married need not obtain parental consent for a second marriage in the States of Alabama, California, Colorado, Florida, Kentucky, Maryland, Minnesota, Nevada, Ohio, Utah, and Virginia. This same provision is found in the law of the District of Columbia.[11] Even though the statutes of the other States do not expressly mention that consent of the parents is not necessary for the contracting of a second marriage, nevertheless this provision is understood, for, according to the laws of all States, emancipation from parental control is effected by means of marriage.[12] Hence in no State of the United States would a minor need the consent of his parents or guardians when the contracting of a second marriage is concerned.

The manner in which the consent of the parents or guardians is to be given varies in different States. Statutes of some States require that the parents or guardians appear personally before the licensing official and there testify that they consent to the marriage of their minor child or ward. In the State of Illinois the parent or guardian must appear personally and make an affidavit testifying to the age of the child. Similar legislation is found in Michigan, Missouri, Nevada, and Rhode Island. In New York, if the parents of the minor live within the State, they must personally appear; if they live outside the State their written consent properly authenticated suffices. Wyoming has the same legislation as New York concerning the manner in which the parents or guardians are to give their consent. The statutes of the vast majority of the States accept either a verbal consent before a civil official or an expression of the consent in writing.[13] In the

---

[10] Vernier, *American Family Laws,* I, 126; cf. *Martindale-Hubbell Law Directory,* II.

[11] Alford, *Jus Matrimoniale,* pp. 58–61; Vernier, *American Family Laws,* I, 121–124.

[12] Vernier, *American Family Laws,* V, 224–257.

[13] Cf. Vernier, *American Family Laws,* I, 121–124.

statutes of Arizona, Colorado, Indiana, and Louisiana no specific form is mentioned as to how the consent of the parents or guardians is to be given.

The State enforces this law concerning the necessity of parental consent for the marriage of minors by withholding a marriage license from the minor until he receives this needed consent. The State then enacts severe penalties in punishment of license officials who would issue a license to a minor without observing the formalities set forth in law. The State also punishes with grave penalties the officiants at such a marriage.[14] This is the only means the State employs in order to enforce this statute. It does not declare that marriages contracted by minors without the knowledge of their parents or guardians or against their will are void or voidable. If the minor is above the minimum age required by the law of the State for marriage, then, regardless of whether parental consent is present or absent, the marriage is valid. Hence the parents or guardians have no right to sue in the civil courts for the annullment of a marriage contracted by their minor child or ward, provided the contracting parties are above the legal marriageable age even though they are below the age of parental consent. Therefore the statutes of the various States, which require parental consent for the marriage of minors below a certain age, do not destroy the common law ruling that such a marriage is valid even though the consent of parents is lacking. The State could alter the common law in this matter by expressly declaring in statute law that the consent of parents or guardians is necessary for the civil validity of a minor's marriage. As yet no State in the United States has in law enacted such a requirement.[15]

---

[14] Alford, *Jus Matrimoniale,* p. 209.

[15] Bishop, *New Commentaries on Marriage, Divorce, and Separation,* I, n. 559; Vernier, *American Family Laws,* I, 120, 126–127; Bouvier's *Law Dictionary,* II, 2098.

CONCLUSIONS

1. It cannot be proved with certainty that the Church in her general law ever required parental knowledge or consent for the validity of the marriage of a minor.

2. In the Decree of Gratian parental consent was not necessary for the validity of the marriage of children except in the case of abduction.

3. Peter the Lombard by his distinction between *sponsalia de praesenti* and *sponsalia de futuro* was the first to demonstrate clearly that parental consent was in no case to be regarded as necessary for the validity of the marriage of minors.

4. The reasons why the Council of Trent considered the marriage of minors contracted without parental consent together with the problem of clandestine marriages were, first, because the chief offenders in the matter of clandestine marriages were minors, and secondly, because in the thought and terminology of the Reformers a clandestine marriage was precisely a union entered into by a minor unknown to his parents or against their will.

5. The only opinion permissible regarding the teaching of the Council of Trent concerning the marriage of minors entered into without the consent of their parents is that such marriages were valid although prohibited and detested by the Church.

6. In the present law of the Church a person, even though he is under twenty-one years of age, may with the consent of those to whom he is subject obtain his own proper domicile.

7. The pastor is obliged to see to it that the guardians of the minor know of and consent to the marriage of their ward; if they are uninformed of or are reasonably opposed to the marriage, the pastor may not assist at the marriage without previously consulting the Ordinary.

8. It is within the legislative competency of the Ordinary to demand by diocesan law that the pastor consult him before

assisting at the marriage of a minor whose parents or guardians are unreasonably opposed to the marriage.

9. Whenever a minor girl leaves with a man for the purpose of marriage without the knowledge of her parents or guardians or contrary to their wishes the crime of abduction is committed, and the man is subject to the penalties of canon 2353.

10. Although canon 2353 does not expressly restrict the opposition of the parents or guardians to a reasonable opposition, nevertheless only their reasonable dissent is to be understood, since canon 1034 considers the celebration of the marriage of minors as licit when the parents are unreasonably opposed.

APPENDIX

PRENUPTIAL INQUIRY RELATIVE TO THE MARRIAGE OF

Bridegroom ....
Name Domicile

Bride ....
Name Domicile

SEPARATE EXAMINATION OF FATHER / MOTHER (OR GUARDIANS) IN CASE OF A MINOR SPOUSE

(In case where pastor is uncertain of parental consent)

(The pastor should propose the questions and write in the answers as given. He should explain to the parents or guardians the sanctity of an oath and the penalties for perjury (canon 2323). The affiant should touch the Holy Gospels while taking the oath in the following formula.)

THE OATH: I........................having acknowledged the nature and sacred character of an oath solemnly swear to tell the whole truth and nothing but the truth in answer to the questions about to be proposed to me.

1. Name? ....Address? ....
   Date of Birth? ....Place of Birth? ....
   Religion? ....Occupation? ....
   Father's name? ....Mother's Name? ....
2. Are you aware that your son / daughter..................intends to contract marriage with...............................?
3. Do you approve of the marriage?.......................
   If not, why are you opposed?..........................
   ....
   ....
4. Are the parties related to each other?...................
   Is there any reason or impediment, public or occult, contrary to the proposed marriage?...............................

5. Has either party contracted a previous marriage?...........
   If so, with whom did this party contract marriage?...........
   Has said marriage been dissolved?.........How?..........
6. Are both parties free and willing to give matrimonial consent?..
   Any coercion or fear?.......................................
7. Are both parties physically fit to enter marriage?...........
   Are they aware of the purpose of marriage?..............
8. Have you anything to add concerning this marriage?........
9. (Read back foregoing testimony; then) Do you solemnly swear to the truth of the above statements which you have made, realizing you are under oath?.......................

Signed..........................

FATHER
MOTHER
(GUARDIAN)

Subscribed and sworn to before me this...................day of ....A. D. 19.... ....

....

PASTOR

(Parish Seal)

BIBLIOGRAPHY

SOURCES

Acta Apostolicae Sedis, Commentarium Officiale, Romae, 1909–

Acta et Decreta Concilii Provincialis Portlandensis in Oregon Quarti, 10 sept. 1932.

Acta et Decreta Sacrorum Conciliorum Recentiorum, Collectio Lacensis, 7 vols., Friburgi Brisgoviae: Herder, 1870–1890.

Acta Sanctae Sedis, 41 vols., Romae, 1865–1908.

Bouscaren, T. Lincoln, *The Canon Law Digest,* 2 vols., Milwaukee: Bruce, 1934–1943.

The Catechism of the Council of Trent, translated into English by the Reverend J. Donovan, Dublin, 1829.

Codex Iuris Canonici Pii X Pontificis Maximi iussu digestus Benedicti XV auctoritate promulgatus, Romae: Typis Polyglottis Vaticanis, 1917.

Codicis Iuris Canonici Fontes cura Emi Petri Card. Gasparri Editi, 9 vols., Romae (postea Civitate Vaticana): Typis Polyglottis Vaticanis, 1923–1939. (Vols. VII, VIII, IX, ed. cura et studio Emi Iustiniani Card. Serédi.)

Collectanea S. Congregationis de Propaganda Fide, 2 vols., Romae: Typographia Polyglotta S. C. de Propaganda Fide, 1907.

Collectio Librorum Iuris Anteiustiniani, ed. P. Krueger—Th. Mommsen–G. Studemund, 7. ed., 3 vols., Berolini: apud Weidmannos, 1923.

Concilii Tridentini Diariorum, Actorum, Epistolarum Tractatuum Nova Collectio, ed. Societas Gorresiana, 13 vols., Friburgi Brisgoviae: B. Herder, 1901–

Corpus Iuris Canonici, ed. Lipsiensis 2. post Aemilii Ludovici Richteri curas ad librorum manu scriptorum et editionis Romanae fidem recognovit et adnotatione critica instruxit Aemilius Friedberg, Lipsiae: ex officina Bernhardi Tauchnitz, 1879–1881. Editio anastatice repetita, Lipsiae: Tauchnitz, 1928.

Corpus Iuris Civilis, editio stereotypa, 3 vols., Berolini: apud Weidmannos, 1928–1929, Vol. I, *Institutiones,* recognovit Paulus Krueger, ed. 15., 1929; *Digesta,* recognovit Theodorus Mommsen, retractavit Paulus Krueger, ed. 15., 1929; Vol. II, *Codex,* recognovit et retractavit Paulus Krueger, ed. 10., 1929; Vol. III, *Novellae,* recognovit Rudolfus Schoell; opus Schoelli morte interceptum absolvit Gulielmus Kroll, ed. 5., 1928.

Decretales D. Gregorii Papae IX, una cum Glossis Restitutae, Romae, 1582.

Decretum Gratiani emendatum et notationibus illustratum una cum glossis, Gregorii XIII, Pont. Max. iussu editum, 2 vols., Romae, 1582.

Friedberg, Aemilius, *Quinque Compilationes Antiquae,* Lipsiae, 1882.

Husslein, J., *Social Wellsprings,* 2 vols., Milwaukee: Bruce, 1940–1942.

Jaffé, Phillipus, *Regesta Pontificum Romanorum ab condita Ecclesia ad annum post Christum natum MCXCVIII,* 2. ed., 2 vols. in 1, correctam et auctam auspiciis Gulielmi Wattenbach curaverunt Kaltenbrunner (33–590), Ewald (590–882), Loewenfeld (882–1198), Lipsiae, 1885–1888.

Liber Sextus Decretalium D. Bonifatii Papae VIII, suae integretati una cum Clementinis et Extravagantibus, earumque Glossis restitutus, Romae, 1582.

Mansi, Joannes, *Sacrorum Conciliorum Nova et Amplissima Collectio,* 53 vols. in 60, Parisiis, 1901–1927.

Monumenta Germaniae Historica, 188 vols., incomplete, Hannoverae, 1826–

———, *Concilia,* Tom. I, *Concilia Aevi Merovingici,* ed. F. Maassen, Hannoverae, 1893.

Potthast, Augustus, *Regesta Pontificum Romanorum, inde ab anno post Christum natum MCXCVIII ad MCCCIV,* 2 vols. in 1, Berolini: Rudolphi De Decker, 1874–1875.

Rituale Romanum Pauli V Pontificis Maximi iussu editum aliorumque Pontificum cura recognitum atque auctoritate Sanctissimi D. N. Pii Papae XI ad normam Codicis Iuris Canonici accomodatum, Ratisbonae, 1937.

S. Romanae Rotae Decisiones seu Sententiae quae . . . prodierunt anno 1909–1931, 23 vols., Romae: Typis Vaticanis, 1912–1939.

Schroeder, H. J., *Disciplinary Decrees of the General Councils: Text, Translation, and Commentary,* St. Louis: B. Herder Book Co., 1937.

Synodus Archidioecesis Sancti Francisci Secunda, 14 oct. 1936, San Francisco: Monitor Publishing Co., 1936.

Synodus Dioecesana Fargensis Prima, 29–30 sept. 1941, Milwauchiae: Ex Typographia Bruce, 1941.

Thesaurus Resolutionum Sacrae Congregationis Concilii, 167 vols., Romae, 1718–1908.

Waterworth, J., *The Canons and Decrees of the Sacred and Oecumenical Council of Trent,* London: C. Dolman, 1848.

REFERENCE WORKS

Alford, Culver Bernard, *Jus Matrimoniale Comparatum,* Romae: Anonima Libraria Cattolica Italiana, 1938.

Appeltern, Victorius ab, *Compendium Praelectionum Iuris Regularis,* 2. ed., Parisiis-Tornaci: Établissements Casterman, 1913.

Aquinas, Saint Thomas, *Commentarium in IV Libros Sententiarum Magistri Petri Lombardi,* ed. Mandonnet, Parisiis: Lethielleux, 1929.

———, *Summa Theologica,* ed. Studii Generalis O. Pr., Ottawa, Canada, 1942.

Artaud, M. Le Chevalier, *Histoire du Pape Pie VII,* 2 vols., Louvain, 1836.

Ayrinhac, H.–Lydon, P. J., *Marriage Legislation in the New Code of Canon Law,* 2. ed., New York: Benziger Bros., 1943.

———, *Penal Legislation in the New Code of Canon Law,* New York: Benziger Bros., 1936.

(Bachofen), Charles Augustine, *A Commentary on the New Code of Canon Law,* 8 vols., St. Louis: B. Herder Book Co., 1931–1938.

Bangen, Ioannes H., *Instructio Practica de Sponsalibus et Matrimonio in Usum Sacerdotum Curatorum,* 4 vols., Monasterii, 1858–1860.

Bastnagel, Clement V., *The Appointment of Parochial Adjutants and Assistants,* The Catholic University of America Canon Law Studies, n. 58, Washington, D. C.: The Catholic University of America, 1930.

Bauduin, G., *De Consuetudine Iure Canonico Dissertatio Canonica,* Lovanii, 1888.

Bellarminus, Card. Robertus, *De Controversiis Christianae Fidei Adversus huius Temporis Haereticos,* 6 vols. in 7, Neapoli, 1856–1860.

Benedictus XIV (Prosper Lambertini), *De Synodo Dioecesana,* libri 13 in 2 tom., Lovanii, 1763.

Bernard, Frank, *Étude Historique et Critique sur le Consentement des Ascendants au Mariage,* Paris: Librairie de la Société du Recueil Général des Lois et des Arrêts, 1899.

Bernardus Papiensis, *Summa Decretalium,* ed. E. A. T. Laspeyres, Ratisbonae, 1860.

Bertolotti, Joseph, *Casus Conscientiae praesertim de Re Morali et Liturgica,* 3 vols., Savonae, 1888.

Beste, Udalricus, *Introductio in Codicem,* 2. ed., Collegeville, Minn.: St. John's Abbey Press, 1944.

Bishop, Joel P., *New Commentaries on Marriage, Divorce, and Separation,* 2 vols., Chicago: T. H. Flood & Co., 1891.

Blat, Albertus, *Commentarium Textus Codicis Iuris Canonici,* 5 vols. in 7, Romae: Collegio "Angelico," 1921–1924; Vol. I, *Normae Generales,* 1921; Vol. II, *De Personis,* 2. ed., 1923; Vol. III, Pars I, *De Sacramentis,* 2. ed., 1924; Vol. V. *De Delictis et Poenis,* 1924.

Bouvier's Law Dictionary, Rawle's third revision, 2 vols., Kansas City, Missouri, and St. Paul, Minnesota, 1914.

Buckland, W. W., *A Textbook of Roman Law from Augustus to Justinian,* 2. ed., Cambridge: The University Press, 1932.

Burdick, William L., *The Principles of Roman Law and Their Relation to Modern Law,* Rochester: The Lawyers Cooperative Publishing Co., 1938.

Calvin's Institutes of the Christian Religion, translated by John Allen, 6. ed., 2 vols., Philadelphia: Presbyterian Board of Publication and Social Work, 1902.

Cappello, Felix M., *Summa Iuris Canonici,* 3 vols., Vol. I, 3. ed., 1938; Vol. II, 3. ed., 1939; Vol. III, 1936, Romae: Apud Aedes Universitatis Gregorianae.

Cappello, Felix M., *Tractatus Canonico-Moralis de Censuris iuxta Codicem Juris Canonici,* 3. ed., Augustae Taurinorum et Romae: Marietti, 1933.

———, *Tractatus Canonico-Moralis de Sacramentis,* 3 vols. in 6, Romae: Marietti, 1928–1933; Vol. I, *De Sacramentis in genere, de Baptismo, Confirmatione et Eucharistia,* 2. ed., 1928; Vol. III, *De Matrimonio,* 3. ed., 1933.

Carberry, John J., *The Juridical Form of Marriage,* The Catholic University of America Canon Law Studies, n. 84, Washington, D. C.: The Catholic University of America, 1934.

Cerato, P., *Matrimonium a Codice I. C. Integre Desumptum,* 4. ed., Patavii: Typis Seminarii Patavini, 1929.

Chelodi, Ioannes, *Ius de Personis iuxta Codicem Iuris Canonici,* ed. altera a Sac. Ernesto Bertagnolli recognita et aucta, Tridenti: Libr. Edit. Tridentum, 1927.

———, *Ius Matrimoniale iuxta Codicem Iuris Canonici,* 3. ed., Tridenti: Libr. Edit. Tridentum, 1921.

———, *Ius Poenale et Ordo Procedendi in Iudiciis Criminalibus iuxta Codicem Iuris Canonici,* Tridenti: Libr. Edit. Tridentum, 1920.

Claeys Bouuaert, F. et Simenon, G., *Manuale Iuris Canonici ad Usum Seminariorum,* 3 vols., Gandae et Loedii: Apud Auctores in Seminariis Gandavensi et Loediensi, Vol. I, 3. ed., 1930; Vol. II, 1931; Vol. III, 3. ed., 1931.

Cloran, Owen M., *A Guide to the Use of the Instruction of the Sacred Congregation of the Sacraments on the Norms To Be Observed by Pastors in Pre-Nuptial Investigations,* Des Plaines, Illinois: St. Mary's Press, 1942.

Cocchi, Guidus, *Commentarium in Codicem Iuris Canonici ad Usum Scholarum,* 5 vols. in 8, Taurinorum Augustae: Marietti, 1922–1930.

Corbett, Percy Ellwood, *The Roman Law of Marriage,* Oxford: Clarendon Press, 1930.

Coronata, Matthaeus Conte a, *Institutiones Iuris Canonici ad Usum Utriusque Clerici et Scholarum,* 5 vols., Taurini (Italia): Marietti, 1928–1936; Vol. I, 1928; Vol. IV, *De Delictis Poenis,* 1935.

Cosci, Christophorus, *De Separatione Tori Coniugalis,* Florentina, 1856.

———, *De Sponsalibus Filiorumfamilias,* Romae, 1766.

Costello, John M., *Domicile and Quasi-Domicile,* The Catholic University of America Canon Law Studies, n. 60, Washington, D. C.: The Catholic University of America, 1930.

Cuiacius, Iacobus, *Opera Omnia, Opera ad Parisiensem Fabrotianem Editionem,* 15 vols., Prati, 1836–1843.

Dauvillier, Jean, *Le Mariage dans le Droit Classique de l'Eglise, depuis le Décret de Gratien (1140) jusq'a la mort de Clement V (1314),* Paris: Recueil Sirey, 1933.

Davis, Henry, *Moral and Pastoral Theology,* 3. ed., 4 vols., London: Sheed and Ward, 1938.

De Angelis, P., *Praelectiones Iuris Canonici ad Methodum Decretalium Gregorii IX Exactae,* 5 vols. in 8, Romae–Parisiis, 1877–1894; Vol. V curavit Nazarenus Gentilini, 1887–1891.

De Becker, Julius, *De Matrimonio Praelectiones Canonicae,* 2. ed., Louvain: Etabliss. Fr. Ceuterick, 1931.

De Meester, Alphonsus, *Juris Canonici et Juris Canonico-Civilis Compendium,* 3 vols. in 4, Brugis: Desclée, 1921–1928.

De Molina, Ludovicus, *De Primogeniorum Hispanorum Origine ac Natura,* Venetiis, 1757.

De Smet, Aloysius, *Tractatus Theologico-Canonicus de Sponsalibus et Matrimonio,* 4. ed., Brugis: Car. Beyaert, 1927.

Devoti, Ioannes, *Institutionum Canonicarum Libri IV,* Romae, 1830.

Doheny, William J., *Canonical Procedure in Matrimonial Cases,* Milwaukee: Bruce Publishing Co., 1938.

Donovan, James J., *The Pastor's Obligation in Pre-Nuptial Investigation,* The Catholic University of America Canon Law Studies, n. 115, Washington, D. C.: The Catholic University of America, 1938.

Drumm, William M., *Hospital Chaplains,* The Catholic University of America Canon Law Studies, n. 178, Washington, D. C.: The Catholic University of America Press, 1943.

Eichmann, Eduard, *Das Strafrecht des Codex Iuris Canonici,* Paderborn: Schöningh, 1920.

Engel, Ludovicus, *Collegium Universi Juris Canonici,* ed. nova, annotationes Barthel Beneventi, Venetiis, 1760.

Erasmus, *Christiani Matrimonii Institutio,* Lug. Batavorum, 1650.

Esmein, *A., Le Mariage en Droit Canonique,* 2. ed., 2 vols., Vol. I rev. by R. Génestal, 1929; Vol. II rev. by R. Génestal and J. Dauvillier, 1935, Paris: Librairie de Recueil Sirey, 1929–1935.

Esswein, Anthony A., *The Extrajudicial Coercive Powers of Ecclesiastical Superiors,* The Catholic University of America Canon Law Studies, n. 127, Washington, D. C.: The Catholic University of America Press, 1941.

Estius, Gulielmus, *In Quatuor Libros Sententiarum Commentaria,* 4 vols. in 2, Parisiis, 1680.

Fagnanus, Prosper, *Commentaria Super Quinque Libros Decretalium,* 5 vols. in 3, Venetiis, 1709.

Fanfani, Ludovicus, *De Iure Parochorum ad normam Codicis Iuris Canonici,* 2. ed., Taurini-Romae: Marietti, 1936.

Farrugia, Nicolaus, *De Matrimonio et Causis Matrimonialibus Tractatus Canonico-Moralis iuxta Codicem Iuris Canonici,* Taurini–Romae: Marietti, 1924.

Feije, Henricus, *De Impedimentis et Dispensationibus Matrimonialibus,* 3. ed., Lovanii, 1885.

Ferraris, Lucius, *Prompta Bibliotheca Canonica, Iuridica, Moralis, Theologica, necnon Ascetica, Polemica, Rubricistica, Historica,* 9 vols.,

Romae: 1885–1889; Ianuarius Bucceroni, S. J. (+ 1918) added the 9th volume to the previous standard set of 8 volumes.

Ferreres, Juan B., *Compendium Theologiae Moralis ad Normam Codicis Canonici,* 14. ed., 3 vols., Barcinone: Eugenius Subirana, 1928.

Ferrero, G., *Ancient Rome and Modern America,* New York: G. P. Putnam's Sons, 1914.

Freisen, Joseph, *Geschichte des canonischen Eherechts bis zum Verfall der Glossenlitteratur,* 2. ed., Paderborn, 1893.

Friedberg, Emil, *Das Recht der Eheschliessung in seiner geschichtlichen Entwicklung,* Leipzig, 1865.

Gasparri, Petrus Card., *Tractatus Canonicus de Matrimonio,* 2. ed., 2 vols., Romae: Typis Polyglottis Vaticanis, 1932.

Genicot, Eduardus, et Salsmans, I., *Institutiones Theologiae Moralis,* 14. ed., 2 vols., Buenos Aires: Dedebec, 1939.

Gonzalez-Téllez, Emmanuel, *Commentaria Perpetua in Singulos Textus Quinque Librorum Decretalium Gregorii IX,* 5 vols. in 4, Lugduni, 1715.

Gougnard, Armandus, *Tractatus de Matrimonio,* 7. ed., Mechliniae: H. Dessain, 1931.

Gutierrez, Ioannes, *Canonicarum Quaestionum Libri Duo,* 3 vols. in 2, Lugduni, 1661.

Heneghan, John J., *The Marriages of Unworthy Catholics: Canons 1065 and 1066,* The Catholic University of America Canon Law Studies, n. 188, The Catholic University of America Press, 1944.

Hervê, J. M., *Manuale Theologiae Dogmaticae,* 4 vols., Vol. IV, 12. ed., Parisiis: Apud Berche et Pagis, 1934.

Hostiensis, Cardinalis (Henricus de Segusia), *Commentaria in Quinque Libros Decretalium,* 5 vols. in 3, Venetiis, 1581.

———, *Summa Aurea,* Venetiis, 1570.

Joannes Andreae, *In Sex Decretalium Libros Novella Commentaria,* 6 vols. in 5, Venetiis, 1581.

Joannis Calvini Opera Quae Supersunt Omnia, ed., Gulielmus Baum–Eduardus Cunitz–Eduardus Reuss, 59 vols. in 58, Brunsvigae, Berolini: Apud C. A. Schwetschke et Filium, 1863–1900.

Joyce, George H., *Christian Marriage,* Heythrop Series: I, London and New York: Sheed and Ward, 1933.

Kay, Thomas H., *Competence in Matrimonial Procedure,* The Catholic University of America Canon Law Studies, n. 53, Washington, D. C.: The Catholic University of America, 1929.

Köstler, Rudolf, *Die väterliche Ehebewilligung, Kirchenrechtliche Abhandlungen* von Dr. Ulrich Stutz, 51. Heft, Stuttgart: Verlag von Ferdinand Enke, 1908.

Laws on Domestic Relations in the 48 States, District of Columbia, England, Australia, the Provinces of Canada, compiled by the Committee on War Work of the American Bar Association, 1943–1944.

Laymann, Paulus, *Theologia Moralis in Quinque Libros Distributa*, ed. nova, Venetiis, 1630.

Leage, R. W., *Roman Private Law Founded on the "Institutes" of Gaius and Justinian*, 2. ed., by C. H. Ziegler, London: Macmillan and Co., 1937.

Leurenius, P., *Forum Ecclesiasticum in quo Ius Canonicum Universum Explicatur*, 5 vols. in 3, Venetiis, 1729.

Luther, M., *Säamtliche Werke*, nach den ältesten Ausgaben kritisch und historisch bearbeitet von Dr. Johann Konrad Irmischer, 67 vols. in 25, Erlangen, 1831–1883.

Maroto, P., *Institutiones Iuris Canonici ad Normam Novi Codicis*, 3. ed., 2 vols., Madrid, 1919.

Martindale–Hubbell, *Law Directory*, 2 vols., 77th annual edition, Summit, N. J.: Martindale-Hubbell, Inc., 1945.

Mascardus, Josephus, *Conclusiones. Omnium Probationum quae in Utroque Iure Quotidie Versantur*, 3 vols., Venetiis, 1593.

McBride, James T., *Incardination and Excardination of Seculars*, The Catholic University of America Canon Law Studies, n. 145, Washington, D. C.: The Catholic University of America Press, 1941.

Michiels, Gommarus, *Normae Generales Iuris Canonici*, 2 vols., Lublin–Polonia: Universitas Catholica, 1929.

———, *Principia Generalia de Personis in Ecclesia*, Lublin–Polonia: Universitas Catholica, 1932.

Migne, Jacques Paul, *Patrologiae Cursus Completus, Series Graeca*, 161 vols., Parisiis, 1856–1866.

———, *Patrologiae Cursus Completus, Series Latina*, 221 vols., Parisiis, 1844–1864.

Mitterer, M., *Geschichte des Ehehindernisses der Entführung im kanonischen Recht seit Gratian*, Görres-Gesellschaft zur Pflege der Wissenschaft im katholischen Deutschland. Veröffentlichungen der Sektion für Rechts-und Sozialwissenschaft, Heft 43, Paderborn, 1924.

Moriarty, Francis E., *The Extraordinary Absolution from Censures*, The Catholic University of America Canon Law Studies, n. 113, Washington, D. C.: The Catholic University of America, 1938.

Mothon, Joseph P., *Institutions Canoniques*, 3 vols., Vol. I, *Des Personnes*, Paris: Société Saint-Augustin, Desclée, De Brouwer, 1922.

Muirhead, J., *The Institutes of Gaius and the Rules of Ulpian*, Edinburgh: T. & T. Clark, 1904.

Muscettula, Franciscus M., *Dissertatio de Sponsalibus et Matrimonio Parentibus Insciis vel Invitis cum Adnotationibus Mazochii et Zech*, Venetiis, 1772.

Nau, Louis J., *Manual on the Marriage Laws of the Code of Canon Law*, 2. ed., New York: F. Pustet Co., 1934.

Navarrus, Martinus (Martin of Azpilcueta), *Opera Omnia in Sex Tomos Distincta*, 6 vols., Venetiis, 1618.

Noldin, H.–Schmitt, A., *Summa Theologiae Moralis iuxta Codicem Iuris Canonici,* 3 vols., Vol. III, 23. ed., Oeniponte: Typis et Sumptibus F. Rauch, 1935.

Oesterle, G., *Praelectiones Iuris Canonici,* 2 vols., Romae: in Collegio S. Anselmi, 1931.

Ojetti, B., *Commentarium in Codicem Iuris Canonici,* 4 vols., Romae: Apud Aedes Universitatis Gregorianae, 1927–1931.

Pallavicini, Cardinalis Pietro Sforza, *Historia Concilii Tridentini,* trans. by Joannes Baptista Giattini, 3 vols., Antverpiae, 1670.

Panormitanus, Abbas (Nicolaus de Tudeschis), *Commentaria in Quinque Libros Decretalium,* 5 vols. in 7, Venetiis, 1588.

Payen, G., *De Matrimonio in Missionibus ac Potissimum in Sinis Tractatus Practicus et Casus,* 2. ed., 3 vols., Zi-ka-wei: Typographia T'OU-SÈ-WÊ, 1935–1936.

Petrovits, Joseph, *The New Church Law on Matrimony,* Philadelphia: John Joseph McVey, 1919.

Petrus Lombardus, *Libri IV Sententiarum studia et cura PP. Collegii S; Bonaventurae in lucem editi,* 2. ed., 2 vols., Ad Claras Aquas: Typographia Collegii S. Bonaventurae, 1916.

Pichler, Vitus, *Jus Canonicum Secundum Quinque Decretalium Titulos Gregorii IX,* 2 vols., Venetiis, 1741.

Pirhing, Ernricus, *Jus Canonicum in Quinque Libros Decretalium Distributum Nova Methodo Explicatum,* 5 vols. in 4, ed. novissima, Dilingae, 1722.

Pistocchi, M., *I Canoni Penali del Codice Ecclesiastico Esposti e Commentati,* Torino–Roma: Marietti, 1925.

Plöchl, Willibald, *Das Eherecht des Magisters Gratianus,* Leipzig: Frank Deuticke, 1935.

Prince, John E., *The Diocesan Chancellor,* The Catholic University of America Canon Law Studies, n. 167, Washington, D. C.: The Catholic University of America Press, 1942.

Probate Act and Rules of the Probate Court of Cook County—Effective January 1, 1940, Published by Edward J. Hughes, Secretary of the State of Illinois.

Prümmer, Dominicus M., *Manuale Theologiae Moralis secundum Principia S. Thomae Aquinatis,* 7. ed., 3 vols., Friburgi Brisgoviae: Herder, 1931–1933.

Ramstein, Matthew, *The Pastor and Marriage Cases,* 2. ed., New York: Benziger Bros., 1938.

Raus, Joannes B., *Institutiones Canonicae iuxta Novum Codicem Iuris,* 2. ed., Lugduni, Parisiis: Vitte, 1931.

Raymundus de Pennafort, Saint, *Summa,* Verona, 1744.

Reiffenstuel, Anacletus, *Jus Canonicum Universum,* 5 vols. in 7, Parisiis, 1864–1870.

Roberts, James B., *The Banns of Marriage,* The Catholic University of America Canon Law Studies, n. 64, Washington, D. C.: The Catholic University of America, 1931.

Robinson, William C., *Elementary Law,* 2. ed., Boston: Little, Brown and Co., 1910.

Roskovány, A. de, *Matrimonium in Ecclesia Catholica,* 4 vols., Pestini (Nitriae): Typis Athenaei, 1870–1882.

Rossi, Joseph, *De Matrimonii Celebratione iuxta Codicem Iuris Canonici,* Romae: F. Pustet, 1924.

Rufinus, *Summa Decretorum,* ed. H. Singer, Paderborn, 1902.

Ryan, Gerald A., *Principles of Episcopal Jurisdiction,* The Catholic University of America Canon Law Studies, n. 120, Washington, D. C.: The Catholic University of America, 1939.

Salucci, Raffaele, *Il Diritto Penale secondo il Codice di Diritto Canonico,* 2 vols., Subiaco: Tipografia dei Monasteri, 1926–1930.

Sanchez, Thomas, *Disputationum de Sancto Matrimonii Sacramento Tomi Tres,* Antverpiae, 1626.

Schmalzgrueber, Franciscus X., *Jus Ecclesiasticum Universum,* 5 vols. in 12, Romae, 1843–1845.

Schröteler, Josef, *Das Elternrecht in der katholisch-theologischen Auseinandersetzung,* München: Neuer Filser-Verlag, 1936.

Sipos, Stephanus, *Enchiridion Iuris Canonici,* Pécs: Typographia "Haladás R. T.," 1926.

Sole, Jacobus, *Praelectiones in Lib. V Codicis Iuris Canonici, De Delictis et Poenis,* Romae: F. Pustet, 1920.

Soto, Dominicus, *In Quartum (quem vocant) Sententiarum,* 2 vols., Venetiis, 1575.

Ter Haar, F., *De Matrimoniis Mixtis Eorumque Remediis,* Taurini–Romae: Marietti, 1931.

The Table Talk of Martin Luther, translated and edited by William Hazlitt, London: George Bell and Sons, 1890.

Toso, Albertus, *Ad Codicem Iuris Canonici Commentaria Minora,* 5 vols., Romae: Marietti, 1921–1934.

Triebs, F., *Praktisches Handbuch des geltenden kanonischen Eherechts in Vergleichung mit dem deutschen staatlichen Eherecht,* Teil I–IV in einem Band, Gesamtausgabe, Breslau: Ostdeutsche Verlagsanstalt, 1933.

Vallensis, Andreas, *Paratitla Iuris Canonici sive Decretalium,* Venetiis, 1732.

Van Hove, A., *Commentarium Lovaniense in Codicem Iuris Canonici,* Vol. I, Tom. II (*De Legibus Ecclesiasticis*), Mechliniae–Romae: H. Dessain, 1930.

Vecchiotti, Septimius, *Institutiones Canonicae,* 19. ed., 3 vols., Taurini: Marietti, 1886.

Vermeersch, A., *Theologiae Moralis Principia, Responsa, Consilia,* 3. ed., 4 vols., Romae: Università Gregoriana, 1937.

Vermeersch, A., et Creusen, J., *Epitome Iuris Canonici cum Commentariis ad Scholas et ad Usum Privatum,* 3 vols., Mechliniae–Romae: H. Dessain, Vol. I, 6. ed., 1937; Vol. II, 5. ed., 1934; Vol. III, 5. ed., 1936.

Vernier, Chester G., *American Family Laws,* 5 vols., Stanford University, Calif.: Stanford University Press, 1931–1938.

Vlaming, Th. M., *Praelectiones Iuris Matrimonii ad Normam Codicis Iuris Canonici,* 3. ed., 2 vols., Bussum in Hollandia: Sumptibus Societatis Editricis Anonymae Olim Paulus Brand, 1919–1921.

Wernz, Franciscus X., *Ius Decretalium,* 6 vols., Romae et Prati, 1898–1905, Vol. IV, *Ius Matrimoniale Ecclesiae Catholicae,* Romae, 1904.

Wernz, F., et Vidal, *Ius Canonicum ad Codicis Normam Exactum,* 7 vols. in 8, Vol. II,. *De Personis,* 3. ed., recognita Philippo Aguirre, 1943; Vol. III, *De Religiosis,* 1933; Vol. V, *Ius Matrimoniale,* 2. ed., 1928; Vol. VII, *Ius Poenale Ecclesiasticum,* 1937, Romae: Apud Aedes Universitatis Gregorianae.

Westermarck, E., *The History of Human Marriage,* London: Macmillan and Co., 1891.

Woywod, S., *A Practical Commentary on the Code of Canon Law,* 6. ed., 2 vols., New York: Joseph F. Wagner, Inc., 1941.

Zitelli, Zephyrinus, *Apparatus Juris Ecclesiastici iuxta Recentissimas Resolutiones S. S. Urbis Congregationum,* Romae, 1886.

ARTICLES

Baumer, A., "De iure poenali pro delinquentibus minoris aetatis in Codice iuris canonici et novissimo schemate Codicis poenalis helvetici."—*Apollinaris,* VI (1933), 453–495.

Browne, M. J., "Questions about Domicile."—*Irish Ecclesiastical Record,* XLVII (1936), 632–634.

———, "Two Cases of Domicile in Relation to Marriage."—*Op. cit.,* XLIX (1937), 416–419.

Brys, J., "De Vicario Oeconomo."—*Collationes Brugenses,* XXIX (1929), 279–281, 398–400.

Cappello, F. M., "De Vicario Substituto."—*Periodica,* XIX (1930), 1*–10*.

———, "Irrogatio Poenae per Modum Praecepti extra Iudicium."—*Periodica,* XIX (1930), 36*-38*.

Claeys Bouuaert, F., "De Vicarii Substituti Constitutione ac Munere."—*Jus Pontificium,* VII (1927), 72–81.

Coucke, V., "Adnotationes."—*Collationes Brugenses,* XXVIII (1928), 253–255.

Creusen, J., "Célébration du mariage, Réponse du 25 Juillet, 1931."—*Nouvelle Revue Theólogique,* LVIII (1931), 827–829.

Crnica, Antonius, "De Lacunis Legis Supplendis ad Normam Codicis J. C."—*Jus Pontificium,* XVI (1936), 182–198; XVIII (1939), 280–292; XIX (1939), 79–89.

Dalpiaz, V., "Num vicariis cooperatoribus competat ipso iure ex can. 476,

§ 6 potestas assistendi matrimoniis in paroecia, cui sunt addicti."—*Consultationes Iuris Canonici,* I, 67–73.

Damen, Corn. Alf., "De Irritatione et Suspensione Votorum Spectato Iure Naturali atque Iure Ecclesiastico Antiquo et Novo."—*Apollinaris,* III (1930), 109–119, 274–295.

De Becker, J., "De Recta Canonis 1098 Codicis Iuris Canonici Interpretatione."—*Ephemerides Theologicae Lovanienses,* IX (1932), 284–291.

De Smet, A., "Recentiores Variationes in re matrimoniali."—*Ephemerides Theologicae Lovanienses,* I (1924), 558–579.

Fallon, M. J., "Domicile of a Wife Who Becomes Insane."—*Irish Ecclesiastical Record,* LVII (1941), 79–84.

———, "Grave Inconvenience Justifying the Celebration of Marriage Without a Priest."—*Irish Ecclesiastical Record,* LIX (1942), 470–471.

Farrugia, Nicolaus, "De Ecclesiastico Domicilio."—*Il Monitore Ecclesiastico,* VII (1935), 312–320.

Gillet, Pierre, "De Exemptione a Patria Potestate."—*Ephemerides Theologicae Lovanienses,* XI (1934), 787–790.

Heneghan, John J., "Civil Marriage License."—*The Jurist,* III (1943), 310–318.

Kinane, J., "Domicile in the New Code."—*Irish Ecclesiastical Record,* XI (1918), 215–231.

———, "Legal or Necessary Quasi-Domicile."—*Irish Ecclesiastical Record,* XXVII (1926), 80–82.

Maroto, P., "Animadversiones."—*Apollinaris,* I (1928), 334–339.

———, "Responsa ad Proposita Dubia 25 iulii 1931."—*Apollinaris,* IV (1931), 381–382.

Noval, J., "De Ratione Corrigendi et Puniendi sive in Judicio sive extra Jure Codicis J. C."—*Jus Pontificium,* II (1922), 147–156; III (1923), 36–40, 204–210.

Oesterle, G., "Elucubratio Historica circa Declarationem Authenticam Can. 1095."—*Jus Pontificium,* VIII (1928), 174–182; IX (1929), 141–158.

O'Donnell, P., "Consent of Parents in Marriage."—*Irish Ecclesiastical Record,* VIII (1887), 633–634.

Piontek, C., "De Acephalis in Iure Canonico."—*Jus Pontificium,* XVII (1937), 171–183.

Prince, John E., "The Chancellor as Delegate of the Bishop."—*The Jurist,* III (1943), 567–586.

Roberti, F., "Quaenam Poenae Applicari Possint per Modum Praecepti."—*Apollinaris,* IV (1931), 294–300.

Roelker, Edward, "The Power to Enact Invalidating Laws."—*The Jurist,* III (1943), 231–257.

Stocchiero, J., "De Jurisdictione Vicariorum Paroecialium."—*Jus Pontificium,* XI (1931), 144–150, 221–231.

———, "Il matrimonio alla presenza d'un vicario del parroco assente"—*Perfice Munus,* VIII (1933), 220–225.

Vermeersch, A., "Annotationes."—*Periodica,* XVIII (1929), 77*–80*.

Vindex (V. Meysztowicz), "Domicilium et Quasi-Domicilium Eorumque Effectus in Codice Iuris Canonici."—*Jus Pontificium,* VI (1926), 34–55, 112–136, 154–158.

Werts, Hilary R., "The Cessation of Invalidation in Grave Difficulty."—*Theological Studies,* IV (1943), 223–248.

PERIODICALS

Analecta Juris Pontificii, Romae, 1855–1869; Parisiis, 1872–1891.

Apollinaris, Romae, 1928–

Collationes Brugenses, Bruges, 1896–

Consultationes Iuris Canonici, Romae: Apud Custodiam Librariam Pontificii Instituti Utriusque Iuris, Vol. I, 1934; Vol. II, 1939.

Ecclesiastical Review, The (originally *The American Ecclesiastical Review*), Philadelphia, Pa. 1889–

Ephemerides Theologicae Lovanienses, Brugis, 1924–

Irish Ecclesiastical Record, Dublin, 1864–

Jurist, The, Washington, D. C., 1941–

Jus Pontificium, Romae, 1921–

Monitore Ecclesiastico, Il, Romae, 1876–

Nouvelle Revue Théologique, Tournai, 1869–

Perfice Munus, Torino, 1926–

Periodica de Religiosis et Missionariis, 8 vols., Brugis, 1905–1919 (Vol. I: 1905, 2. ed., 1911; II and III: 1907, 2. ed., 1911; IV: 1909, 2. ed., 1913; V: 1911, 2. ed., 1913; VI: 1912; VII: 1912–1914; VIII: 1919); from 1920: *Periodica de Re Canonica et Morali utile praesertim Religiosis et Missionariis,* 7 vols., Brugis, 1920–1927 (Vol. IX: 1920; X and XI: 1922–1923; XII: 1923–1924; XIII: 1924–1925; XIV: 1925–1926; XV: 1926–1927); from 1927: *Periodica de Re Morali, Canonica, Liturgica,* Brugis (1927–1936) et Romae (1937–), Vol. XVI, 1927–

Theological Studies, The America Press, New York, N. Y., 1940.

ABBREVIATIONS

AAS—*Acta Apostolicae Sedis.*

ASS—*Acta Sanctae Sedis.*

Coll. Lac.—*Acta et Decreta Sacrorum Conciliorum Recentiorum, Collectio Lacensis.*

C.—*Codex* (Iustinianus).

Collectanea S. C. P. F.—*Collectanea Sacrae Congregationis de Propaganda Fide.*

D.—*Digestum* (Iustinianum).

ER—*The Ecclesiastical Review.*

ETL—*Ephemerides Theologicae Lovanienses.*

Fontes—*Codicis Iuris Canonici Fonte cura . . . Gasparri editi.*

I—*Institutiones* (Iustinianae).

IER—*Irish Ecclesiastical Record.*

JE—Jaffé, *Regesta Pontificum Romanorum* (edited by P. Ewald: from 590 to 882).

JK—Jaffé, *op. cit.* (edited by F. Kaltenbrunner: from 33 to 590).

JL—Jaffé, *op. cit.* (edited by S. Loewenfeld: from 882 to 1198).

JP—*Jus Pontificium.*

Mansi—Mansi, J. D., *Sacrorum Conciliorum Nova et Amplissima Collectio.*

MGH—*Monumenta Germaniae Historica.*

MPG—Migne, *Patrologiae Cursus Completus, Series Graeca.*

MPL—Migne, *Patrologiae Cursus Completus, Series Latina.*

N—*Novellae* (Iustinianae).

PCI—Pontificia Commissio ad Codicis Canones authentice interpretandos.

Potthast—Potthast, Augustus, *Regesta Pontificum Romanorum.*

S. C. C.—Sacra Congregatio Concilii.

S. C. de Prop. Fide—Sacra Congregatio de Propaganda Fide.

S. C. de Sacr.—Sacra Congregatio de disciplina Sacramentorum.

S. C. S. Off.—Sacra Congregatio Sancti Officii.

S. R. R. Dec.—*Sacrae Romanae Rotae Decisiones seu Responsa* (from 1909).

ALPHABETICAL INDEX

BIOGRAPHICAL NOTE

Cletus Francis O'Donnell was born August 22, 1917, in Waukon, Iowa. After completing his primary education in the parish school of Holy Cross, Chicago, Illinois, he entered Quigley Preparatory Seminary of the Archdiocese of Chicago, graduating in June, 1935. In the fall of that year he entered St. Mary of the Lake Seminary, Mundelein, Illinois. There he received the degree of Master of Arts. He was ordained to the Sacred Priesthood on May 3, 1941. Following a year of parochial work in Our Lady of Lourdes parish, Chicago, he enrolled in the School of Canon Law at the Catholic University of America in September, 1942. In May, 1943, he received the degree of the Baccalaureate in Canon Law, and the degree of the Licentiate in Canon Law in May, 1944.

CANON LAW STUDIES*

1. Freriks, Rev. Celestine A., C.PP.S., J.C.D., Religious Congregations in Their External Relations, 121 pp., 1916.
2. Galliher, Rev. Daniel M., O.P., J.C.D., Canonical Elections, 117 pp., 1917.
3. Borkowski, Rev. Aurelius L., O.F.M., J.C.D., De Confraternitatibus Ecclesiasticis, 136 pp., 1918.
4. Castillo, Rev. Cayo, J.C.D., Disertacion Historico-Canonica sobre la Potestad del Cabildo en Sede Vacante o Impedida del Vicario Capitular, 99 pp., 1919 (1918).
5. Kubelbeck, Rev. William J., S.T.B., J.C.D., The Sacred Penitentiaria and Its Relation to Faculties of Ordinaries and Priests, 129 pp., 1918.
6. Petrovits, Rev. Joseph J. C., S.T.D., J.C.D., The New Church Law on Matrimony, X-461 pp., 1919.
7. Hickey, Rev. John J., S.T.B., J.C.D., Irregularities and Simple Impediments in the New Code of Canon Law, 100 pp., 1920.
8. Klekotka, Rev. Peter J., S.T.B., J.C.D., Diocesan Consultors, 179 pp., 1920.
9. Wanenmacher, Rev. Francis, J.C.D., The Evidence in Ecclesiastical Procedure Affecting the Marriage Bond, 1920 (Printed 1935).
10. Golden, Rev. Henry Francis, J.C.D., Parochial Benefices in the New Code, IV-119 pp., 1921 (Printed 1925).
11. Koudelka, Rev. Charles J., J.C.D., Pastors, Their Rights and Duties According to the New Code of Canon Law, 211 pp., 1921.
12. Melo, Rev. Antonius, O.F.M., J.C.D., De Exemptione Regularium, X-188 pp., 1921.
13. Schaaf, Rev. Valentine Theodore, O.F.M., S.T.B., J.C.D., The Cloister, X-180 pp., 1921.
14. Burke, Rev. Thomas Joseph, S.T.D., J.C.D., Competence in Ecclesiastical Tribunals, IV-117 pp., 1922.
15. Leech, Rev. George Leo, J.C.D., A Comparative Study of the Constitution "Apostolicae Sedis" and the "Codex Juris Canonici," 179 pp., 1922.
16. Motry, Rev. Hubert Louis, S.T.D., J.C.D., Diocesan Faculties According to the Code of Canon Law, II-167 pp., 1922.
17. Murphy, Rev. George Lawrence, J.C.D., Delinquencies and Penalties in the Administration and the Reception of the Sacraments, IV-121 pp., 1923.

* **Below n. 100 only numbers 25 and 57 are still available. Beginning with n. 100 only the following numbers are unavailable: Nos. 100–118 inclusive, and also n. 122.**

18. O'REILLY, REV. JOHN ANTHONY, S.T.B., J.C.D., Ecclesiastical Sepulture in the New Code of Canon Law, II-129 pp., 1923.
19. MICHALICKA, REV. WENCESLAS CYRILL, O.S.B., J.C.D., Judicial Procedure in Dismissal of Clerical Exempt Religious, 107 pp., 1923.
20. DARGIN, REV. EDWARD VINCENT, S.T.B., J.C.D., Reserved Cases According to the Code of Canon Law, IV-103 pp., 1924.
21. GODFREY, REV. JOHN A., S.T.B., J.C.D., The Right of Patronage According to the Code of Canon Law, 153 pp., 1924.
22. HAGEDORN, REV. FRANCIS EDWARD, J.C.D., General Legislation on Indulgences, II-154 pp., 1924.
23. KING, REV. JAMES IGNATIUS, J.C.D., The Administration of the Sacraments to Dying Non-Catholics, V-141 pp., 1924.
24. WINSLOW, REV. FRANCIS JOSEPH, O.F.M., J.C.D., Vicars and Prefects Apostolic, IV-149 pp., 1924.
25. CORREA, REV. JOSE SERVELION, S.T.L., J.C.D., La Potestad Legislativa de la Iglesia Catolica, IV-127 pp., 1925.
26. DUGAN, REV. HENRY FRANCIS, A.M., J.C.D., The Judiciary Department of the Diocesan Curia, 87 pp., 1925.
27. KELLER, REV. CHARLES FREDERICK, S.T.B., J.C.D., Mass Stipends, 167 pp., 1925.
28. PASCHANG, REV. JOHN LINUS, J.C.D., The Sacramentals According to the Code of Canon Law, 129 pp., 1925.
29. PIONTEK, REV. CYRILLUS, O.F.M., S.T.B., J.C.D., De Indulto Exclaustrationis necnon Saecularizationis, XIII-289 pp., 1925.
30. KEARNEY, REV. RICHARD JOSEPH, S.T.B., J.C.D., Sponsors at Baptism According to the Code of Canon Law, IV-127 pp., 1925.
31. BARTLETT, REV. CHESTER JOSEPH, A.M., LL.B., J.C.D., The Tenure of Parochial Property in the United States of America, V-108 pp., 1926.
32. KILKER, REV. ADRIAN JEROME, J.C.D., Extreme Unction, V-425 pp., 1926.
33. MCCORMICK, REV. ROBERT EMMETT, J.C.D., Confessors of Religious, VIII-266 pp., 1926.
34. MILLER, REV. NEWTON THOMAS, J.C.D., Founded Masses According to the Code of Canon Law, VII-93 pp., 1926.
35. ROELKER, REV. EDWARD G., S.T.D., J.C.D., Principles of Privilege According to the Code of Canon Law, XI-166 pp., 1926.
36. BAKALARCZYK, REV. RICHARDUS, M.I.C., J.U.D., De Novitiatu, VIII-208 pp., 1927.
37. PIZZUTI, REV. LAWRENCE, O.F.M., J.U.L., De Parochis Religiosis, 1927. (Not Printed.)
38. BLILEY, REV. NICHOLAS MARTIN, O.S.B., J.C.D., Altars According to the Code of Canon Law, XIX-132 pp., 1927.
39. BROWN, MR. BRENDAN FRANCIS, A.B., LL.M., J.U.D., The Canonical Juristic Personality with Special Reference to its Status in the United States of America, V-212 pp., 1927.

40. Cavanaugh, Rev. William Thomas, C.P., J.U.D., The Reservation of the Blessed Sacrament, VIII-101 pp., 1927.
41. Doheny, Rev. William J., C.S.C., A.B., J.U.D., Church Property: Modes of Acquisition, X-118 pp., 1927.
42. Feldhaus, Rev. Aloysius H., C.PP.S., J.C.D., Oratories, IX-141 pp., 1927.
43. Kelly, Rev. James Patrick, A.B., J.C.D., The Jurisdiction of the Simple Confessor, X-208 pp., 1927.
44. Neuberger, Rev. Nicholas J., J.C.D., Canon 6 or the Relation of the Codex Juris Canonici to the Preceding Legislation, V-95 pp., 1927.
45. O'Keefe, Rev. Gerald Michael, J.C.D., Matrimonial Dispensations, Powers of Bishops, Priests, and Confessors, VIII-232 pp., 1927.
46. Quigley, Rev. Joseph A. M., A.B., J.C.D., Condemned Societies, 139 pp., 1927.
47. Zaplotnik, Rev. Johannes Leo, J.C.D., De Vicariis Foraneis, X-142 pp., 1927.
48. Duskie, Rev. John Aloysius, A.B., J.C.D., The Canonical Status of the Orientals in the United States, VIII-196 pp., 1928.
49. Hyland, Rev. Francis Edward, J.C.D., Excommunication, Its Nature, Historical Development and Effects, VIII-181 pp., 1928.
50. Reinmann, Rev. Gerald Joseph, O.M.C., J.C.D., The Third Order Secular of Saint Francis, 201 pp., 1928.
51. Schenk, Rev. Francis J., J.C.D., The Matrimonial Impediments of Mixed Religion and Disparity of Cult, XVI-318 pp., 1929.
52. Coady, Rev. John Joseph, S.T.D., J.U.D., A.M., The Appointment of Pastors, VIII-150 pp., 1929.
53. Kay, Rev. Thomas Henry, J.C.D., Competence in Matrimonial Procedure, VIII-164 pp., 1929.
54. Turner, Rev. Sidney Joseph, C.P., J.U.D., The Vow of Poverty, XLIX-217 pp., 1929.
55. Kearney, Rev. Raymond A., A.B., S.T.D., J.C.D., The Principles of Delegation, VII-149 pp., 1929.
56. Conran, Rev. Edward James, A.B., J.C.D., The Interdict, V-163 pp., 1930.
57. O'Neill, Rev. William H., J.C.D., Papal Rescripts of Favor, VII-218 pp., 1930.
58. Bastnagel, Rev. Clement Vincent, J.U.D., The Appointment of Parochial Adjutants and Assistants, XV-257 pp., 1930.
59. Ferry, Rev. William A., A.B., J.C.D., Stole Fees, V-136 pp., 1930.
60. Costello, Rev. John Michael, A.B., J.C.D., Domicile and Quasi-Domicile, VII-201 pp., 1930.
61. Kremer, Rev. Michael Nicholas, A.B., S.T.B., J.C.D., Church Support in the United States, VI-136 pp., 1930.
62. Angulo, Rev. Luis, C.M., J.C.D., Legislation de la Iglesia sobre la intencion en la application de la Santa Misa, VII-104 pp., 1931.

63. Frey, Rev. Wolfgang Norbert, O.S.B., A.B., J.C.D., The Act of Religious Profession, VIII-174 pp., 1931.
64. Roberts, Rev. James Brendan, A.B., J.C.D., The Banns of Marriage, XIV-140 pp., 1931.
65. Ryder, Rev. Raymond Aloysius, A.B., J.C.D., Simony, IX-151 pp., 1931.
66. Campagna, Rev. Angelo, Ph.D., J.U.D., Il Vicario Generale del Vescovo, VII-205 pp., 1931.
67. Cox, Rev. Joseph Godfrey, A.B., J.C.D., The Administration of Seminaries, VI-124 pp., 1931.
68. Gregory, Rev. Donald J., J.U.D., The Pauline Privilege, XV-165 pp., 1931.
69. Donohue, Rev. John F., J.C.D., The Impediment of Crime, VII-110 pp., 1931.
70. Dooley, Rev. Eugene A., O.M.I., J.C.D., Church Law on Sacred Relics, IX-143 pp., 1931.
71. Orth, Rev. Clement Raymond, O.M.C., J.C.D., The Approbation of Religious Institutes, 171 pp., 1931.
72. Pernicone, Rev. Joseph M., A.B., J.C.D., The Ecclesiastical Prohibition of Books, XII-267 pp., 1932.
73. Clinton, Rev. Connell, A.B., J.C.D., The Paschal Precept, IX-108 pp., 1932.
74. Donnelly, Rev. Francis B., A.M., S.T.L., J.C.D., The Diocesan Synod, VIII-125 pp., 1932.
75. Torrente, Rev. Camilo, C.M.F., J.C.D., Las Procesiones Sagradas, V-145 pp., 1932.
76. Murphy, Rev. Edwin J., C.PP.S., J.C.D., Suspension Ex Informata Conscientia, XI-122 pp., 1932.
77. MacKenzie, Rev. Eric F., A.M., S.T.L., J.C.D., The Delict of Heresy in its Commission, Penalization, Absolution, VII-124 pp., 1932.
78. Lyons, Rev. Avitus E., S.T.B., J.C.D., The Collegiate Tribunal of First Instance, XI-147 pp., 1932.
79. Connolly, Rev. Thomas A., J.C.D., Appeals, XI-195 pp., 1932.
80. Sangmeister, Rev. Joseph V., A.B., J.C.D., Force and Fear as Precluding Matrimonial Consent, V-211 pp., 1932.
81. Jaeger, Rev. Leo A., A.B., J.C.D., The Administration of Vacant and Quasi-Vacant Episcopal Sees in the United States, IX-229 pp., 1932.
82. Rimlinger, Rev. Herbert T., J.C.D., Error Invalidating Matrimonial Consent, VII-79 pp., 1932.
83. Barrett, Rev. John D. M., S.S., J.C.D., A Comparative Study of the Third Plenary Council of Baltimore and the Code, IX-221 pp., 1932.
84. Carberry, Rev. John J., Ph.D., S.T.D., J.C.D., The Juridical Form of Marriage, X-177 pp., 1934.
85. Dolan, Rev. John L., A.B., J.C.D., The Defensor Vinculi, XII-157 pp., 1934.

86. HANNAN, REV. JEROME D., A.M., S.T.D., LL.B., J.C.D., The Canon Law of Wills, IX-517 pp., 1934.
87. LEMIEUX, REV. DELISE A., A.M., J.C.D., The Sentence in Ecclesiastical Procedure, IX-131 pp., 1934.
88. O'ROURKE, REV. JAMES J., A.B., J.C.D., Parish Registers, VII-109 pp., 1934.
89. TIMLIN, REV. BARTHOLOMEW, O.F.M., A.M., J.C.D., Conditional Matrimonial Consent, X-381 pp., 1934.
90. WAHL, REV. FRANCIS X., A.B., J.C.D., The Matrimonial Impediments of Consanguinity and Affinity, VI-125 pp., 1934.
91. WHITE, REV. ROBERT J., A.B., LL.B., S.T.B., J.C.D., Canonical Ante-Nuptial Promises and the Civil Law, VI-152 pp., 1934.
92. HERRERA, REV. ANTONIO PARRA, O.C.D., J.C.D., Legislacion Ecclesiastica sobra el Ayuno y la Abstinencia, XI-191 pp., 1935.
93. KENNEDY, REV. EDWIN J., J.C.D., The Special Matrimonial Process in Cases of Evident Nullity, X-165 pp., 1935.
94. MANNING, REV. JOHN J., A.B., J.C.D., Presumption of Law in Matrimonial Procedure, XI-111 pp., 1935.
95. MOEDER, REV. JOHN M., J.C.D., The Proper Bishop for Ordination and Dimissorial Letters, VII-135 pp., 1935.
96. O'MARA, REV. WILLIAM A., A.B., J.C.D., Canonical Causes for Matrimonial Dispensations, IX-155 pp., 1935.
97. REILLY, REV. PETER, J.C.D., Residence of Pastors, IX-81 pp., 1935.
98. SMITH, REV. MARINER T., O.P., S.T.Lr., J.C.D., The Penal Law for Religious, VII-169 pp., 1935.
99. WHALEN, REV. DONALD W., A.M., J.C.D., The Value of Testimonial Evidence in Matrimonial Procedure, XIII-297 pp., 1935.
100. CLEARY, REV. JOSEPH F., J.C.D., Canonical Limitations on the Alienation of Church Property, VIII-141 pp., 1936.
101. GLYNN, REV. JOHN C., J.C.D., The Promoter of Justice, XX-337 pp., 1936.
102. BRENNAN, REV. JAMES H., S.S., M.A., S.T.B., J.C.D., The Simple Convalidation of Marriage, VI-135 pp., 1937.
103. BRUNINI, REV. JOSEPH BERNARD, J.C.D., The Clerical Obligations of Canons 139 and 142, X-121 pp., 1937.
104. CONNOR, REV. MAURICE, A.B., J.C.D., The Administrative Removal of Pastors, VIII-159 pp., 1937.
105. GUILFOYLE, REV. MERLIN JOSEPH, J.C.D., Custom, XI-144 pp., 1937.
106. HUGHES, REV. JAMES AUSTIN, A.B., A.M., J.C.D., Witnesses in Criminal Trials of Clerics, IX-140 pp., 1937.
107. JANSEN, REV. RAYMOND J., A.B., S.T.L., J.C.D., Canonical Provisions for Catechetical Instruction, VII-153 pp., 1937.
108. KEALY, REV. JOHN JAMES, A.B., J.C.D., The Introductory Libellus in Church Court Procedure, XI-121 pp., 1937.

109. McManus, Rev. James Edward, C.SS.R., J.C.D., The Administration of Temporal Goods in Religious Institutes, XVI-196 pp., 1937.
110. Moriarty, Rev. Eugene James, J.C.D., Oaths in Ecclesiastical Courts, X-115 pp., 1937.
111. Rainer, Rev. Eligius George, C.SS.R., J.C.D., Suspension of Clerics, XVII-249 pp., 1937.
112. Reilly, Rev. Thomas F., C.SS.R., J.C.D., Visitation of Religious, VI-195 pp., 1938.
113. Moriarty, Rev. Francis E. C.SS.R., J.C.D., The Extraordinary Absolution from Censures, XV-334 pp., 1938.
114. Connolly, Rev. Nicholas P., J.C.D., The Canonical Erection of Parishes, X-132 pp., 1938.
115. Donovan, Rev. James Joseph, J.C.D., The Pastor's Obligation in Prenuptial Investigation, XII-322 pp., 1938.
116. Harrigan, Rev. Robert J., M.A., S.T.B., J.C.D., The Radical Sanation of Invalid Marriages, VIII-208 pp., 1938.
117. Boffa, Rev. Conrad Humbert, J.C.D., Canonical Provisions for Catholic Schools, VII-211 pp., 1939.
118. Parsons, Rev. Anscar John, O.M.Cap., J.C.D., Canonical Elections, XII-236 pp., 1939.
119. Reilly, Rev. Edward Michael, A.B., J.C.D., The General Norms of Dispensation, XII-156 pp., 1939.
120. Ryan, Rev. Gerald Aloysius, A.B., J.C.D., Principles of Episcopal Jurisdiction, XII-172 pp., 1939.
121. Burton, Rev. Francis James, C.S.C., A.B., J.C.D., A Commentary on Canon 1125, X-222 pp., 1940.
122. Miaskiewicz, Rev. Francis Sigismund, J.C.D., Supplied Jurisdiction According to Canon 209, XII-340 pp., 1940.
123. Rice, Rev. Patrick William, A.B., J.C.D., Proof of Death in Prenuptial Investigation, VIII-156 pp., 1940.
124. Anglin, Rev. Thomas Francis, M.S., J.C.D., The Eucharistic Fast, VIII-183 pp., 1941.
125. Coleman, Rev. John Jerome, J.C.D., The Minister of Confirmation, VI-153 pp., 1941.
126. Downs, Rev. Joseph Emmanuel, A.B., J.C.D., The Concept of Clerical Immunity, XI-163 pp., 1941.
127. Esswein, Rev. Anthony Albert, J.C.D., Extrajudicial Penal Powers of Ecclesiastical Superiors, X-144 pp., 1941.
128. Farrell, Rev. Benjamin Francis, M.A., S.T.L., J.C.D., The Rights and Duties of the Local Ordinary Regarding Congregations of Women Religious of Pontifical Approval, V-195 pp., 1941.
129. Feeney, Rev. Thomas John, A.B., S.T.L., J.C.D., Restitutio in Integrum, VI-169 pp., 1941.
130. Findlay, Rev. Stephen William, O.S.B., A.B., J.C.D., Canonical

Norms Governing the Deposition and Degradation of Clerics, XVII-279 pp., 1941.

131. Goodwine, Rev. John, A.B., S.T.L., J.C.D., The Right of the Church to Acquire Property, VIII-119 pp., 1941.

132. Heston, Rev. Edward Louis, C.S.C., Ph.D., S.T.D., J.C.D., The Alienation of Church Property in the United States, XII-222 pp., 1941.

133. Hogan, Rev. James John, A.B., S.T.L., J.C.D., Judicial Advocates and Procurators, XIII-200 pp., 1941.

134. Kealy, Rev. Thomas M., A.B., Litt.B., J.C.D., Dowry of Women Religious, IX-152 pp., 1941.

135. Keene, Rev. Michael James, O.S.B., J.C.D., Religious Ordinaries and Canon 198, V-164 pp., 1942.

136. Kerin, Rev. Charles A., S.S., M.A., S.T.B., J.C.D., The Privation of Christian Burial, XVI-279 pp., 1941.

137. Louis, Rev. William Francis, M.A., J.C.D., Diocesan Archives, X-101 pp., 1941.

138. McDevitt, Rev. Gilbert Joseph, A.B., J.C.D., Legitimacy and Legitimation, X-247 pp., 1941.

139. McDonough, Rev. Thomas Joseph, A.B., J.C.D., Apostolic Administrators, X-217 pp., 1941.

140. **Meier, Rev. Carl Anthony, A.B., J.C.D., Penal Administrative Pro**cedure Against Negligent Pastors, XI-240 pp., 1941.

141. Schmidt, Rev. John Rogg, A.B., J.C.D., The Principles of Authentic Interpretation in Canon 17 of the Code of Canon Law, XII-331 pp., 1941.

142. Slafkosky, Rev. Andrew Leonard, A.B., J.C.D., The Canonical Episcopal Visitation of the Diocese, X-197 pp., 1941.

143. Swoboda, Rev. Innocent Robert, O.F.M., J.C.D., Ignorance in Relation to the Imputability of Delicts, IX-271 pp., 1941.

144. Dubé, Rev. Arthur Joseph, A.B., J.C.D., The General Principles for the Reckoning of Time in Canon Law, VIII-299 pp., 1941.

145. McBride, Rev. James T., A.B., J.C.D., Incardination and Excardination of Seculars, XX-585 pp., 1941.

146. Król, Rev. John T., J.C.D., The Defendant in Contentious Trials, XII-207 pp., 1942.

147. Comyns, Rev. Joseph J., C.SS.R., A.B., J.C.D., Papal and Episcopal Administration of Church Property, XIV-155 pp., 1942.

148. Barry, Rev. Garrett Francis, O.M.I., J.C.D., Violation of the Cloister, XII-260 pp., 1942.

149. Bolduc, Rev. Gatien, C.S.V., A.B., S.T.L., J.C.D., Les Études dans les Religions Cléricales, VIII-155 pp., 1942.

150. Boyle, Rev. David John, M.A., J.C.D., The Juridic Effects of Moral Certitude on Pre-Nuptial Guarantees, XII-188 pp., 1942.

151. **Canavan, Rev. Walter Joseph, M.A., Litt.D., J.C.D., The Profes**sion of Faith, XII-143 pp., 1942.

152. Desrochers, Rev. Bruno, A.B., Ph.L., S.T.B., J.C.D., Le Premier Concile Plénier de Québec et le Code de Droit Canonique, XIV-186 pp., 1942.
153. Dillon, Rev. Robert Edward, A.B., J.C.D., Common Law Marriage, X-148 pp., 1942.
154. Dodwell, Rev. Edward John, Ph.D., S.T.B., J.C.D., The Time and Place for the Celebration of Marriage, X-156 pp., 1942.
155. Donnellan, Rev. Thomas Andrew, A.B., J.C.D., The Obligation of the Missa pro Populo, VII-131 pp., 1942.
156. Eltz, Rev. Louis Anthony, A.B., J.C.D., Cooperation in Crime, XII-208 pp., 1942.
157. Gass, Rev. Sylvester Francis, M.A., J.C.D., Ecclesiastical Pensions, XI-206 pp., 1942.
158. Guiniven, Rev. John Joseph, C.SS.R., J.C.D., The Precept of Hearing Mass, XIV-188 pp., 1942.
159. Gulczynski, Rev. John Theophilus, J.C.D., The Desecration and Violation of Churches, X-126 pp., 1942.
160. Hammill, Rev. John Leo, M.A., J.C.D., The Obligations of the Traveler According to Canon 14, VIII-204 pp., 1942.
161. Haydt, Rev. John Joseph, A.B., J.C.D., Reserved Benefices, XI-148 pp., 1942.
162. Huser, Rev. Roger John, O.F.M., A.B., J.C.D., The Crime of Abortion in Canon Law, XII-187 pp., 1942.
163. Kearney, Rev. Francis Patrick, A.B., S.T.L., J.C.D., The Principles of Canon 1127, X-162 pp., 1942.
164. Linahen, Rev. Leo James, S.T.L., J.C.D., De Absolutione Complicis In Peccato Turpi, 114 pp., 1942.
165. McCloskey, Rev. Joseph Aloysius, A.B., J.C.D., The Subject of Ecclesiastical Law According to Canon 12, XVII-246 pp., 1942.
166. O'Neill, Rev. Francis Joseph, C.SS.R., J.C.D., The Dismissal of Religious in Temporary Vows, XIII-220 pp., 1942.
167. Prince, Rev. John Edward, A.B., S.T.B., J.C.D., The Diocesan Chancellor, X-136 pp., 1942.
168. Riesner, Rev. Albert Joseph, C.SS.R., J.C.D., Apostates and Fugitives from Religious Institutes, IX-168 pp., 1942.
169. Stenger, Rev. Joseph Bernard, J.C.D., The Mortgaging of Church Property, 186 pp., 1942.
170. Waldron, Rev. Joseph Francis, A.B., J.C.D., The Minister of Baptism, XII-197 pp., 1942.
171. Willett, Rev. Robert Albert, J.C.D., The Probative Value of Documents in Ecclesiastical Trials, X-124 pp., 1942.
172. Woeber, Rev. Edward Martin, M.A., J.C.D., The Interpellations, XII-161 pp., 1942.
173. Benko, Rev. Matthew Aloysius, O.S.B., M.A., J.C.D., The Abbot *Nullius,* XIV-148 pp., 1943.

174. Christ, Rev. Joseph James, M.A., S.T.L., J.C.D., Dispensation from Vindicative Penalties, XIV-285 pp., 1943.

175. Clancy, Rev. Patrick M. J., O.P., A.B., S.T.Lr., J.C.D., The Local Religious Superior, X-229 pp., 1943.

176. Clarke, Rev. Thomas James, J.C.D., Parish Societies, XII-147 pp., 1943.

177. Connolly, Rev. John Patrick, S.T.L., J.C.D., Synodal Examiners and Parish Priest Consultors, X-223 pp., 1943.

178. Drumm, Rev. William Martin, A.B., J.C.D., Hospital Chaplains, XII-175 pp., 1943.

179. Flanagan, Rev. Bernard Joseph, A.B., S.T.L., J.C.D., The Canonical Erection of Religious Houses, X-147 pp., 1943.

180. Kelleher, Rev. Stephen Joseph, A.B., S.T.B., J.C.D., Discussions with Non-Catholics: Canonical Legislation, X-93 pp., 1943.

181. Lewis, Rev. Gordian, C.P., J.C.D., Chapters in Religious Institutes, XII-169 pp., 1943.

182. Marx, Rev. Adolph, J.C.D., The Declaration of Nullity of Marriages Contracted Outside the Church, X-151 pp., 1943.

183. Matulenas, Rev. Raymond Anthony, O.S.B., A.B., J.C.D., Communication, a Source of Privileges, XII-225 pp., 1943.

184. O'Leary, Rev. Charles Gerard, C.SS.R., J.C.D., Religious Dismissed After Perpetual Profession, X-213 pp., 1943.

185. Power, Rev. Cornelius Michael, J.C.D., The Blessing of Cemeteries, XII-231 pp., 1943.

186. Shuhler, Rev. Ralph Vincent, O.S.A., J.C.D., Privileges of Regulars to Absolve and Dispense, XII-195 pp., 1943.

187. Ziolkowski, Rev. Thaddeus Stanislaus, A.B., J.C.D., The Consecration and Blessing of Churches, XII-151 pp., 1943.

188. Heneghan, Rev. John Joseph, S.T.D., J.C.D., The Marriages of Unworthy Catholics: Canons 1065 and 1066, XVI-213 pp., 1944.

189. Carroll, Rev. Coleman Francis, M.A., S.T.L., J.C.L., Charitable Institutions.

190. Cieslük, Rev. Joseph Edward, Ph.B., S.T.L., J.C.L., National Parishes in the United States.

191. Coburn, Rev. Vincent Paul, A.B., J.C.D., Marriages of Conscience, XII-172 pp., 1944.

192. Connors, Rev. Charles Paul, C.S.Sp., A.B., J.C.D., Extra-Judicial Procurators in the Code of Canon Law, X-94 pp., 1944.

193. Coyle, Rev. Paul Raymond, A.B., J.C.D., Judicial Exceptions, X-142 pp., 1944.

194. Fair, Rev. Bartholomew Francis, A.B., S.T.L., J.C.L., The Impediment of Abduction.

195. Gallagher, Rev. Thomas Raphael, O.P., A.B., S.T.Lr., J.C.D., The Examination of the Qualities of the Ordinand, X-166 pp., 1944.

196. Gannon, Rev. John Mark, S.T.L., J.C.D., The Interstices Required for the Promotion to Orders, XII-100 pp., 1944.

197. Goldsmith, Rev. J. William, B.C.S., S.T.L., J.C.D., The Competence of Church and State over Marriage—Disputed Points, X-128 pp., 1944.
198. Goodwine, Rev. Joseph Gerard, A.B., S.T.B., J.C.D., The Reception of Converts, XIV-326 pp., 1944.
199. Kowalski, Rev. Romuald Eugene, O.F.M., A.B., J.C.D., Sustenance of Religious Houses of Regulars, X-174 pp., 1944.
200. McCoy, Rev. Alan Edward, O.F.M., J.C.D., Force and Fear in Relation to Delictual Imputability and Penal Responsibility, XII-160 pp., 1944.
201. McDevitt, Rev. Vincent John, Ph.B., S.T.L., J.C.L., Perjury.
202. Martin, Rev. Thomas Owen, Ph.D., S.T.D., J.C.D., Adverse Possession, Prescription and Limitation of Actions: The Canonical "Praescriptio," XX-208 pp., 1944.
203. Miklosovic, Rev. Paul John, A.B., J.C.L., Attempted Marriages and Their Consequent Juridic Effects.
204. Mundy, Rev. Thomas Maurice, A.B., S.T.L., J.C.D., The Union of Parishes, X—164 pp., 1945.
205. O'Dea, Rev. John Coyle, A.B., J.C.D., The Matrimonial Impediment of Nonage, VIII-126 pp., 1944.
206. Olalia, Rev. Alexander Ayson, S.T.L., J.C.D., A Comparative Study of the Christian Constitution of States and the Constitution of the Philippine Commonwealth, XII—136 pp., 1944.
207. Poisson, Rev. Pierre-Marie, C.S.C., A.B., Ph.L., Th.L., J.C.L., Droits Patrimoniaux des Maisons et des Églises Religieuses.
208. Stadalnikas, Rev. Casimir Joseph, M.I.C., J.C.D., Reservation of Censures, X-141 pp., 1944.
209. Sullivan, Rev. Eugene Henry, S.T.L., J.C.D., Proof of the Reception of the Sacraments, X—165 pp., 1944.
210. Vaughan, Rev. William Edward, J.C.D., Constitutions for Diocesan Courts, X-210 pp., 1944.
211. Paro, Rev. Gino, S.T.D., J.C.L., The Right of Apostolic Legation.
212. Balzer, Rev. Ralph Francis, C.P., J.C.L., The Computation of Time in a Canonical Novitiate.
213. Dougherty, Rev. John Whelan, A.B., S.T.L., J.C.L., De Inquisitione Speciali.
214. Dziob, Rev. Michael Walter, J.C.L., The Sacred Congregation for the Oriental Church.
215. Eidenschink, Rev. John Albert, O.S.B., B.A., J.C.L., The Election of Bishops in the Letters of Pope Gregory the Great.
216. Gill, Rev. Nicholas, C.P., J.C.L., The Spiritual Prefect in Clerical Religious Houses of Study.
217. Hynes, Rev. Harry Gerard, S.T.L., J.C.D., The Privileges of Cardinals, XII-183 pp., 1945.
218. McDevitt, Rev. Gerald Vincent, S.T.L., J.C.D., The Renunciation of an Ecclesiastical Office, XIV—179 pp., 1946.

219. MANNING, REV. JOSEPH LEROY, J.C.L., The Free Conferral of Offices.
220. MEYER, REV. LOUIS G., O.S.B., A.B., S.T.B., J.C.D., Alms-Gathering by Religious, XII—163 pp., 1946.
221. O'DONNELL, REV. CLETUS FRANCIS, M.A., J.C.L., The Marriage of Minors.

www.ingramcontent.com/pod-product-compliance
Lightning Source LLC
LaVergne TN
LVHW050254080826
844660LV00012B/638

* 9 7 8 0 8 1 3 2 2 4 0 5 3 *